Theory and Practice of Education:
An Introduction

Theory and Practice of Education: An Introduction

M. E. Downey and A. V. Kelly

University of London, Goldsmiths' College

99503

Harper & Row, Publishers
London   New York   Evanston   San Francisco

First published 1975
Reprinted 1976
Published by Harper & Row
28 Tavistock Street, London WC2E 7PN

Standard Book Number 06-318037-5 (cloth)
Standard Book Number 06-318038-3 (paper)

Typeset by Red Lion Setters, London
Printed in Great Britain by
Butler & Tanner Ltd, Frome and London

Contents

Introduction

Although the picture is a good deal more cheering than it was even ten years ago, the theoretical basis of the practice of education is still far from satisfactory. The study of education which all teachers in training undergo has often appeared to have so little relevance to educational practice that it has come to be regarded by some people as an academic study which can be pursued for its own sake. In rejecting this kind of study, many teachers have abandoned any kind of theoretical study of education and, as a result, since there can be no practice without principles of some kind, their practice has been founded on nothing more substantial than folk-lore, intuition or even passing whims and fancies. They complain that the voice of the practising teacher is not heard in the councils at which major educational decisions are made, but forget that these decisions must be based on theoretical considerations of a kind which they have explicitly and even proudly rejected. Decisions at that level, therefore, are made either under the urgings of some ideological view promulgated by whatever political faction happens to be in power, as has been the case with the comprehensivization of secondary education, or on the basis of scientific evidence culled from some other field such as psychology or sociology which has only a partial contribution to make to any educational issue, as was the case with the establishment of selective forms of secondary education. The fundamental problem is that no one has ever been quite clear what Education Theory is.

The term 'theory' seems to have at least three different meanings. In the first place, it is most commonly used to refer to an explanation of a group of related scientific phenomena, as when we speak of the theory of radiation. In this kind of context, it denotes a set of interconnected hypotheses that have been framed in order to describe and explain a particular series of natural phenomena. The word 'theory' is also used, however, to refer to a body of doctrine, a collection not of descriptions but of prescriptions, intended not to explain but to guide action. It is in this sense that the word is used when we speak of such things as Marxist theory, where the concern is to offer a coherent body of opinion, a 'philosophy'. Finally, we find the term used in an intermediate sense, in which it does no more than to pick out a related body of problems, as when we speak of the theory of knowledge. Here we are neither referring to an explanatory system nor to any particular set of views; we are merely indicating the relatedness of certain kinds of problem.

Much of the difficulty that has surrounded Education Theory arises from the fact that no one has been clear into which of these categories to put it, or, indeed, whether it fits into any of them. Some have seen it as being a kind of scientific theory, an attempt to frame hypotheses to explain certain phenomena. They have been attracted, therefore, as we have seen, to the scientific theories of psychology or sociology and the result of this has been that their view of educational problems has been one-sided and inadequate and their practice consequently misguided. A scientific theory is concerned, as we saw, to describe and explain; it may even be used as a basis for prediction, although in the case of the human sciences this is fraught with particular difficulties; but alone it can never provide guides for action; practical decisions must be made also in the light of other considerations. Any view of education, therefore, that excludes such considerations because it is taken from the standpoint of any of these disciplines will be a warped and dangerous view, as the history of the development of the educational system in Britain can reveal.

Others have, therefore, taken the view that Education Theory involves the generation of bodies of doctrine, collections of more or less coherent prescriptions as to what teachers and schools ought to be doing. This approach has led to the production of a great deal of what has rightly been castigated as 'mush' or 'beautiful thoughts' and has done more than anything else to bring educational theory into disrepute. As a result, it has in recent years been rejected entirely in favour of a more rigorous and differentiated study of the 'foundation' or 'contributory' disciplines of education, in particular philosophy, psychology and sociology. Unfortunately, this seems to have been an over-reaction, a rejection of the baby with the bath water. For the merit that the prescriptive approach did have was that it injected into discussions of education a sense of purpose, an awareness that education is a practical activity and some ideas about what teachers and schools ought to be doing, of a kind that can never come from the sciences of psychology or sociology or from the analytical processes of the philosopher. This element is vital if Education Theory is to have full relevance for educational practice.

In fact, it seems that Education Theory has elements of it in all the three kinds of theory that we delineated. It denotes a range of problems, those practical problems that teachers and others concerned with the practice of education need to give thought to and to make decisions about; it needs to offer some set or sets of views that may help us to decide on the directions in which these decisions are to take us; and it must also contain a proper and rigorous scientific basis to ensure that these decisions are theoretically sound and consistent with whatever evidence is available.

If this is what Education Theory is or ought to be, two things seem to be required to ensure that it offers the teacher the support he needs. In the first place, it must start and end with the problems that the practice of education throws up; it must be firmly rooted in the school and the classroom and must have a direct practical relevance to all aspects of the teacher's work. Without this, it is the study of something else and not of education, which is after all a practical activity. Secondly, if it is to deal adequately with issues of this kind, its approach must not lean too heavily on other disciplines or bodies of theory devised for other purposes. We have already commented on the disastrous consequences of basing educational decisions only on psychological or sociological considerations. We must add our conviction that it is not enough that the study of education should draw on all relevant disciplines separately. A much more concerted approach than that is needed. It is not what each individual discipline or subject has to contribute to any particular issue that is interesting, important and useful; it is the combined effect of them that is needed, along with something more, a full account of and allowance for the aims and purposes of our activities.

Lastly, both of these objectives must be achieved without loss of rigour. We must not return to the days of 'mush' or 'beautiful thoughts' unless it be to sort out the mush and find a sound basis for the beautiful thoughts. We should now be entering a further stage in the development of educational theory when it can stand in its own right as a rigorous body of theoretical knowledge that all teachers can respect and profit from in the practice of their profession.

It is towards that end that this book has been written. We hope that it will link theory to practice and bring a coherence to the theory itself in a way that will not only help students of Education to pass their examinations but will also improve their professionalism as teachers. We hope too that it will prove of value to practising teachers and will lead to a better understanding of some of the highly complex professional tasks they must undertake.

We have tried to focus, therefore, on those aspects of Education Theory that are directly relevant to the practice of the teacher in the classroom. All areas of Education Theory should have such relevance for the work of the schools but, since some selection had to be made, we felt it appropriate here to concentrate on those areas which are of immediate import for the individual teacher. We have begun with an examination of some of the ways in which the judgements teachers make of their pupils and the attitudes they have towards them can determine the progress those pupils will make in their education. We have then gone on to consider in more detail some of the most significant aspects of these judgements and attitudes — the views the teacher holds about the nature of intelligence and the kinds of ability he values, his approach to the problem of motivating his pupils, the multiple impact of language differences, the methods of control that he favours and his attitudes to questions of freedom and authority and relationships generally. We have then considered some of the questions that need to be asked about the curriculum, since the current trend towards an increased individualization of educational provision places responsibility on the individual teacher for many decisions in this area that hitherto were taken for him by those who drew up syllabuses of various kinds. Finally, since one of the main themes running through most of the current thinking about education, its content, its organization and its methods, is the ideological issue of educational equality, we felt it necessary to conclude our discussion with an examination of some of the major implications of that debate for educational practice.

If we have failed to attain our objectives, we hope that this will be attributed to our own inadequacies rather than to any fundamental weakness in the view of Education Theory from which we start, since it is our conviction that unless something is done to establish the study of Education along the lines we have indicated, both the theory and the practice of Education will continue to be held back from their proper development.

Our thanks are due to those colleagues at Goldsmiths' College and in the London Institute of Education generally whose commitment to this approach to the study of Education and continuing contributions towards its development have encouraged us in what we have tried to do. In particular, however, we must record our gratitude to John Handford and Keith Thompson whose constructive and supportive comments on the first draft of the text not only enabled us to improve it in a number of important ways but also gave us renewed energy and confidence. We hope that all will feel that their efforts have been and will continue to be worthwhile.

M. E. Downey
A. V. Kelly
London, December 1974

I Teachers' Judgements of Children

In attempting to introduce students and teachers to ways of studying the theory and practice of Education that we have tried to develop in recent years we hope to emphasize several points. Firstly, that it is of great importance to begin by considering the practical classroom issues which are of concern to all teachers; secondly, to examine the theoretical issues which arise out of such practical problems and then to suggest any appropriate guidance which might be drawn from such theoretical considerations on empirical evidence.

It is for these reasons that we have chosen to discuss judgements of children as the topic of our first chapter. This is a task which, as we shall see, is central to all aspects of a teacher's work. The judgements he makes necessarily affect any of his dealings with children: the ways in which he assesses their ability and progress, selects work for them or helps them to further their own interests, encourages them towards an appreciation of standards of excellence.

Young teachers may feel somewhat daunted by the idea of judging children and reluctant to see this as part of their teaching task. But an analysis of the implications of judging other people will make clear that judgement of others enters into every kind of human interaction. When we meet a person for the first time we form some sort of impression of him immediately; our first impressions lead us to put him into a category, based on our past experience of other people. For instance, we make up our minds quickly whether he looks pleasant or angry, easily approachable or someone to be approached with caution, whether he looks sad or happy, and so on. Whether these impressions are right or not we discover during further social intercourse with him, but if we were not able to form some kind of judgement about the sort of person we are about to enter into conversation with, we should probably be very inept in our dealings with him. It is thus inevitable that judgements are formed early, but whether they are long lasting, appropriate, open to revision or modification involves all kinds of problems.

If we accept that forming impressions or judgements of other people is an integral part of any kind of social interaction, we can see that it must necessarily be part of a teacher's task. A teacher has to sum children up as people in order to know how to treat them when he is first getting to know them; in order to know what kind of provision to make educationally and what kind of work to plan for them, he has to make a rough and ready assessment of their abilities; to see whether they have learnt anything, he again has to judge their progress. Or on a more formal level, teachers are required to make judgements of children in written form - hence a more permanent one - when they complete record cards, write end-of-term reports, testimonials or references. Judging and assessing children seems then to be an integral and necessary part of teaching which cannot be avoided. If we now consider some of the practical problems raised by the whole issue of judging, assessing and evaluating others, we shall see that this part of a teacher's work is just as important as his understanding of motivation, intelligence, his knowledge of his subject matter and of child development.

The impressions teachers form of their pupils as individuals and the judgements they make of their abilities and progress are naturally subjective: the human being making the judgement is not a measuring instrument to be calibrated and read with any degree of accuracy. It is therefore logically impossible to talk of right or accurate judgements since no precise criteria can be set up to determine this accuracy. Probably it is more appropriate to talk of making a just or fair judgement; this implies making only those inferences from an individual's behaviour for which we have some direct evidence from observation. If a teacher is assessing a child's ability or attitude towards school he must ensure that what he infers is based on what he himself has seen: to say that a child's learning will be impeded because he has a poor grasp of English and cannot use language fluently is nearer the truth if a teacher is familiar with his work, has conversed with him and listened to him in conversation with his peers than if he merely infers that his use of language will be poor because he knows that the child comes from a lower working class background. To make indirect inferences of this nature is highly inaccurate and easily leads to the labelling of a child with no substantial evidence to support the view. The more direct the source of evidence, the more objectively accurate the judgement is likely to be. If a teacher does pay keen attention to what he observes he will also be ready to recognize and accept changes in his pupils. All too often the unfavourable reputations children gain at one stage in their school career are shaken off only with great difficulty because the teacher is not observant of change in his pupils' attitudes, interests or application. It is easy to interpret a person's behaviour so that it fits into one's preconceived picture of him, and this clearly must be avoided if judgements are not to be unfair and misleading. Since a teacher has to be so careful of interpreting his own evidence from direct sources he must be even more wary of unquestioningly accepting other people's judgements as valid.

As suggested earlier, a teacher has to make judgements of children's abilities, interests, aptitudes to help him to plan appropriate work for them and to adopt an appropriate teaching style. In other words, one essential feature of making judgements is that they should be helpful and relevant educationally. It is not helpful, for example, to class pupils as 'dull', 'slow', if all this means is that a label has been attached to them to explain to others why the teacher is achieving no success with such pupils, or even to convince himself that their dullness is a reason for not trying harder to help them learn. Far more to the point would be a specific comment about a specific difficulty; for instance, if a child has difficulty with reading, it is unhelpful just to call him a slow reader, but helpful to note specific vowel combinations for example that cause him difficulty and hinder his progress, because this kind of judgement helps a teacher to plan specific remedial work.

Judgements made of children must not only be helpful but also relevant: to make judgements in terms of home background, social class, race or religion is usually irrelevant to the task in hand - that of educating children. It is clearly helpful to understand something of children's home background in a multicultural classroom, since family traditions, upset perhaps by a new environment, can have important repercussions on a child's attitude towards and understanding of school, but it is usually irrelevant to call upon such factors as a ready explanation of underachievement.

We have mentioned so far that judgements must be helpful to the teachers who make them, but they are sometimes intended to be helpful to others: other teachers, parents and even children themselves. Teachers' detailed records of children's work and progress are written not only to guide their own planning, but also to show those who take over the class the following year how far each child has progressed in various skills and curriculum topics. The scant clichés such as 'could do better', 'very good', are obviously of very little help at all and, if anything, serve to stereotype children for those who read the reports. If record cards are to be of help they must necessarily be detailed, since only detailed information can reflect careful scrutiny of evidence from direct observation, as previously emphasized. It is sad to note that very few secondary schools adopt an internal system of record keeping such as has been described; it is even worse to note the archaic report forms that many teachers laboriously fill in at the end of the school year with only sufficient space for what is usually a well-worn cliché for each subject. These reports are supposed to inform parents of their children's progress and presumably also to help the children themselves. If reports were more detailed and informative they would surely encourage parents to take greater interest in their children's progress.

Judgements made of children to children are usually on the spot comments relating to attitudes, effort and so on and are associated with approval, disapproval, praise or blame. This is clearly a two-way process: a child must be in a position to make his own comments to the teacher and feel at liberty to say if he feels unfairly treated, or that the teacher has overlooked some of his best efforts.

It has been seen so far that judgements are not only necessary for social interaction but are also inevitable. We simply could not deal with the barrage of information about people impinging upon us if we did not relate each new experience to what we already know. In other words, we see each new experience as similar to or dissimilar from others we have undergone in the past: we thus form categories into which we tentatively slot our present experiences perhaps altering the category as we obtain more evidence or information about the person we are judging or more cues from his behaviour itself. It is this process that Schutz[1] refers to as 'typification' and Berger and Luckman[2] call 'typificatory schemes'. Berger and Luckman suggest that whereas most of our experience of other people takes place in face to face situations, we apprehend them or form impressions of them also by means of typificatory schemes which we have built up in the past for example 'redheads', 'Englishmen', 'culturally deprived children' (our examples). These typifications affect our interaction with the person concerned so that he becomes a typical redhead, having all the characteristics we have learnt by direct or indirect experience to associate with redheads, unless his behaviour intervenes and challenges this view, that is, unless he behaves atypically. Thus unless challenged, these typifications will hold until further notice and will determine our actions towards that person. One serious problem is that very often a challenge goes unnoticed because the typification we have made has become too rigid to be modified: a teacher seeing an immigrant child as one doomed to failure because of language difficulties is likely to class him as ESN and to disregard evidence of ability (Coard, 1971).[3] Once a typification has been provided, the label attached to a child to be judged very often leaves a teacher to search for cues in that child's behaviour which correspond to characteristics he has been led to expect. Thus the typification becomes confirmed and has consequences for the teacher's attitudes towards the child; since interaction is an active process these attitudes on the part of the teacher are likely to have repercussions on the child's behaviour and school progress.

A brief review of some of the recent literature on educability will enable us to examine some of the assumptions that teachers make about the relationship between educability and social class, ability, race and even sex. We can then consider the implications of some of these assumptions for pupils' school achievement and behaviour in class and go on to ask why teachers' assumptions or typifications should have the effect they do.

Becker (1952),[4] drawing on interviews he had with sixty teachers in Chicago schools, shows how teachers classify children according to their notion of an ideal pupil. This ideal pupil is one who cooperates with the teacher, enabling him to do his job successfully: he is typically eager to learn, he behaves well, is neatly and tidily dressed and does not offend the teacher's sense of propriety. This type of pupil, according to the teacher's own accounts, tends to come from middle or upper middle class homes. Once a picture of an ideal pupil has been formed, those deviating from the ideal are perceived as less acceptable. They are less easy to teach, less well behaved in class and even less morally acceptable to teachers. Becker's teachers tended to classify their pupils into three groups: the upper (ideal) group; the middle group, coming mainly from lower middle and upper working class strata of society, and the bottom group, belonging mainly to the lower social strata. The middle group were judged to be nice, docile children, not very bright, yet easy to get on with and well behaved. The bottom group were considered very difficult, hostile to work with, lazy, dull, badly behaved, untidily dressed and even morally unacceptable to the teachers. Thus it was only with the upper group that the teachers felt really sure of success (and we must remember that success was seen in terms of satisfying the overall school requirements of completing the syllabus satisfactorily). Becker's study draws attention to the way in which teachers tend to classify children in terms of a perceived relationship between social class and educability. In this discussion he does not go further to look at possible consequences of this classification, except to note the constant movement of teachers away from schools where they are likely to encounter pupils like those in the bottom group. But we must also ask how the teacher's image of these pupils when he does teach them affects his handling of them. This issue will be discussed later in the light of further empirical studies.

Since Becker's paper was written in 1952 extensive research has been carried out both in this country and the USA to show how working class children are at a disadvantage compared with middle class children in school achievement and educational opportunity. Much of the work done in the 1950s and early 1960s (see Chapters III and VII on Motivation and Equality) set out to show the extent of these differential opportunities and in fact there is substantial evidence of working class failure, which was attributed to poor home backgrounds, lack of parental interest and insufficient encouragement. Pre-school programmes were set up in the USA to compensate for inferior home backgrounds, in the hope that 'disadvantaged' children would catch up before they came to school. A question which was raised only later was whether the school contributed towards the failure of these children, and if so, how it did. From the late 1960s on we find a series of investigations both in this country and in the USA which aim to answer this question. Fuchs for example (1968)[5] in the USA carried out a small scale study of probationary teachers in New York slum schools, in an attempt to show how teachers (perhaps inadvertently) help children to fail. A detailed account of one young teacher's experiences in a slum school illustrates the point. The teacher began her work in the school by trying to examine her own methods critically and attributing children's failure to her own lack of experience and expertise. But very soon she was persuaded (reluctantly) by more experienced teachers that the cause of failure lay not with her, but in the inferior home backgrounds from which the children came. Children were thus being typified as failures right at the beginning of their school career because of their home background. As Fuchs says: 'the slum school system's tacit belief that social conditions outside the school make such failures inevitable *does* make such failures inevitable'. Furthermore, children are tracked (or streamed in our terminology) right from the beginning, thus receiving labels which will follow them right through their school career and will result in differential teaching which serves only to widen the gap even more between those judged as able, indifferent or poor at the age of six.

Rist (1970),[6] aware of the dearth of studies attempting to explain exactly how the school helps to reinforce the class structure of society reports results of an observational study of one class of ghetto children from the time they entered kindergarten to half way through their third year of schooling. As soon as they entered school, they were placed by their teacher in reading groups which reflected the social class composition within the whole group. These groups remained over the two and a half years of study and the teacher's differential behaviour towards each group was noticeable. Thus she had made initial presuppositions about the children on the basis of how she perceived their social background; these typifications were to have clear consequences for their socialization into the school system. Rist suggests the following stages in this process of differentiation and its consequences: the teacher (as in Becker's study) has an ideal type of pupil in mind, possessing those characteristics necessary for success; since the criteria could not be based on any kind of school attainment (as the children had only just entered school) the characteristics were related to social class. Thus early in their school career a subjective evaluation was being made as to the presence or absence of these desired characteristics and children were grouped accordingly; from then on, groups were treated differently according to whether they were seen as fast or slow learners. Markedly less attention and encouragement were offered to the slow group who in any case were not expected to succeed. Patterns of interaction between the teacher and children thus became rigid; later on in their school career the whole process would repeat itself but this time based on supposed evidence of success or failure - actual performance in reading. But we may ask what had contributed towards the success or failure of these children.

British studies reveal a similar tendency on the part of teachers to correlate educability with social class. Part of the NFER project[7] initiated in 1958 to study children's reading progress was concerned with teacher's attitudes towards children's home background, their expectations of children and their assessments of children's reading ability and their actual performance on a standardized reading test. Teachers' subjective assessments, based on their records of book level reached by each child, suggested that children from middle and upper working class areas had a noticeably higher reading ability than those in lower working class areas. Middle class pupils were rated highest. However, when tested on a standardized reading test (NFER's *National Survey 7+ Reading Attainment Test*) this marked difference was not apparent. Lower working class children were still inferior to the other two groups but there was no marked difference between middle class and upper working class children. It is possible then that teachers' assessments reflect the standards they themselves apply to pupils from different social environments: all working class children are expected to perform less well than middle class children, so they do, it seems. But are they in fact not given higher level books in the reading scheme? Are they held back because they are expected to be slow?

The studies referred to so far show how teachers categorize children according to what they know (or think they know) about their social background. Yet another important basis upon which teachers form their typifications of pupils is the school stream in which they are placed. In fact, stream and social class are often confounded or even taken to be parallel. Keddie (1971)[8] shows how the 'knowledge' teachers have of children, or the way in which they judge their ability is based on the stream in which they are placed as well as the social class from which they come. The ideal pupil is one who is seen to be easiest to teach, who is like the teacher and who accepts what the teacher offers unquestioningly. He presents no problems in class, works quietly and independently, doing what the teacher wants. He belongs to an A stream and stems from a middle class background. The less than ideal or problematic pupil is the one who questions what the teacher offers, demands to know the point of the activity and in fact is generally seen as unlike the teacher. As a participant observer in a large comprehensive school Keddie studied the progress of a Humanities Course designed to be taught as an undifferentiated programme across the whole ability range to a fourth year group, and eventually to be examined by mode 3 of the CSE and O level. She tries to show how, in fact, although the avowed aims of the course are to develop autonomy and independence, to allow children to work at their own speed and to learn to think for themselves, in practice it seems to be designed for an ideal pupil who already exists - the A stream pupil, who because of his middle class background already possesses the desired characteristics. Thus these pupils accept a new subject with a different label (Humanities, Socialization) which they readily take over from the teachers; the problem pupils are the C streamers who accept it less readily and want to recognize the content as History, Biology and so on with which they are more familiar.

One of the points of particular interest in the study is the way context affects teachers' typifications. Keddie sees teachers at the planning stage as acting within an *educationist context,* basing their ideas on what they deem theoretically desirable. In this context they hold ability and social class separate, condemning streaming and differentiation by ability because they are socially divisive. But in the other context in which they work, with a practical orientation, the *teacher context,* these ideals tend to be forgotten. Ability and social class are confused; treatment of pupils is different according to their stream. For example, teachers admit to preparing different material according to the stream they are going to teach even though the programme was designed to be taught right across the ability range; they even admit to insufficient preparation for the C streamers on the assumption that these pupils won't notice and won't ask questions. They are prepared to answer questions asked by A stream pupils which they would gloss over with C streamers as trivial, irrelevant or disruptive. Different kinds of behaviour and application are accepted and even expected, according to stream.

Further evidence showing how teachers typify pupils according to stream is found in the work of Hargreaves (1967)[9] and Lacey (1970)[10] both of whom based their observations on secondary schools in which they worked. In studying social relationships between teachers and boys in four fourth year streams in a secondary modern school, Hargreaves shows the gradual deterioration of relationships and segregation which seems to follow upon streaming. Pupils are judged as different in ability at the beginning of their secondary school career and are streamed accordingly. Interestingly enough, although teachers perceive the separate streams as homogeneous in ability, they are in fact, according to IQ scores, less homogeneous than when they were first grouped in this way (for example in the second year the D stream contained no boys with IQs above the median, whereas by the fourth year there were six). But this differentiation, now embedded in the organization of the school, has repercussions for other aspects of the pupils' behaviour. Because they come to see themselves as different (this self image is obviously reinforced by teachers' attitudes towards different streams), their relationships deteriorate so that there is marked hostility between the A and D stream pupils. As Hargreaves comments, academic and delinquescent subcultures develop, one subculture perceiving the other as a negative reference group, so that hostility and lack of communication between the two groups becomes marked. Teachers too have grown to expect little of their D stream pupils who adapt to these lower expectations with lowered aspirations and diminished interest in the school. Not only do teachers expect less of the D stream pupils academically, but they also expect them to behave badly and accordingly discriminate against them for example where school holiday trips are concerned. Little wonder then that their hostile attitude grows. Hargreaves is at pains to point out that it would be dangerous to generalize these findings to other secondary schools and this caution must be respected. But certainly the possible implications must not be overlooked.

Lacey's study takes place within a grammar school where boys are segregated on the basis of first year examination results into four streams before the beginning of their second year. Just as in Hargreaves' study, we see how the initial process of differentiation on the part of the teachers has repercussions for the boys' behaviour. Pupils in separate streams see themselves as progressively different, as is seen from a study of changing friendship patterns. Their interest and attitudes towards school, their acceptance of school values, as well as participation in extra-curricular activities takes on a different character according to whether they have been placed in a high or low stream. Lacey refers to this differentiation amongst pupils as polarization. He describes it as 'a process of subculture formation in which the school-dominated normative culture is opposed by an alternative culture . . . the antigroup culture' whose members reject school values, indulge in antisocial activities and so on.

Again it would be unwise to assume that streaming in all secondary schools would have similar repercussions as at Hightown Grammar described by Lacey. However these two field studies serve to draw our attention to some of the undesirable repercussions that can follow where teachers are tempted to typify children and when the ensuing categories become part of the structure of the school. Progressive retardation of those placed in lower streams leads to the following sequence of processes: reduced teacher expectations of low stream pupils, with less demanding academic tasks set for them; pupils' own level of aspiration is lowered because of lack of academic challenge and adequate or appropriate incentives; a sense of present and future failure follows, leading to an even more reduced level of aspiration, motivation and performance.

If differentiation in the form of streaming were removed, would these undesired consequences also be alleviated? Would the removal of formal institutionalized categories that are established within the school also result in the absence or reduction of unfair typifications made by teachers?

We have already seen however that even in classes of younger children where streaming does not take place (NFER study: Goodacre, 1968)[11] there is a tendency to typify according to perceived social class and consequently to assume a correlation between social class and ability, even where it does not manifestly exist. Some of Barker-Lunn's findings (1970)[12] show that teachers can in effect stream within their classes, very often with an assumed social class relationship, even when the school is formally unstreamed. The fact that children's progress can be affected by teachers' initial categorizations of them and assumptions about their ability and future chances of success, regardless of the way in which segregation is formally organized, still poses the all-important question to which an answer will be sought later: how exactly *do* typifications have the effect they do?

But before we come to the crucial question, it would be interesting to consider race as a further basis on which typifications are formed. It has long been recognized that immigrant children, new to British schools from their countries of origin, unfamiliar with the English language, the organization of British schools and methods of teaching as well of the way of British life in general are likely to be at a disadvantage in school achievement in comparison with native children. This disadvantage should in fact apply only to first generation immigrants whose difficulties might be predominantly linguistic. Yet should second and third generation children of immigrant parents experience similar problems when they have grown up in the same neighbourhood as their British peers, learning the same language, be it a Cockney or Liverpool dialect? Coard's study (1971)[13] suggests that their educational disadvantage lies not so much in their actual ability or the actual language they use as in their perceived ability. Teachers, Coard suggests, in his highly impassioned monograph, typify them as being low in ability, speaking a language inappropriate for school learning and it is thus the teachers themselves who help them to fail. Coard quotes figures obtained from the ILEA showing that a disproportionate number of West Indian children are placed in ESN schools: 28 per cent of all pupils in their ESN schools are immigrants, compared with only 15 per cent in ordinary ILEA schools. Further analysis of these figures is indeed alarming, since it reveals 75 per cent of all immigrants in ESN schools are West Indian even though West Indians form only half the immigrant population in ordinary schools. Since ESN schools are designed to enable less able children to cope with their low abilities and to make the best of them, Coard was forced to ask whether all these West Indian children needed to be socialized to a low scholastic achievement in this way or whether they had been wrongly placed because they were inappropriately judged by their teachers.

The West Indian child is seen to suffer under several crucial handicaps: firstly, low teacher expectations which affect the degree of help and encouragement his teacher is ready to offer; secondly the effect of low teacher expectations upon his own self-image and abilities, which in turn reduces his motivation to succeed in school, because he feels certain of failure. These effects are very reminiscent of those we found operating with lower working class British children. The West Indian child may be at an even greater disadvantage because of the widely held belief (supported by the views and interpretations of the evidence offered by Jensen[14] and Eysenck[15]) that negroes are in any case genetically inferior to whites. Whereas the explanation of working class failure is seen to lie in adverse home conditions and the rather patronizing argument that such children could have done better in more favourable conditions is permitted, the assumption that negroes are genetically inferior leads those who make it to the smug conclusion that whatever the school did for them, they could never succeed.

At the beginning of this chapter it was argued that some sort of categorization or typification was necessary and inevitable in any kind of social interaction. Several empirical studies were then examined to illustrate some of the bases on which teachers tend to typify children. However the consequences of such categorizations were found to be undesirable in that they had adverse repercussions for pupils' school careers.

Does this mean then that for some children typification is bound to have adverse effects which cannot be avoided? It would be useful to summarize the particular effects which typification by social class, stream and race can have upon pupils in order to see how undesirable consequences might be avoided. One highly useful concept to draw upon is Becker's notion of the ideal pupil. But by implication, any pupil who does not conform to this ideal is automatically a deviant in some way. He deviates from the ideal in terms of behaviour, being judged as unruly, disruptive in class; he is not expected to behave as well as the ideal pupil and in fact fulfils these expectations. Hargreaves' D stream boys are in fact unpopular with their peers if they conform to the teachers' standards of acceptable behaviour. Attitudes towards school of those pupils labelled as failures or belonging to an anti-school group tend to deteriorate so that they refuse to participate even in those activities which they enjoy and excel at. Because their status in school is low, they seek recognition elsewhere, often prematurely adopting adult roles, as did Lacey's pupils who drank and smoked on the school premises and refused to wear school uniform. With their rejection of school values and norms goes their rejection of anything the school might offer in terms of achievement and qualification. Teachers expect them to work slowly, to find difficulty in understanding material that is accepted by the ideal pupil, thus they are presented with less demanding tasks, their aspirations and motivation are reduced and eventually their performance is lowered. The self-fulfilling prophecy has indeed taken effect: pupils have conformed to the picture of themselves presented to them by their teachers. Naturally the same effect works positively: children of whom high expectations are made live up to these (A stream children succeed: does this mean that teachers were justified in placing them in an A stream or that teachers' expectations raised their aspirations, resulting in superior performance?) To talk of the effects of a self-fulfilling prophecy must involve some discussion of a pupil's self-image. If he sees himself as a failure, he becomes one. But what helps to create this self-image?

If we accept Mead's[16] notion of the self as a process rather than a structure, that is something constantly changing and developing during the course of the individual's interaction with other people, particularly with those who are important to him, we can see that the way in which he learns to see himself is influenced partly by the way in which others see him and act towards him. Because this concept of the self is essentially an active process, the individual is seen as acting towards the world and others in it, interpreting what confronts him and organizing his action accordingly.

If we consider this notion of the self in relation to pupils' self concepts in the classroom it follows that a child can only construct his self concept by reference to the behaviour of other people towards him, both teachers and peers. Interactionist theory (the framework within which Mead writes) predicts that children perceived unfavourably by teachers and peers will develop unfavourable self concepts, since through interaction they learn to see themselves as others see them - unfavourably.

Nash (1973)[17] working within this framework, put this hypothesis to the test in his study of teacher expectation. On the basis of preliminary observations made in a small primary school over a period of a year, he set out to discover whether pupils' self concepts, as illustrated by their behaviour in class, would vary according to the way in which they were judged by teachers. His hypothesis was that the behaviour of children in classes where they are perceived favourably by the teacher would be different from where they are perceived unfavourably. An investigation of how pupils behaved towards teachers they encountered in their first year of secondary schooling confirmed the hypothesis. Children who admitted to 'playing up' in class with those teachers they did not get on with and judged to be too soft or boring behaved well and were said to behave well by teachers who judged them more favourably. Nash suggests that teachers' expectations will also affect pupils' academic behaviour in a similar way in so far as the teacher's interaction with any pupil will contribute towards his self-concept. A further empirical investigation supported this view: children were asked to rate themselves and others according to their relative position in class. With very few exceptions their own estimate of their relative position in class corresponded to the teacher's view of them. It is interesting to note that when Nash examined friendship groupings, he found that cliques were made up predominantly of children either unfavourably or favourably perceived by their teacher. It seems then that teachers' views of children also affect their friends' views and expectations of them, so that an unfavourable self-image derived from teachers' views is even more reinforced by peers' views. Hargreaves too noted in his study of fourth year boys that those perceived unfavourably by teachers tended to form friendships with one another and not with those judged favourably by teachers and vice versa. Very few friendship bonds were found between A and D stream boys.

Pidgeon (1970)[18] has indicated two ways in which a teacher's attitudes and perceptions might influence pupils' behaviour: firstly, if he regards certain parts of his curriculum content to be above a pupil, he simply will not attempt to teach it, but will select something less demanding (*cf.* Keddie, 1970); secondly, if a pupil is led to believe that he is capable of little, he will have low expectations of himself, low motivation and consequently will achieve little. Nash's study lends support to these views: through their interaction with teachers, pupils discover the teachers' views of them by the way in which teachers treat them.

Bearing this in mind, we might argue that it is simply not feasible to say that lower working class children or West Indian immigrants perform poorly in school *because* they come from poor backgrounds unless we can confirm that they *still* perform poorly even when teachers behave towards them in exactly the same way as they behave towards children from higher social classes born of British parents. This clearly is an assumption that has never been tested, and in fact would be difficult to test, since subtle cues teachers might give to indicate a different judgement of their pupils are difficult to observe and record. But until such an investigation has been made it is dangerous to make such a judgement in good faith.

The discussion so far has shown how typifications made of pupils become embedded in the social context of the school and are developed and confirmed by social interaction. However there is another important category of influences which affect the way we as human beings judge others, which is just as relevant to teachers and pupils in school. A study of some aspects of person perception will show how certain factors affect an individual's judgement in addition to the way in which his judgements are affected by the social context. Interpersonal perception can be described as the forming of judgements by people about others, especially those judgements which concern us as social beings; such judgements are concerned with the ways in which people react and respond to others in thought, feeling and action. Whereas people tend to form snap impressions of others, taking an immediate dislike to another on first sight, for example, in a rather intuitive manner, most of the judgements we make are by inference, both from available evidence and from general principles we hold about human behaviour. It is partly because interpersonal perception is largely inferential that such factors within an individual can have such a distorting effect on his final judgement.

But before we examine this process at work in the classroom, it is useful to look at some of the features of perception in general. The way in which we perceive other people is necessarily different from our perception of objects, in that person perception is a two-way process: merely by perceiving another and interpreting his behaviour, we have an effect on the very behaviour we are observing which in turn affects our interpretation of it, whereas objects do not change when we perceive them. Object perception is a one-way process. Yet in spite of the fact that people change and usually have more emotional significance for us than objects, there is no fundamental difference between object and person perception since in both cases we use cues available to us and make inferences on the basis of such cues.

When we meet another person for the first time, as for instance, when a teacher confronts a new class of children at the beginning of the school year, he has certain cues immediately available to him - physical cues such as physique, dress, hair colour and style. These are static features in that they do not change under our scrutiny, and although they are of little actual value in helping to form accurate judgements, they nevertheless are used. When Secord (1958)[19] presented subjects with still photographs of people and asked them to describe the personalities of those represented in the photographs, most subjects did so readily and without apparent difficulty, producing surprisingly uniform descriptions. There do seem to be facial stereotypes which can help produce a distorted judgement based on no further evidence. Swarthy complexions tend to be disliked and unpleasant characteristics attributed to their owners. The kind of stereotype liked or disliked will of course depend on the context and even on fashion and current approval. It is sad to note in this connection, Coard's observation that his black pupils drew themselves as white; both negro and white pupils refused to see their teacher as black (although he was) because black skin apparently in the social context in which he was working was disliked and had unpleasant connotations. Stereotypes exist about physique, suggesting that fat people are conceived as happy, fun-loving, and thin people as anxious (Strongman and Hart, 1968);[20]

about voice, accent and dialect; about clothes and hairstyle (Gibbins, 1969).[21]
If teachers are equally susceptible to such stereotypes as the subjects tested
in the laboratory, inferences they make about their pupils are likely to be
wildly inaccurate and unfair. Dynamic cues such as facial expression, posture,
movement, gestures, rate of speech and intonation offer a similar array
available to the teacher on first meeting his class. But although these offer
some kind of information helping to create a first impression, they are
highly unreliable if further evidence is not available.

Luchins (1959)[22] confirms that first impressions tend to be long lasting
but are not the most accurate. Experiments showed that the first of two
conflicting descriptions of a boy determined the final impression but that the
second description tended to be ignored. It is to some extent reassuring that
the rigidity of first impressions can be reduced by warning the person making
the judgement of its dangers. If teachers are made aware of the misleading
nature of first impressions, they can be on their guard and ready to accept
further evidence. However, first impressions can easily be created by others'
prior judgements. Kelley (1950)[23] informed one group of students that a
speaker was a cold person, another group that he was a warm person, thus
creating prior expectations (or a mental set) for them. This mental set duly
had its effects in that those expecting a cold speaker saw him as such and
participated less in discussion than did the other group. Moreover their
impression of him was rigidly held and was not altered by subsequent
evidence. There are clearly many occasions when teachers are exposed to a
mental set of this kind created by others: in staffroom gossip where teachers
prepare a new colleague for troublemakers (Hargreaves, 1972)[24]; from
reports and record cards made available to him. Impressions offered by
others are particularly undesirable when we remember that children do in
fact behave differently according to the way in which teachers treat them
(Nash, 1973).[25] To be influenced by another teacher's impressions would
mean that the newcomer picked out and interpreted cues from a child's
behaviour that conformed to a prior judgement with the result that similar
teacher-pupil interaction would be perpetuated.

Kelley's study suggested that within a cluster of characteristics detected
in a person there is a central feature which is likely to affect one's whole
picture of him: a person described as warm was seen as generally acceptable
and likeable, for example. Asch (1946)[26] had already identified such a central
dimension and found in fact that whereas terms like warm and cold do seem
to colour one's whole picture of the person being judged, others like polite,
blunt are less central in that they have little effect on other dimensions. This
halo effect, as it has been called, seems to be a consistent feature of the way
in which most people make judgements of others; since most people expect

their ideas about others to be consistent, they expect those they rate highly on a valued trait to possess other positive traits to a similar degree.

If this is a general feature of person perception, then its implications for teachers are obvious: a teacher who sets high store by neatness, tidiness, well-spokenness, politeness might well perceive a child possessing these characteristics as more assiduous, interested and highly motivated than one devoid of them. Jackson (1964)[27] suggested that well-spoken, neatly dressed children tended to be found in A streams. Is this because they conform to the teacher's image of an A stream stereotype or because more intelligent children *are* neatly dressed and so on? Related to the halo effect is the tendency to base one's judgements on a logical error, that is to suppose that the possession of one characteristic automatically implies another. Such traditional beliefs as 'all redheads are hot tempered probably originated in this way. This kind of error can be perpetuated by accidental reinforcement: the case of one redhead who is in fact hot-tempered confirms the view previously held; from then on one notices redheads who have this characteristic, but not those devoid of it. Such impressions can also be confirmed by particular authority sources: many falsely held assumptions surely stem from one's parents whose word in early childhood is not doubted.

Just as in object perception, the way we judge other people can be affected by our needs and values. Several laboratory experiments have shown that where subjects value high status, they see those holding positions of high status as more powerful, more influential than those of lower status, even in the absence of any objective evidence (Thibaut and Riecken, 1955).[28] Similarly we tend to judge favourably those who fulfil our needs. Could it be that a teacher who feels a particular need for success and fear of failure will tend to judge more favourably on all characteristics those children who do well and thus satisfy the teacher's need for success? The likelihood of this is certainly strong enough for teachers to be aware of its possible dangers.

One question arising from this discussion of person perception is whether there are certain types of people who are more susceptible to such influences and less aware of them than others. It seems that everyone is *likely* to be affected by mental set, first impressions, halo effect, but that some people are more ready to recognize further evidence than others and to alter their judgements accordingly. Adorno *et al.* (1950)[29] in a large scale study of personality along an authoritarian-democratic continuum, identified the authoritarian type as one who, amongst other characteristics, tends to hold stereotyped views of other people, failing to recognize individual characteristics, once he has labelled a person and slotted him into a pre-existing category. If a teacher uses such categories as 'working class children', 'the culturally deprived', 'West Indian immigrants' and attributes certain characteristics to all those he sees as belonging to any of these groups, his judgements are bound to be biased. Stereotypes are in fact wrong most of the time and are over inclusive. People holding them will not recognize contrary evidence: Frenkel-Brunswik (1948)[30] describes such people as being 'intolerant of ambiguity', meaning that such people are not ready to accept new evidence if it is inconsistent with ideas they already hold and are slow even to perceive change. A further unfortunate attribute of the authoritarian type is that he is not self-reflective; he tends to shy away from analyzing his own feelings, motives, reasons for action and so is less likely to question the validity of the views he holds.

This fairly comprehensive picture of ways in which teachers' judgements can be distorted, and of their implications for children's development and achievement may seem rather daunting to a young teacher whose fear of making some of the mistakes warned against in this chapter could be so great that he would rather avoid making judgements at all than lay himself open to some of the consequences outlined here. But as was said earlier judging other people and forming impressions of them is not only an integral and inevitable part of human social life, it is also part of the teacher's responsibility. Rather than to shy away from making judgements it is important to attempt to make them, exercising care and discrimination, fully aware of how they might be made rigid by the social context and institutionalized nature of the school, and how they might be distorted by factors acting upon the individual. It is important to distinguish between the kinds of judgement being made - for instance, assessment of performance which is an integral part of teaching and estimation of effort or interest a child is putting into his work. This, as we see in the discussion of motivation, is far more difficult to do with any degree of accuracy and it is all too easy to imply some sort of moral failure on the part of a child who is deemed not to be trying as hard as he ought. Again, this does not mean that teachers should ignore motivational issues: it implies that encouragement is always worthwhile and that failure on the part of a child is not necessarily to be seen as reprehensible. It is very important not to confuse judgements of performance with judgements of worth as a person. A child is not better or worse as a person because he can read well or fails to learn to read, because he gains a higher or a lower intelligence test score or because he is deemed capable or otherwise of obtaining O levels. Yet because our society is achievement oriented, intelligence, often equated with academic success, is highly valued, and although as a concept it is morally neutral, it might mistakenly become associated with moral acceptability.

If in making judgements of children, teachers are to avoid this confusion, it is highly important for them to remember that respect for persons is an essential part of education, part of the teacher-pupil relationship. The notion of respect for persons involves treating children as individuals, recognizing and valuing their personal characteristics. It follows then that to see them simply as members of a category could result in overlooking these individual characteristics. For a child to develop and function as a person, he needs to be treated as one; he needs to be able to develop the kind of self concept that allows him to regard himself as of value. To treat children as persons in their own right, who are able to develop this kind of self image, involves regarding them as responsible for their own actions and therefore having some control over what they do. To see children as passive entities whose destiny is shaped by influences beyond their control is to lose sight of their power to be autonomous. Children who are regarded as doomed failures because of their lower working class background are not being accorded due respect because firstly they are being placed in a category where all members supposedly share common characteristics, and secondly they are not considered to have any control over their own future. If many of them are not *seen* to be able to determine their own career and in the school context are given less encouragement to do so, many will inevitably fail, thus conforming to the working class pattern, reinforcing the stereotype and confirming the self-fulfilling prophecy.

Included in the concept of developing autonomy is the notion of coming to terms with constraints imposed upon one's freedom, including one's own limitations. To be allowed to try, but then to fail, helps children to learn what their strengths and weaknesses are. It would be foolish to assume that all children could be equally successful at all things; part of developing as a person is to realize where one can succeed, but also to acknowledge that there are standards of excellence one might not reach and nevertheless to value others' achievements. For a teacher to prevent a child from attempting something that he thinks the child will fail at, is to omit to treat him as an autonomous being or to show him respect as an individual. However children do need some guidance from adults as to what they might be able to achieve; they need to know what the tasks involve that they hope to tackle and need to be encouraged to estimate their own abilities realistically. It would surely be just as misguided to let children think they could achieve what for them would be impossible as to prevent them from ever trying because of some preconceived notion of their abilities held by the teacher. The sad cases of children who for many years aspire to be doctors or teachers when they cannot cope very adequately even with the basis skills of literacy and numeracy acts as a reminder that one of the most important reasons for assessment and judgement by teachers is to help children to gain a realistic picture of their own capabilities and to make the most of them, while at the same time accepting their limitations. Recognizing and accepting one's own limitations is not incompatible with acknowledging standards of excellence in areas where one is not highly competent; if comparison between individuals is avoided, especially where it implies differential worth of persons, then it should be possible to achieve this idea in practice.

The main issues discussed in the rest of this book will be illuminated by those outlined in this chapter. Classification or categorization of children as those sharing common characteristics is clearly at stake in practical issues of equality and fairness. If we accept that justice means treating children similarly if they are the same, yet differently according to differences relevant to education, we imply that we are able to judge children in such a way as to pick out these differences or similarities - yet, as we have learned in this discussion, such assessment cannot be made without an awareness of its problems. Problems of categorization and assessment again arise when curriculum issues are considered. If different curricula are chosen as suitable for different groups of children, can we be sure that children's abilities and interests have been appropriately assessed? One of the problems created by a differentiated curriculum is that knowledge becomes hierarchically structured and some kinds of knowledge valued more highly than others. It can easily follow that children allowed access to so-called high status knowledge are deemed more worthy as persons than those offered mere 'common sense' knowledge (Barnes, 1969;[31] Young, 1970).[32]

The importance of flexibility in assessing children, readiness to accept fresh evidence in forming impressions or making judgements of them cannot be overemphasized since such judgements affect all our activities in school.

REFERENCES

1. A. Schutz, Collected Papers, Nijhoff, 1962, vol.1.
2. P.L. Berger and T. Luckman, *The Social Construction of Reality,* Penguin, 1966
3. B. Coard, *How the West Indian Child is Made Educationally Subnormal in the British School System,* New Beacon Books, 1971
4. H.S. Becker, 'Social class variations in the teacher-pupil relationship'. In *School and Society,* B. Cosin *et al.* (eds.), Routledge and Kegan Paul with Open University Press, 1952
5. E. Fuchs, 'How teachers learn to help children fail', *Transactions,* 1968, reprinted in *Tinker, Tailor . . . The Myth of Cultural Deprivation,* N. Keddie (ed.), Penguin, 1973
6. R.C. Rist, 'Student social class and teacher expectations: the self-fulfilling prophecy in ghetto education', HER, 1970
7. E. Goodacre, 'Teachers and their pupils' home background', NFER, 1968
8. N. Keddie, 'Classroom knowledge'. In *Knowledge and Control,* M.F.D. Young (ed.), Collier-Macmillan, 1971

9. D.H. Hargreaves, *Social Relations in a Secondary School,* Routledge and Kegan Paul, 1967
10. C. Lacey, *Hightown Grammar: The School as a Social System,* Manchester University Press, 1970
11. Goodacre, *op. cit.*
12. J.C. Barker-Lunn, 'Streaming in the primary school', NFER, 1970
13. Coard, *op. cit.*
14. A.R. Jensen, 'How much can we boost IQ and scholastic achievement?' HER, 1967
15. H.J. Eysenck, *Race, Intelligence and Education,* Temple Smith, 1971
16. G.H. Mead, see H. Blumer, 'Sociological implications of the thoughts of G.H. Mead *A.J.S.,* 1965-6', vol.71. In *School and Society, op.cit.*
17. R. Nash, *Classrooms Observed,* Routledge and Kegan Paul, 1973
18. D.A. Pidgeon, *Expectation and pupil performance,* NFER, 1970
19. B. Secord, 'The role of facial features in interpersonal perception'. In R. Tagiuri and L. Petrullo (eds.), *Person Perception and Interpersonal Behaviour,* Stanford University Press, 1958
20. K.T. Strongman and C.J. Hart, 'Stereotyped reactions to body build', *Psychological Reports,* 1968
21. K. Gibbins, 'Communication aspects of women's clothes and their relation to fashionability', *B.J. Soc.Clin.P.,* 1967
22. A.S. Luchins, 'Primary-recency in impression formation'. In *Order of Presentation in Persuasion,* Yale University Press, 1959
23. H.H. Kelley, 'The warm-cold variable in first impressions of persons', *J. Person,* 1950
24. D.H. Hargreaves, *Interpersonal Relations in Education,* Routledge & Kegan Paul, 1972
25. Nash, *op. cit.*
26. S.E. Asch, 'Forming impressions of personality', *Journal of Abnormal Social Psychology* 1946
27. B. Jackson, *Streaming: an Education System in Miniature,* Routledge & Kegan Paul, 1964
28. J.W. Thibaut and A.W. Riecklin, 'Some determinants and consequences of the perception of social causality', *Journal of Personality,* 1955
29. T.W. Adorno, E. Frenkel-Brunswik, D.J. Levinson and R.N. Sanford, *The Authoritarian Personality,* Harper and Row, 1950
30. E. Frenkel-Brunswik and R.N. Sanford, 'The anti-semitic personality: a research report'. In E. Simmel (ed.), *Anti-semitism - A Social Disease,* International University Press, 1948
31. D. Barnes *et al. Language, the Learner and the School,* Penguin, 1969
32. M.F.D. Young, 'An approach to the study of curricula as socially organized knowledge.' In *Knowledge and Control, op.cit.*

II Concepts of Intelligence

We saw in the last chapter some of the ways in which teachers judge children
and some of the dimensions on which they judge them. Although not the sole
aim of education - and some might argue, not even the main aim - nevertheless
the development of children's intellectual abilities is something that most
teachers hope to promote. If this is the case, judgements have to be made
about children's abilities so that an understanding of what these involve is
essential if children are to be fairly assessed.

For most teachers the term 'intelligence' is associated primarily with
notions of testing or measuring intellectual ability by some kind of
standardized test. Few pause to consider that measurement itself assumes
one particular concept of intelligence, but it is not the only one and perhaps
not even the most important one. The same teachers would not feel, however,
that they had to know a child's IQ (test score) in order to say whether he
usually acted intelligently in the playground or laboratory for instance. A still
further issue is at stake when teachers are planning appropriate work for their
pupils where one of their aims is usually to promote intellectual development. This does not mean to help them gain a higher test score, but to
develop the ability to grasp relationships, to think logically and to deal
effectively with their environment to the best of their ability. These everyday
issues with which teachers are faced indicate at least two different
perspectives from which mental growth or intelligence can be viewed: the
psychometric view, concerned with the measurement of abilities, and the
developmental view, concerned with the structure of abilities. Which
approach to mental growth is adopted by investigators depends on the
purposes of the investigation, but if teachers are to use theories of mental
growth to guide practice they must see the two perspectives as essentially
complementary, not contradictory. Both approaches provide useful starting
points for the assessment and interpretation of human mental abilities on the
one hand and afford practical guidance in planning of work, assessing
children's progress on the other, provided that teachers understand the basis
of the theoretical framework.

But before we go on to look at these two broad theoretical perspectives,
it will be useful to look at the very general concept of intelligence, which is
both evaluative and descriptive. It is used evaluatively in that it is considered
a prized ability - it is thought better (more valuable) to be intelligent than

unintelligent for obvious reasons. It must be stressed however that the term 'intelligence' is a *morally* neutral one; there is nothing inherently moral in being highly intelligent. Such misuse or misunderstanding of the term can have unfortunate repercussions for those about whom judgements are being made. In a school system that values intelligence and achievement above all else, teachers might easily be misled into judging an intelligent pupil as a better person all round.

If on the other hand, we use the term 'intelligence' purely descriptively we need to know what characteristics are being picked out, and how to recognize intelligent behaviour.

Ryle[1] suggests that to act intelligently is to think about what one is doing; thus it would not be possible to act intelligently by accident or by chance. A young child for example might accidentally do something that for his age would appear exceptionally intelligent, but if it were not incorporated into his learning patterns and were not repeatable - if he could not yet learn from his own experience, this would not count as intelligent behaviour, but only a chance happening. Thinking about what one is doing is clearly seen in the performance of motor skills which very often give the appearance of being performed automatically, as if by habit. Yet it is only because the performer has thought about what he was doing in learning the skill that he can cope with disruptions, even serious ones, without a subsequent breakdown in performance. A skilled driver is usually able to cope with an unexpected hazard on the road because he is thinking about his actions even though performance under normal conditions appears so smooth as to be deceptive.

It is important not to confuse the ability to carry out a complex skill which has been learnt, with *any* kind of complex routine. MacIntyre[2] suggests that this would be a mark of intelligent behaviour; if it is, then the statement must certainly be qualified. Sticklebacks carry out highly complex routines as in courting and mating behaviour, yet this is instinctive and unadaptable rather than intelligent. Similarly obsessives perform such complex routines that one minor false step causes them to go back to the beginning of the whole ritual again - hardly intelligent behaviour since it is both maladaptive and unadaptable. This kind of complex routine fails to be intelligent because it betrays no intentionality or purpose. It is merely fixed and rigid and could not be adapted to suit any particular purpose.

It seems then that intelligent behaviour must be intentional and that it must be adaptable to a specific purpose in the mind of the person himself. A machine could be programmed to carry out apparently purposeful activities but could not be called intelligent on these grounds. Behaviour judged as intelligent must of course be related to the age of the person concerned or to any special problems that he has. Thus it would not be particularly intelligent of a normal adult to climb on to a stool to get an object out of reach, but it would be considered intelligent for a two-year old to do so.

It is a sad fact that all too often physically handicapped children are considered to belong to a different species when judgements of intelligence are are being made. One eleven-year old blind pupil was praised as highly intelligent because she showed she could count the number of studs on an upholstered armchair - an ability we should not consider remarkable in a normal six-year old.

If intelligent behaviour is marked by intentionality, adaptability, the ability to profit from experiences, the ability to think about what one is doing, these criteria might provide teachers with a useful frame of reference within which to observe children in situations other than classroom ones - around the school, on their way to and from school, in the playground, on the playing fields etc. But not all the information needed in order to assess children's behaviour is observable. What must also be discovered is why children act as they do and whether they have their own reasons for action. These issues necessarily lead to a discussion of motivation and reasons for action.

The criteria suggested however do emphasize the active nature of learning; it is not enough for children to develop intelligence, but also to *use* it to think for themselves in every kind of situation not only in school. If children are taught to think for themselves in school, that is, are taught to develop independence in this respect then there is every hope that regardless of ability differences they will continue to use their intelligence and to act as rational human beings after they have left school.

The two theoretical perspectives on the nature of intelligence can now be discussed in detail, together with some of their implications for education.

Psychometry is concerned with mental measurement. The main interests of psychologists such as Galton, Spearman, Burt lay in examining individual differences in measured intelligence and in attempting to discover what kinds of abilities go to make up what we call intelligence. Around the turn of the century there arose a pressing educational need to detect those children who, because of apparent dullness, were not able to profit from normal schooling. When Binet was asked in 1904 by the Paris Education Authorities to assist in discovering such children, he began to develop individual tests of ability designed specifically to rank children of the same age according to their relative brightness. Without going into detail on the history of mental testing, suffice it to note that many more individual and later group tests were developed for similar purposes: The Army 'Alpha and Beta' tests in 1916 to test and place recruits to the US Army; after the war and in the 1920s such tests were used to help to select bright children for secondary schools, able adults for Civil Service positions and for similar selective entrance purposes. They were designed then to measure certain cognitive abilities which were thought to be largely independent of direct teaching and although it was never claimed that purely innate capacity could be measured, the tests were assumed to give some indication of a child's innate ability to reason.

Some definitions of intelligence reveal the kinds of ability intended to be tapped by such tests. Burt's definition of intelligence (1955)[3] as an 'innate, all-round cognitive ability' suggests firstly an emphasis on abilities a child is born with although in a later article (1966)[4] Burt reminds his critics that he never denied the importance of environment. Secondly it implies that these abilities are of a general, non-specific nature (*cf.* Spearman's 'g' factor) and thirdly that they are cognitive only, excluding by definition motivational elements.

Vernon (1969)[5] sees intelligence as referring mainly to the ability to grasp relationships and to think symbolically again with an emphasis on the cognitive side. But we must remember that a person's inclinations and motivation are probably just as important in determining his achievements, including achievement on an intelligence test, as his abilities. Stott (1966)[6], for example, suggests that a child's ability to solve any problems, including those in an intelligence test, depends partly on the 'effectiveness motivation' he has developed in the past. This issue will be raised again in our discussion of motivation in Chapter III. Since however it is far easier to observe and measure what a person can do than to assess his willingness to do it, the effort he puts into it or his reasons for doing it, psychologists have tended to concentrate on the cognitive and neglect the motivational components of intelligence. It is therefore interesting to come across an early definition of intelligence by Wechsler (1944)[7] who includes 'acting purposefully' in his definition. This neglected area of motivation will be discussed later.

In order later to discover how the concept of intelligence a teacher holds might affect his educational practices it will be useful here to pursue some further issues raised by a psychometric approach to intelligence and, in particular, the debate over the relative overriding importance of innate or environmental influences on the development of intelligence which became known as the nature-nurture controversy. Experimental data, adduced to support each side of the argument, was gathered largely from twin studies. If test scores of identical twins correlate highly whether the children were brought up in the same family or in a totally different environment, then it could be argued that environment must have little if any influence on measured intelligence. Burt's results (1966)[8] showed that despite wide differences in the environmental conditions of the identical twins in his sample who were brought up separately the correlations for intelligence test scores were notably high: Rho = 0.874 as compared with 0.925 for those brought up together. His conclusion was that intelligence, when adequately assessed, is largely though not entirely dependent on genetic constitution. Newman *et al.* (1937)[9] in the USA found far lower correlations for the scores of identical twins brought up separately: for twins brought up together Rho = 0.91; for pairs brought up apart Rho = 0.67.*

Much research was devoted to the exploration of the determinants of correlations between test scores. Burt's critical summary of twin studies (1966) shows the kind of argument presented. More recently the nature-nurture debate has been reopened in a different context - that of racial differences. Jensen's outspoken article (1969)[10] on racial differences in measured intelligence, with its implications of negro inferiority, was followed by a series of attacks on his assumptions, methodology and conclusions. What originated in the 1930s as a theoretical discussion on the relative importance of genetic and environmental determinants of intelligence seems to have been revived as an ideological and even political debate over the supposed intellectual inferiority of some races, the point of which it is difficult to see since it offers no help to teachers who have to deal with particular children rather than with generalities.

The risks involved in a limited interpretation by teachers of this kind of finding cannot be overemphasized. If it is assumed that intelligence is largely innately determined then it could easily follow that these innate differences can be accurately measured at a given age; on the basis of measured intelligence children might then be offered a different kind of education according to what was supposed to be their innate fixed intellectual capacities, as indeed was suggested by the Norwood Committee in 1943.[11] Yet further implications for a differential educational programme would arise in our now multiracial society, namely that the intellectual status of various immigrant groups could be assessed and a programme offered them according to test results. It is in fact Bernard Coard's contention (1971)[12] that West Indian children are made ESN in English schools because, as indicated by their measured ability, they are capable only of limited educational achievement. Yet since no psychologist denies the effect of environmental interaction, however small, on the development of intelligence, surely the task of teachers is to understand the nature of environmental influences since the school's job is to create an educational environment even though it can do nothing about innate capacities.

*The values of Rho range from +1 to -1; for general purposes, a value greater than 0.5 in either direction suggests a high degree of correspondence.

Hebb's view of intelligence A and B[13] suggests the importance of early stimulation for future growth. He conceives of intelligence A as the innate potential for development; this is the genetic component and since it can never be observed or measured, is purely a hypothetical construct. Intelligence B is seen as 'the functioning of a brain where development has gone on'. Intelligence A then gives the potential for growth, but is manifested only if and when growth takes place; since growth is not the same as maturation it depends on some sort of nurture in the form of environmental stimulation. Hebb's own work on brain damaged patients suggested that early stimulation was most important; those suffering from later brain damage were far less impaired in terms of thought processes and problem solving than those who suffered similar damage early in life.

This hypothesis received confirmation from two further sources, again by work stemming from Hebb's laboratory. Experimental groups of rats were reared in a 'stimulating' environment, that is one where the animals had freedom to roam and explore, where plenty of interesting objects were provided to arouse curiosity. Control groups were reared in a restricted environment, that is in cages where they had little freedom and no new objects to explore. On subsequent tests, the experimental groups were found to be superior in maze learning (a kind of rodent intelligence test). The wide variety of stimulus variation experienced by the experimental animals early in life had given them a head start over the impoverished controls.

The second source of positive evidence supporting the early stimulation hypothesis was the vast amount of work on sensory deprivation, or reduced sensory input, to use the later and more accurate term.[14] Subjects (humans and various kinds of animal) deprived of sensory stimulation (visual or auditory input; tactile stimulation) in early life were found to remain permanently retarded while even adult subjects (as in the well known coffin experiments) showed impaired vision, impaired problem solving ability etc. for some time after they emerged from the restricted and monotonous environment to which they had agreed to be subjected.

If then early stimulation is required for the functioning brain to grow, as it seems certainly is the case, this suggests that however small the effect of the environment might be on the development of innate potential as compared with an inborn component, it is the quality and nature of the environmental influences that are important. And for teachers concerned with practice no less than psychologists concerned with providing a theoretical explanation, the important question is: what exactly is it that makes an environment stimulating for a particular child at a particular stage of development?

This sort of question which arises from Hebb's work seems to provide a useful link with our other broad perspective on intelligence - the developmental approach of Piaget. It is partly because of the influence of Piaget's work that educators have begun to think of intelligence as more than a mental faculty which simply matures as children grow up. Piaget[15] has conceived intelligence in terms of a cumulative building up of complex schemata through the impact of the growing organism and the environment on one another. It is important to consider the origins of the Piagetian approach to intelligence and to remember that whereas intelligence tests were practical tools used to obtain data for educational purposes, Piaget's tasks were designed to test his hypotheses about the child's thinking and concept development. They were intended to explore and reveal differences which became apparent at various stages in any one child's development and were concerned therefore with intra-individual rather than inter-individual differences.

The Piagetian conception of intelligence is then essentially developmental and structural in nature. In his system, intelligence is broadly conceived as an adaptation to the physical and social environment. Since it is developmental, it shows the acquisition of knowledge (in terms of adaptation to the environment) along certain stage sequences. As children develop and interact with their environment, the structures built at an earlier stage evolve gradually into an integral part of the structure of a later stage. For example, an infant first learns very slowly about the permanence of objects - that a ball he has been playing with does not cease to exist when he cannot see it. This notion of permanence, his first step towards invariance of objects, is necessary to the notion of conservation of quantity which is learned during the stage of concrete operations. If the learning of one concept (in our example, permanence) is essential to the understanding of more complex concepts at a later stage of development then it follows that the sequence of development must remain constant. The permanence of objects could not be learnt *after* conservation of quantity since the understanding of permanence is a necessary condition of conservation. Similarly concrete operations form a basis upon which formal operations can later be learnt. To understand the notion of ratio the child has to be able to compare different quantities and consider them in relation to one another rather than an absolute.

In Piaget's detailed description of the stages through which children pass from birth onwards, it emerges that what is of particular interest to him is not so much the products of thought, such as the answer a child gives to a conservation problem, but the processes of thought, namely the methods children use to respond to their environment or the kinds of attempts they make to solve problems set them. This suggests a qualitative approach to the development of intelligence characteristic of the interest in developmental sequences within any one child rather than a quantitative approach concerned with comparing measured differences between children.

The period of sensory motor or practical intelligence is characterized by a gradual moving away from a world in which the self is undifferentiated from the environment, to one which the child can experience and begin to understand through his actions. He comes to this understanding by first of all making purely perceptual and motor adjustments to objects about him. During this period (lasting for roughly the first two years of the child's life) he is seen to develop from an organism governed purely by his reflexes to a human being whose behaviour is beginning to show intentionality. A young infant will for example first look at his own hands when he drops an object he is playing with and only gradually after much experience in handling objects will he begin to search for it when it is no longer in sight. But he is so far able only to perform actions, not represent them; his understanding of the world is limited to his own physical interaction with it. When he begins to go beyond the purely motor stage, the beginnings of some symbolic representation are apparent.

The child now enters the stage of pre-operational thought in which he no longer has to rely on action alone but can cope with representation. One example of representation is pretending: a child who pretends that a newspaper is a pillow will lie down with his head on it and 'go to sleep'. The pre-operational period is characterized still by egocentrism: a child cannot imagine what an object would look like from a different angle - he would draw it as it looks to him if asked to imagine himself in another position; he still tends to centre on only one aspect of a situation, such as the height of a column of water, disregarding its breadth. Thought at this stage tends to be static because the child cannot understand the link between successive conditions and see them as a coherent whole. It is not unnaturally very similar to sensory motor intelligence upon which it is based.

But as the child begins to decentre, i.e. to be able to focus upon more than one aspect of a situation simultaneously and to see things from other points of view he gradually develops the notion of invariance without which more mature logical thought cannot proceed. During this period he shows the first signs of being able to deal with the potential as well as the actual in that he can predict what *will* be the case even if he has not yet experienced it (if confronted with say a series of straws of different lengths placed in order from short to long, he will be able to predict

accurately that to continue the series he will need a longer one). But he
still cannot say what *might* be the case; he cannot yet deal with the
hypothetical which properly belongs to the stage of formal operations.
Indeed this is probably the most important general characteristic of formal
operational thought. Only as a result of being able to deal logically with
reality, the concrete, the here and now, can the adolescent, as he now is,
conceive of reality as a part of what might be. At this stage he has already
come to grips with the problem of stabilizing what he senses to the wider
issues of imagining and hypothesizing. This implies that he must set up a
series of hypotheses which in turn he confirms or rejects. This process
clearly rests on the notion of invariance which he has already learnt and
on the ability to perform combinatorial operations (as in the metal rod
experiment).[16] Similarly classification, seriation, correspondence which he
learnt at the concrete stage now enable him to develop propositional
thinking: he is able to spot the logical flaw in the following by being able
to form sets and subsets; that is to classify.

> All Xs are Ys
> Here is a Y
> Therefore it is an X

According to Piaget's scheme then a child is seen as developing through
several stages of thinking, each more complex than the last and each one
built upon and incorporating the previous one. Piaget postulates no fixed
age limits for this development but maintains that the sequence is
constant. The ages he suggests give only very rough guidance. Nor does he
imply that everyone goes through all the stages and finally achieves formal
operations. Many adults stop short of this. Development does not come
about by maturation alone, although it is a maturational process. A child
of four could not cope with propositional logic for example. It has been
stressed all along that it is through interaction with the environment that
the child develops his ability to think, or his intelligence; environment
clearly plays an important part, but Piaget insists that creating a richer
environmental experience for the child will not of itself accelerate his
intellectual growth.

   We are now in a position to be able to compare and contrast the
Piagetian and psychometric approaches to the theoretical study of
intelligence[17] and then consider their applications to education. Certain
conceptual similarities become apparent when the origins of intelligence
are considered. The controversy over the contribution of genetic factors
to intelligence for instance has already been highlighted in studies taking a
psychometric approach. Attempts have even been made to assess the
proportion of intelligence attributable to genetic factors.

Piaget too although he does not lay the same kind of emphasis on the problem acknowledges the importance of genetic factors for the development of intelligence. It follows from an acceptance of genetic factors as part of intelligence that maturation also plays an important part. Piaget as we have seen puts more emphasis on this than do the psychometricians.

In both approaches rationality stands out as the most central characteristic of intelligence. The ability to reason is being tested by such problems as CAT:KITTEN as DOG: ?   which shows whether the child can perceive relationships; in items such as the odd-man-out type the child is required to recognize which items belong to one class and which is excluded, showing whether he can classify. Or again he is required to continue a number series to show whether he can perceive relationships between numbers, for example 1, 4, 13, 40, 121. . . . For Piaget reasoning or logical thinking is the essence of mature intelligence; he is concerned not only to find out whether children can give a rational solution to a problem but also and mainly to investigate the thought processes children adopt in trying to solve the problem.

The two approaches also show a methodological similarity in that their means of investigation are not strictly experimental. Experimental treatment would be inappropriate for a psychometric approach since setting up control and experimental groups of human beings and contriving conditions to influence the development of intelligence would clearly raise ethical issues. The nearest approximation to this is seen in the purely experimental techniques adopted by Hebb in his animal studies and in the work he prompted in the field of sensory deprivation both of which have a bearing on studies of intelligence. Investigations of intelligence test scores are, as with twin studies, correlational. For Piaget's work traditional experimental methods as such would be quite inappropriate since he is concerned with individuals, not broad differences between groups of individuals. Thus a clinical or natural history approach where the adult talks to one or very few children lends itself most appropriately to his aims.

Although the two approaches do not suggest fundamental differences in the nature of intelligence they do nevertheless examine intelligence from two different perspectives; such differences can be found in the nature of the genetic component, the course of mental growth, the relative parts played by nature and nurture and the nature of the environment in early mental development. Both acknowledge some genetic determinant and yet the function of this is seen differently. For Piaget this genetic determinant refers to the stage sequence notion: the individual is constitutionally programmed to pass through the stages in an invariant order, though neither the rate nor the age at which he does so is fixed. In the psychometric approach the genetic determinant is taken to result from the chance combination of genes at conception - chance, because each parent contributes only half his genetic components to the infant. As mentioned earlier, a major part of measured intelligence in later life is attributed to this genetic factor (*cf.* Hebb's intelligence A).

Furthermore the approaches differ in what they observe about mental growth. Piaget is interested in the nature of mental structures and examines how new abilities arise out of earlier ones; he is concerned with the quality of mental growth and the processes of thought. Mental growth is seen quite differently from a psychometric perspective which lays more empahsis on the rate of growth than its nature. Using correlational methods and data it is claimed to be possible to predict at the age of 4 with 50 per cent accuracy the level of measured intelligence at the age of 17; and at 8 with 80 per cent accuracy. This kind of statistical calculation led to the assumption that measured intelligence at the age of 11 would predict with almost complete accuracy the level of intelligence at 17 - which may well be statistically correct. What does not follow, as practice has shown, is that the level of intelligence at 16 or 17 will correlate highly with school achievement. Tests are of course constructed using scaled items which tap different levels or quality of thought. But differences are concealed in the final numerical score, since points are given for the correct answer rather than for the type of answer or process of reasoning.

The nature-nurture controversy has already been discussed in relation to the psychometric approach where proportion of variants in intellectual ability has been attributed separately to heredity or environment. In contrast to this rather static view Piaget sees the contributions of nature and nurture as active in the way they control various mental activities. In his view we inherit the processes of assimilation and accommodation. Assimilation processes are prompted from within (nature), whereby the individual takes in new experiences from the outside and adapts or accommodates to them, thus building new schemata by revising or restructuring his former knowledge. Accommodation processes are thus affected by the environment. The two are constantly interacting (the process of equilibration) and depending on the particular mental activity, their relative contribution will fluctuate. Symbolic play such as pretending is largely assimilative whereas imitation by its very nature is largely a matter of accommodation.

A fourth important difference is seen between the two approaches in the emphasis placed on the role of the environment in early mental development. Hebb as we have seen lays enormous stress on an environment rich in variation of experience in the early years. Yet further research has shown the importance of health factors for mental growth even before birth, for example the diet of the mother during pregnancy and of the infant from three to six months after birth (Harrell *et al.*, 1955;[18] Stoch, 1967);[19] oxygen availability at birth. It is established too that certain diseases and drugs during pregnancy can have a serious retarding effect on the mental development of the baby. Young infants have been shown to need a rich variety of visual, tactile and motor experiences. A child needs to explore his environment to become familiar with different sizes, shapes, weights; he needs to gain different tactile experiences and to recognize by touch what is hard, soft, furry in texture; what is cold, hot etc. To profit from a stimulating environment he needs a background of security as a base and the freedom to explore, unencumbered, what is around him in order to find out what his world is like and how it works. The emphasis on early experience as will be seen later led indirectly to the introduction of pre-school enrichment programmes for so-called deprived children. If evidence of a positive and negative nature suggests that certain factors retard mental growth and certain others tend to accelerate it, it follows that this information could be useful in guiding favourable child-rearing techniques and planning early school programmes.

Piaget's view of the role of the environment in development is rather different, in that it is built into his whole conception of intelligence. By stressing the biological nature of the development of intelligence, with its emphasis on maturation, he does not reduce the importance of environmental interaction. On the contrary, his theory is based on the notion that intellectual development cannot take place without interaction with the environment; intelligence for him *means* constructing one's knowledge of the world; therefore environmental factors are the medium through which intelligence can develop at all; it must therefore be influenced by the constraints of this medium. But although environmental interaction forms an integral part of the growth of intelligence, Piaget does not acknowledge that an increased concentration of specific environmental experiences, as in training techniques, can accelerate mental growth since it is constrained by biological and maturational factors. Experimental attempts have been made to contradict this view (Churchill, 1958)[20] but results remain equivocal, although Sigel *et al.* (1966)[21] found that special experience helped children who were at a transitional stage. Cross cultural evidence supports the invariants of the stage sequence notion; yet different kinds of experience seem to suggest a retarding effect in some areas (Greenfield, 1966).[22]

Now that the characteristics of the two perspectives have been outlined,

together with their similarities and differences it is appropriate to examine
their educational implications. It is a pity that in most introductory
textbooks of educational psychology under the chapter heading
'Intelligence' we find only a discussion on intelligence testing with an
outline of the psychometric conception of intelligence. It is not surprising
if teachers come to hold this as the only approach, since work on Piaget
is almost always discussed in a quite different section of the book, under
the heading of 'Development of thinking' or 'Concept development in
young children' or simply 'The work of Jean Piaget'. However changes that
have been taking place in schools over recent years, particularly in the
education of young children, bear evidence to the impact of Piaget's work
on educational practice.

First however let us explore the implications of the psychometric view
for selection and grouping, teaching method, the curriculum and
motivation. If intelligence is thought to be determined largely by innate
factors, then it follows that children of different abilities can be sorted out
by some kind of test and if it is deemed appropriate to teach the same
'kinds' of children together in a homogeneous class, to group like abilities
together for educational purposes. This would be possible, however, only
if tests could predict fairly reliably what a child's ability would be like
some years in the future. Evidence to support the reliability of prediction
is found for example in the work of Bloom,[23] though contrary evidence is
quoted by Vernon.[24]

It was this interpretation of intelligence that influenced the Norwood
Committee when they made their recommendations for the future of
secondary education in 1943.

Tripartism thus became the dominant pattern of secondary education
after 1944 although it was not built into the Education Act of that year.
And indeed it seemed at the time a logical argument to say that if children
do differ in ability then it was only fair to treat them differently. On this
kind of argument equality of educational opportunity seemed to be based,
as we shall see in Chapter VII; unfortunately many other factors were
overlooked, not least the effects of environmental influences on test
performance and measured intelligence. Not only were children selected
for different kinds of education, but once in the supposedly appropriate
secondary school, they were again grouped by ability into streams designed
to create classes of a fairly narrow ability range, so that the teacher's job
would be easier in that all children would learn at the same pace. Junior
schools too were affected by the new system of secondary selection:
streaming was even more widely practised than before, so that children in
A streams could race ahead to secure coveted selective places in grammar

schools.

Grouping children like this, both within the school and within the system, led not surprisingly to the attachment of ability labels to children. The A streams were the intelligent who could do well and who needed stimulating work and experienced teachers; the lowest streams were those who by nature were low on the intelligence scale and could never be expected to achieve very much in school. Teachers' judgements tended to be influenced by such expectations, as later research has shown (Goodacre, 1968;[25] Rist, 1970;[26]) so that even without their awareness possibly they tended to underestimate those labelled as 'dull', to provide less interesting and stimulating work for them in the firm belief that whatever they did for the children, they would never be able to learn: a fixed view of intelligence in the extreme.

Ability differences soon came to be associated with social class; teachers expected children from middle class families to be bright. As Jackson (1964)[27] and Douglas (1964)[28] showed, a preponderance of middle class children yet very few lower class children found themselves in A streams.

Intelligence tests as so far developed seem to test mainly those abilities (for example, certain kinds of verbal ability) which middle class children develop apparently more easily than those from the lower working class. Such test results tend to confirm the link between class origin and measured ability. Measured intelligence was now no longer a statistical construct; it was fast becoming a social construct, with all the overtones of labelling and typification which have recently been brought into the limelight by sociologists.

During the 1950s attention turned from the innate roots of intelligence to the importance of environmental factors during the early years. One of the consequences of this recognition was the interpretation of the failure of working class children who did not develop as their early potential had predicted in terms of lack of stimulation in the home. As a result children who failed in school, especially lower working class children, came to be known as deprived or even culturally deprived (Riessman, 1962).[29] Intellectual stimulation was thought to be so meagre in some families that even those innate abilities with which a child was endowed could not develop sufficiently for him to profit very much from the education provided for him. Ample research, as we shall see in Chapter VII, showing how working class pupils failed to gain places in an A stream or a grammar school, left school early, failed to seek opportunities offered by further education, all lent support to the deprivation hypothesis. The picture was a very pessimistic one: if a child, especially a girl, happened to be born into a large lower working class family as a middle child she would stand little chance of developing her intelligence and profiting from education (Little and Westergaard, 1964).[30]

In the USA research of a different kind was sparked off by this same deprivation hypothesis: if early environment is so important for the development of intelligence, the argument ran, and there are many families who do not or cannot provide their young children with appropriate stimulation in the early years, then the school must intervene and do it for them. In this way were launched intervention or compensatory programmes such as Headstart, High Horizons etc., where children were given special preschool experience intended to rouse them intellectually and compensate for the deficiencies of the home, thus preparing them for school proper. This practical approach showed a more optimistic attitude than did some of the research being done in Britain at the same time. Yet early intervention programmes failed because they were founded on a mistaken view of cultural deprivation. Children may well have come from an intellectually stultifying environment, but the way to salvation was not to be via a different culture, the mainstream culture of white Americans imposed upon all children. Bernstein (1968)[31] came near a solution when he suggested that what was needed was not compensatory education but education itself.

To consider now the effects of a psychometric view of intelligence within the classroom. Since in this view it is not intellectual development that is stressed but rather the accumulation of knowledge and skills to be assessed quantitatively, teaching tends to be largely instructional; knowledge is selected by the teacher and directly imparted to pupils who are passive learners, absorbing what is offered to them and reproducing what the teacher knows, if they are successful; or, if they are failures, they are passive non-participants in what goes on in the classroom. This model of teaching sees the teacher as the one who does most of the talking - he it is who takes the opportunity of using, practising and extending his language skills, rather than his pupils who are required to give one word answers to specific questions.

Curriculum content is selected for children according to their ability. The former sentiments of the Norwood Committee still seem to be followed in many secondary schools where the A stream or band is offered an 'academic' curriculum including one or more foreign languages, perhaps also Latin; specialized courses in Physics, Chemistry, Biology in addition to the basic traditional curriculum subjects such as Mathematics, English, History, Geography. Little opportunity is given to these pupils to pursue practical subjects such as Handicraft, Art, Home Economics, Child

Welfare etc., which are reserved for the less able who are not expected to be able to cope with the supposedly more theoretical disciplines. Thus develops a hierarchical view of the curriculum with a stratification of knowledge of the kind criticized by Young (1971).[32]

Motivation on this view is usually extrinsic. Children learn because of the reward to be gained in the form of examination successes, prizes, general approval. If they do become interested in what they learn for its own sake this is probably a chance matter.

Piaget's view of intelligence as developmental implies a very different model of education: one whose function is to guide the developing child through the stages of intellectual growth, providing him with an appropriately structured curriculum in terms of learning sequences, yet allowing him freedom to discover and structure knowledge for himself. This naturally has implications also for teaching method, motivation and assessment. Unlike the psychometric approach which allows children to be grouped and taught as a group according to measured ability, what follows from the developmental approach is essentially individualized teaching and learning. Not all children of a given age level have reached the same level of cognitive development, nor indeed does an individual child show the same cognitive structures or develop at the same rate across all fronts, and he may be at one stage in one conceptual area and at a different one in another. To try to teach a whole class of children as if they were all at one stage in everything is to deny the importance of individual rates of growth as revealed by Piagetian research: for those children who are not yet ready to cope with the concepts involved the content will mean little and they will make little or no progress; for those who have already mastered those concepts it will mean nothing but repetition of what they already know, with little or no novelty to activate their minds. Learning on this model of intelligence must by its very nature then be individualized; and since the classroom is the environment in school with which the child interacts to structure his intelligence, teaching methods must allow for this interaction. Discovery and enquiry methods are best suited to this but to offer optimum opportunities for intellectual growth, the material must be geared to the child's own stage of development. Again, the appropriate dimension of discovery is important. As Richards (1973)[33] reminds us, discovery learning need not always be at a concrete level as it is for younger children. Adolescents discover too but symbolically through the use of language, by exploring hypotheses either alone or in cooperation with their peers.

We saw that on our other model it was the teacher who did most of the talking in the classroom, in imparting knowledge to children and questioning them on specific points of fact. Since children's language conveys their thought (although it is not synonymous with thought) to listen and to get to understand children's language is one of the first priorities of a teacher. Children's modes of thinking make them in a way cognitive aliens to adults so in order to diagnose the stage of thinking they have reached, teachers clearly must learn to communicate with children and from what they say, infer what their conceptual world is like - the method Piaget himself used. The younger the child, the more tortuous his thinking and the more bizarre his world will appear to adults (in a child's world for example the sun and moon follow him as he is walking along; dreams fly in thorugh the window; everything that moves is alive) and unless the teacher is able to talk to the child at his own level no appropriate discourse will develop during which he can confront a child, when he is ready, with the illogicalities of his own thought, thus creating cognitive conflict and preparing the way for the child to pass on to the next stage. Questioning is thus at a premium since this can reveal to a child an inherent conflict in his *own* argument. Judicious questiqning serves to orient the child towards inconsistencies in his own thinking or phenomena that might otherwise be overlooked or even taken for granted. This kind of questioning is very different from that employed by teachers who merely want to find out whether a child has learnt (or can repeat) what he, the teacher, has just said. The contrast between the two kinds of questioning reveals the difference between the child as an active learner and as a passive automaton parroting the right answers. The language children use can however sometimes conceal lack of understanding of the underlying concepts. Sigel (1961) has shown how children's understanding of the concept 'brother' is far from complete until they have acquired the notion of reciprocity (i.e. realized that they can also be a brother); similarly Jahoda (1963)[34] has revealed children's partial understanding of concepts of nationality.

Teaching methods must however be geared not only to the stage of conceptual development of the learner but also to the nature of the subject matter. Once a teacher has diagnosed the child's level of conceptual functioning he has to be able to select appropriate content to build into the learning situation. This means having a clear understanding of the structure and organization of the areas of knowledge that lend themselves to this kind of analysis. Piaget's work offers most useful guidance in the field of science (especially physical sciences) and Mathematics; his own use of material in these areas to explore children's thinking can offer some direct guidance;[35] but principles of the stage sequence concept can be applied also to other curriculum areas such as

Geography (space), Religion, History (time).[36, 37] Possibly the idea of sequential structure can also be applied to areas hitherto unexplored in this way, such as children's understanding of the tragic. Certainly Piaget's own work in the sphere of moral development is of enormous help to teachers generally and might form the basis of any programme of moral education designed for schools.[38]

In Piaget's view learning is a continuous process; if teachers acknowledge that children are learning something all the time, even if apparently not what they had planned for them to learn, then the question of motivation is rather different from one where teachers are asking why children learn or what they can do to help children to learn or even to make them learn. Children inevitably learn by being in contact with an environment with which they interact. Motivation then comes to be built into the very process of living in a physical or social environment and coming to terms with it. Provided a child is made aware of discrepancies and inconsistencies in his growing consciousness of his world, the cognitive dissonance thus created spurs him on to resolve the conflict and attain a more complex stage of thought. Cognitive conflict can be seen as a kind of intrinsic motivation, provided that children recognize the existence of such a conflict (*cf.* Frank, 1964).[39]

In assessing what children have learnt it would be quite inappropriate to use a right/wrong answer technique. On a Piagetian view children's answers are rarely completely wrong but show only partial understanding. Before he learns that left and right are relative terms, for example, a child will use them as absolutes, as they are in fact in the context of right hand/ left hand. But such reasoning is not wrong, only limited. On the other hand, a right answer might score a point if a child's knowledge were being assessed quantitatively, but as we have seen right answers frequently conceal misunderstandings. So rather than evaluating children's answers as right or wrong it is more appropriate to perceive them (value them) as an expression of the child's current stage of mental reasoning since it is only in this way that the next step can be gauged. Evaluation itself seems to play a different function here: on the Piagetian model it serves as a guide for the teacher in planning and structuring future learning sequences for the individual child; whereas from a psychometric perspective evaluation serves, because of its quantitative nature, to compare individuals with others.

So far this discussion of intelligence has centred round the ability to think rationally, to learn from experience, to perform concrete or formal operations. The investigation of individual differences in abilities has been one of the main concerns of psychologists working within the psychometric framework, yet they have pursued an interest in the quantitative rather than qualitative differences, attempting to measure and compare individuals in a scalar fashion. Examination of the content of intelligence tests however has revealed little of qualitative difference between individuals' modes of thinking and little that is of an obviously creative nature.

Before the 1950s little interest had been shown by psychologists, or in general by teachers, in creative performance. If an outstanding individual was generally acknowledged as a genius in his own field he was thought to be endowed with certain qualities that ordinary people did not have. In the 1950s however there was a surge of interest in creativity, especially on the part of psychologists, some of whom such as Guilford saw creativity as a national investment in various spheres of scientific enquiry, the space race in particular. He describes creative behaviour as including 'such activities as inventing, designing, contriving, composing and planning. People who exhibit these types of behaviour to a marked degree are recognized as being creative' (1950).[40] Creativity and creative productivity were thought to extend far beyond the domain of measured intelligence and consequently attempts were made to trace the relationship between intelligence and creativity. Those making this attempt (for example Guilford, 1950, 1959;[41] Getzels & Jackson, 1962)[42] were so influenced by the psychometric framework within which they were working that their their efforts were concentrated on attempts to demonstrate that performance on tests requiring unusual, original or remote responses was independent to a certain extent of performance on conventional tests of intelligence. This quest for easily objectifiable testing and scoring procedures directed attention towards measurement of something for which oddly enough no appropriate criteria had been established. Open ended tests were thus designed to assess creativity, yet how to recognize creativity had been given very little attention.

One of the best known studies of creativity and intelligence is that of Getzels and Jackson (1962)[43] who attempted to differentiate two groups of adolescents on the basis of (1) their scores on conventional intelligence tests such as the Binet or WISC and (2) their scores on open ended tests, constructed specially for the study and based on the work of Guilford. These tests including problems of word association, unusual uses, hidden shapes, fables and making up problems were designed to reveal the creativeness of the adolescents. Creative thinking, observed from the performance of the subjects, was characterized by the ability to ' produce new forms, to risk conjoining elements that are customarily thought of as independent and dissimilar, to go off in new directions . . . the ability to free (oneself) from the usual, to diverge from the customary . . . to enjoy the risk and uncertainty of the unknown'. Getzels and Jackson compare these tendencies with those of the non-creative performers, who tended to focus on the usual, to shy away from the risk and uncertainty of the unknown and to seek out the safety and security of the known, with Guilford's factors of convergent and divergent thinking.

On the basis of the data produced by the test scores Getzels and Jackson were able to distinguish two groups; a high creativity group (subjects in the top 20 per cent on creativity measures but below the top 20 per cent on intelligence measures) and a high intelligence group (top 20 per cent in intelligence, below the top 20 per cent in creativity measures) though as might be expected, the scores were not completely independent. The experimenters then proceeded to look for further differences between the two groups, such as differences in school achievement, popularity, personality traits, but the interesting feature of this study in the present context is that the characteristics of creative behaviour were deduced from the students' performance on certain tests rather than tests being compiled to assess creative performance for which criteria had previously been set up. Guilford (1959)[44] had suggested criteria by which to recognize creative or divergent thinking which could then be expressed in a quantifiable form. These were fluency (including word-, associational-, expressional-, and ideational- fluency), spontaneous flexibility and originality. In commenting on appropriate testing procedures Guilford says for example of ideational fluency that 'sheer quantity is the important consideration; quality need not be considered so long as responses are appropriate'.

Interesting as this kind of work may be, it does not help to answer some some questions of real importance for education. Teachers need to know whether creative promise can be discovered in children and whether creative talents can be promoted in school. But the ability to attain high scores on open ended tests has not been shown to bear any relationship to a child's ability to write a poem, paint a picture, invent a mechanical device, build a model or indeed to perform any of those activities which a layman might call creative. Nor can the tests predict creative performance later in life. The ability to give an unusual answer to a test question may reveal a difference in willingness to take risks or even a desire to appear bizarre. The fact that convergent thinkers do not give unusual answers does does not mean that they have no creative ability. After all to some highly intelligent children the test may simply appear trivial and not worth bothering with.

To raise questions about creativity in education or even different modes of thinking requires further analysis of the concept of creativity. As we

have seen, intelligence is far more than performance on a test; similarly
creativity must be more than test performance. What is needed then for
the understanding of the relationship between creativity and intelligence is
some kind of conceptual reorientation.

Jackson and Messick (1965)[45] attempt to construct a hierarchical
model of creative responses which seems to go much further than previous
attempts in picking out what might be called a creative performance.
Intelligent responses they suggest are characterized as being correct in
that they satisfy objective criteria and operate within the constraints of
logic and reality. Creative performances by comparison are more difficult
to recognize because they have to satisfy subjective criteria and and are
thus open to a wide variety of judgemental standards. Jackson and Messick
use the term 'good' to characterize such creative responses and attempt to
analyze what constitutes the good in this sense. Their first prerequisite for
a creative response or performance, whether it relates to an artistic or
scientific product, is the novel, the unusual - unusual that is by comparison
with other products of the same class. A young child's painting for example
might show features that are unusual for children of his age but would not
surprise us in an adult's work. For a creative response to be merely unusual
though is not enough; it might be nothing more than odd or bizarre or even
totally inappropriate. Appropriateness then is a second or higher order
criterion; thus to be creative a product must be both unusual and yet
appropriate to the context. But at this stage the level of creative excellence
must be examined. To distinguish levels of creative excellence requires two
further criteria: that of transformation of ideas or materials to overcome
conventional restraints and condensation of meaning and association. These
criteria are both difficult to define and to recognize. Transformation involves
not just a restructuring of old ideas but a creation of new forms that
generate reflection and wonder in the observer and stimulate him to further
thought. Condensation is characteristic of the very highest levels of creative
performance; it implies an intensity and concentration of meaning
(intellectual or emotional) that can evoke constant contemplation - such as
Tolstoy's *War and Peace* or a mature Haydn symphony. Children's creative
performances clearly will seldom reach such levels but nevertheless this
analysis comes nearer to setting out criteria that teachers might find useful in
judging a creative production or creative thought than the brief hints that
psychologists had previously offered before plunging into a morass of test
procedures and data.

As Elliot[46] reminds us, creativity has traditionally been associated
with the creation of something quite new, as if out of nothing. Such a
concept of creativeness stems clearly from the divine myth of creation

but a newer concept of creativeness allows far more flexibility in what can be included as creative acts, products or thinking. This newer concept sees creativeness as developing novel ideas and either using them to solve problems for which there is no adequate response in terms of existing knowledge, methods or techniques or simply making them available to others. This notion of creativity can be thought of as part of what we understand by imaginativeness.

It seems from this kind of analysis then that all teachers should discover what creativity means to them and what could count as a creative response in any particular sphere of children's activity and learning. This kind of approach is surely far more profitable than attempting to measure certain test responses where one's thinking can so easily become enmeshed in the intricacies of scoring and standardizing. As soon as a testing approach is adopted the notion of comparability in creativity arises. This of all areas in education is surely not one where an element of competitiveness is at all appropriate. It is interesting to remember, as with intelligence, that the term creativity can be used descriptively as well as evaluatively. If we are merely describing a child's thinking as being creative, we wish to point out certain characteristics of that style of thinking without implying that it is better than any other style. In using the term evaluatively, it implies that creative thinking is something worthwhile and something that we want to promote in children. Whereas teachers would clearly not want to promote or develop any kind of learning or skill that they did not consider worthwhile it would be a mistake to undervalue those achievements which were not considered creative in favour of those that were. After all, in order to be creative at a high level of excellence, a person must have mastered certain basic skills and have acquired a certain verifiable body of knowledge. A boy cannot be creative in the design workshop for example unless he knows something of the properties of the materials he is using and recognizes the constraints they impose upon his freedom to create; similarly he cannot work upon his materials until he has mastered certain skills and techniques of handling the appropriate tools. Just as there has been a danger of associating moral values with intelligence, a morally neutral term, a similar risk can arise with creativity. Not all children are as creative as others, just as not all are equally intelligent. But those who are less creative (or less intelligent) are not worse people for that.

In recent years in nearly all statements made by teachers, psychologists, educationists, about the need for flexibility in education there has been some criticism - at times very heated and at times justifiable - about the iniquities of an education system, both in this country and in the USA which requires conformity, conventionality and regurgitation of knowledge in a passive way rather than imaginative and creative thinking which, as some research has shown, has even been frowned upon.

Getzels and Jackson (1962)[47] in their comparison of high creativity and high intelligence groups of adolescents found for example that teachers preferred to teach the high intelligence pupils, although the scholastic achievements of the high creativity group were as good; they found their unconventionality, their tendency to ask unexpected questions and to raise issues that teachers had not anticipated, rather irksome. Further investigation revealed that the attitudes of the high IQ pupils bore a far closer relationship to those of their teachers than did the attitudes of the high creativity group. Perhaps it is hardly surprising that teachers favour pupils whose attitudes are congruent with their own. Hasan and Butcher (1966),[48] replicating the Getzels and Jackson study with Scottish schoolchildren found the same - that teachers preferred the highly intelligent pupils in their classes to the highly creative ones. Torrance (1967)[49] found that creative or divergent boys were not very popular with their classmates and gained the reputation of being silly. Divergent girls for some reason escaped this labelling: do children have sex role expectations of their peers where creativity is concerned? Haddon and Lytton (1968)[50] found that children with creative ideas are popular with their peers in primary schools that adopt informal methods and individual learning, whereas in more formal schools high IQ pupils are more popular.

This last finding raises two particularly interesting questions: firstly whether the difference between convergent and divergent or creative thinkers is largely a difference of personality; and secondly whether certain kinds of school do more than others to promote creative thinking. If divergent thinking is marked partly by the ability to produce novel and unusual ideas and to offer several possible solutions to a problem instead of preferring just one, it suggests that these people are more flexible, more tolerant of ambiguity, and less conventional than convergers. Getzels and Jackson did find their high creatives showed unconventionality and independence of judgement. Judged by the norms of their teachers, they were seen as deviant to some extent, valuing those qualities which were important to them as persons - such as a keen sense of humour - higher than those which might lead to worldly success. Hudson in this country (1966)[51] investigated some of the personality ramifications of convergers and divergers in sixth forms of grammar and public schools. Convergers by contrast with divergers tended to insist on respect for authority, to value obedience, to adopt a conventional manner of dress, speech etc. They did not feel hampered, as divergers did, by the limits of a school syllabus, presumably welcoming its guidance. These pupils tended to choose predominantly Science and Mathematics for their

A level subjects. It must be remembered, in making a distinction between the two groups, that there is no clear cut-off point. Convergers are those who show a *bias* in this direction; in Hudson's study they were those who gained a higher score on an intelligence than on open-ended tests regardless of how high each score was.

However if some pupils do show a bias towards convergence and others a bias towards divergence it is interesting to discover whether schools can and do cater for both. A school system which is geared towards the passing of examinations and the attainment of qualifications, especially at secondary level, would seem to emphasize the ability to produce right answers or perhaps what the examiner wants; thus convergent thinking would tend to be at a premium. Anxiety on this count, stimulated by such as Guilford and Torrance in the USA and by Hudson, Haddon and Lytton in this country, has served to alert teachers to the dangers of undervaluing one type of thinking. If teachers are less favourably disposed towards divergent children, these children may soon learn to conceal such originality as they have by withdrawing into themselves. Thus potential creativity is stunted early.

Schools however are not all the same in their social climate or aspirations. Haddon and Lytton (1968)[52] compared two types of primary school, one using more conventional formal methods with an emphasis on achievement, rigid timetabling and instruction, and the other a more progressive type of school, placing great emphasis upon self-initiated and creative learning. The schools were matched for socio-economic status and the children for verbal reasoning scores. Children in the informal schools showed higher scores on open ended tests than those in the formal schools. Whether these are tests of true creative thinking is in doubt, but the indication that some children were more willing to venture unusual answers does perhaps reflect the freedom to learn that they had experienced in their schools where they moved freely about the classroom, had free access to the school library and worked much of the time without supervision.

Critics of the traditional authoritarian type of education who have been writing recently within a sociological framework have contrasted two opposing paradigms in the social sciences which have formed a pattern for education (Esland, 1971).[53] One is the psychometric paradigm which as we have seen in our discussion of different concepts of intelligence has been concerned with intelligence testing and a consequent imputation to children of specified levels of academic potential and achievement. This view diverts attention from children's thought processes and individual differences in modes of thinking and has led to a passive view of learning in which the individuality of the pupils, their interpretation of their world, and the meanings they attach to their learning experiences have been neglected. The phenomenological paradigm which Esland and others would like in its place is one which is concerned with individual ways of knowing, where an active rather than a static notion of the mind is emphasized. Processes of thought are 'seen to be part of a highly complex personal system of interpretations, intentions and recollections' (Esland, 1971).[54] This view of development suggests that learning is a growth process, subject to an individual personalized interpretation and that the mind is capable of unlimited development in many directions.

This view of education with its interest in classroom interaction without directions from a teacher, would seem to provide an important conceptual and practical framework, not only for cognitive development along Piagetian lines, but also for the growth of creative thinking. In suggesting what practical action teachers might take if they wish to create a school climate favourable to the development of creative thinking and abilities, Torrance (1967)[55] makes suggestions that anticipate just those attitudes being advocated by Esland and others within a phenomenological framework in the sociology of education. Torrance's suggestions are that teachers should be respectful of children's unusual questions and ideas, showing them that these ideas have value; that they should provide opportunities for self-initiated learning and for periods of non-evaluated practice, indicating that whatever children do may be of some value and is not constantly going to be assessed by some absolute criterion of correctness set up by teachers. This emphasizes not only the need to value children in their own terms, by acknowledging the worth of common sense knowledge they bring with them into the classroom, but also acknowledges the importance of freedom and flexibility to develop and grow. These seem to be the cornerstones of both cognitive and creative development.

REFERENCES

1.   G. Ryle, *Concept of Mind,* Hutchinson, 1967, ch.2
2.   A. MacIntyre and P.H. Nowell-Smith, 'Purpose and intelligent action'. *Proc. of Arist. Soc. Suppl.,* vol.34, 1960
3.   C. Burt, 'The evidence for the concept of intelligence', *British Journal of Educational Psychology,* 1955, pp. 158-77
4.   C. Burt, 'The genetic determination of differences in intelligence', *British Journal of Psychology,* 1966, pp. 137-53
5.   P.E. Vernon, *Intelligence and Cultural Environment,* Methuen, 1969, p.10.
6.   D.H. Stott, 'Commentary on "The genetic determination of differences in intelligence: a study of monozygotic twins reared together and apart", by Cyril Burt', *British Journal of Psychology,* 1966, pp. 423-33
7.   D. Wechsler, 'The measurement of adult intelligence', p.3, 1944. Quoted by

T.R. Miles, contribution to 'Intelligence testing and the theory of intelligence', *British Journal of Educational Psychology.* 1957
8.   C. Burt, 1966, *op.cit.*
9.   H.H. Newman, F.N. Freeman and K.J. Holzinger, *Twins: a Study of Heredity and Environment,* Chicago University Press, 1937
10. A.R. Jensen, 'How much can we boost IQ and scholastic achievement?' *Harvard Education Review,* 1969
11. *Norwood Report,* HMSO, 1943
12. B. Coard, *How the West Indian Child is Made Educationally Sub-normal in the British School System,* New Beacon Books, 1971
13. D.O. Hebb, *The Organization of Behaviour,* Wiley, 1949
14. See, for example, W.H. Bexton, W. Heron and T.H. Scott, 'Effects of decreased variations in the sensory environment', *Canadian Journal of Psychology,* 1954, S. Smith and W. Lewty, 'Perceptual isolation using a silent room', *Lancet,* 1954, H. Leiderman, 'Sensory deprivation', *A.M.A. Arch. Internal Medicine,* 1958. All referred to in M.D. Vernon's *Psychology of Perception,* Penguin, 1962
15. See J.H. Flavell, *The Developmental Psychology of Jean Piaget,* Van Nostrand, 1963
16. J.H. Flavell, *op.cit.,* (metal rod and pendulum experiments), p.348-9
17. D. Elkind, *Children and Adolescents,* Oxford University Press, 1970, ch.8
18. R.F. Harrell *et al., The Effect of Mothers' Diet on the Intelligence of the Offspring,* New York Teachers College, Columbia, Bureau of Publications, 1955.
19. M.B. Stoch, 'The effect of undernutrition during infancy on subsequent brain growth and intellectual development', *South African Medical Journal,* 1967
20. E.M. Churchill, 'The number concepts of the very young child', *Leeds University Res. and Stud.,* nos. 17 and 18, 1958
21. I.E. Sigel, A. Roeper and F.H. Hooper, 'A training procedure for the acquisition of Piaget's conservation of quantity', *British Journal of Educational Psychology,* 1966
22. P.M. Greenfield, 'On culture and conservation' in J. Bruner *et al., Studies in Cognitive Growth,* Wiley, 1966, ch.11
23. B.S. Bloom, *Stability and Change in Human Characteristics,* Wiley, 1964, ch.3
24. P.E. Vernon, *op.cit.,* p.78-9
25. E. Goodacre, 'Teachers & their pupils' home background', NFER, 1968
26. R.C. Rist, 'Student social class and teacher expectations: the self-fulfilling prophecy in ghetto education', *Harvard Education Review, 1970*
27. B. Jackson, *Streaming: an Educational System in Miniature,* Routledge & Kegan Paul, 1964
28. J.W.B. Douglas, *The Home and the School,* MacGibbon & Kee, 1964
29. F. Riessman, *The Culturally Deprived Child,* Harper & Row, 1962
30. A. Little & J. Westergaards, 'The trend of class differentials in educational opportunity in England and Wales', *British Journal of Sociology,* 1964
31. B. Bernstein, 'Education cannot compensate for society', *New Society,* 1970. In *Language and Education,* Routledge & Kegan Paul with Open University Press, 1972
32. M.F.D. Young, 'An approach to the study of curricula as socially organised knowledge'. In *Knowledge and Control,* M.F.D. Young (ed), Collier-Macmillan, 1971
33. C. Richards, 'Third thoughts in discovery', *Educational Review,* 1973

34. G. Jahoda, 'The development of children's ideas about country and nationality', *British Journal of Educational Psychology*, 1963
35. For an account of Piaget's work relevant to mathematical and scientific concepts see K. Lovell, *The Growth of Basic Mathematical & Scientific Concepts in Children*, University of London Press, 1961
36. See R. Hallam, 'Piaget and the teaching of history', *Educational Research*, 1969, R. Hallam, 'Piaget and moral judgements in history', *Educational Research*, 1969, E.A. Peel, 'Understanding school material', *Educational Review*, 1972, Prior, 'The place of maps in the junior school', Birmingham University dissertation, 1959
37. R. Goldman, 'Researches in religious thinking', *Educational Research*, 1964
38. J. Piaget, *The Moral Judgement of the Child*, Routledge & Kegan Paul, 1932
39. Frank, quoted by J. Bruner in 'The course of cognitive growth', *American Psychologist*, 1964
40. J.P. Guilford, 'Creativity', *American Psychologist*, 1950. In Cashdan (ed.), *Personality Growth and Learning*, Longman with Open University Press, 1972
41. J.P. Guilford, 'Traits of creativity' in P.E. Vernon (ed.), *Creativity*, Penguin, 1970
42. J.W. Getzels and P.W. Jackson, *Creativity and Intelligence*, Wiley, 1962
43. J.W. Getzels and P.W. Jackson, *op.cit.*
44. J.P. Guilford, *op.cit.*, 1959
45. P.W. Jackson and S. Messick, 'The person, the product and the response: conceptual problems in the assessment of creativity', *British Journal of Educational Psychology*, 1969
46. R.K. Elliott, 'The concept of creativity', *PPES of Great Britain*, 1971
47. J.W. Getzels and P.W. Jackson, *op.cit.*
48. P. Hasan and H.J. Butcher, 'Creativity and intelligence: a partial replication with Scottish children of Getzels' and Jackson's study', *British Journal of Psychology* 1966
49. E.P. Torrance, 'Give the devil his dues' in J.C. Gowan *et al*, *Creativity: its Educational Implications*, Wiley, 1967
50. F.A. Haddon and H. Lytton, 'Teaching approach and the development of divergent thinking abilities in primary schools', *British Journal of Educational Psychology*, 1968
51. L. Hudson, *Contrary Imaginations*, Penguin, 1966
52. F.A. Haddon and H. Lytton, *op.cit.*
53. G.M. Esland, 'Teaching and learning as the organisation of knowledge' in M.F.D. Young (ed.), *Knowledge and Control*, Collier-Macmillan, 1971
54. G.M. Esland, *ibid.*
55. E.P. Torrance, *op.cit.*, 1967

III Motivation and Learning

The discussion of intelligence and abilities in the last chapter was concerned with one group of preconditions for learning. But to have the ability does not mean that children will in fact learn; they have also to wish to learn, to have some interest in what they are learning and to have some kind of aspirations in terms of mastery, whether of skills or a body of knowledge. In discussing motivation we shall thus be concerned with examining children's willingness to learn, the efforts they expend and the reasons they have for doing what they do.

Motivation is in many ways difficult to assess because there is no easy way of objectifying children's actions. When a teacher writes 'Could do better with more effort' on a child's report, what does he mean by this statement? How does he know what effort the child is putting into his activities? What does 'more' effort mean? On the other hand, how does a teacher know that a child is trying hard when he comments that 'X tries hard but finds the subject difficult'?

It seems that intelligence or the use of intelligence is very closely related to this question of motivation, so that the two must, if they are going to make any practical sense, be considered together. It was noted in the previous chapter that very few definitions of intelligence referred to a motivational factor. Stott (1966)[1] criticizes Burt's view of intelligence as an 'innate, general, cognitive factor' for the very reason that it omits all reference to motivation. Stott argues that the ability a child reveals in solving problems such as those set before him in an intelligence test depends partly upon 'the strength of his intrinsic motivations during the early stages of his development'. He suggests that the ability to solve problems depends partly on the extent to which he has in the past engaged in problem solving which in turn depends upon his 'effectiveness-motivation'. A child without the confidence or desire to widen the scope of his effectiveness in this way will thus remain at a low level of cognitive development. The difficulty lies in distinguishing the influence of motivation from that of ability. It seems that neither can be effective unless developed in early childhood. Suffice it to say at this point that motivation has been a neglected factor; later in the discussion some further psychological ramifications of this will be examined.

Before pursuing further conceptual issues in this area or examining empirical evidence that could give teachers some guidance in the classroom, we must consider some of the questions that teachers would like answered when faced with problems of motivation. The questions that do concern teachers seem to be of two main kinds: those referring to what has happened in the past and those concerning what might happen in the future. Questions referring to the past are raised when children behave unexpectedly or abnormally (either compared with their own usual behaviour or with that of their peers) or when they fail to meet teachers' expectations or standards set for them. For example a child who is normally a model of punctuality and who suddenly arrives late for school several days in succession makes a teacher ask what the cause of his lateness is. A child who interrupts others in class, perhaps disturbing them when they are absorbed in what they are doing or even destroying some piece of work, will make the teacher ask what is wrong with the deviant: what has got into him? Or again if a child is failing to learn to read, teacher will ask what is making him fail or what is preventing him from learning. All such questions seem to require a causal explanation, as if there were some force at work making a child late, some demon inside him making him disruptive or some barrier preventing him from learning to read. It is as if the child concerned were being made to behave in certain ways either against his will or without his awareness.

The other kinds of question are those concerning what is going to happen in the future: 'what are you doing that for?' 'what are you aiming at?' 'what have you in mind?' Questions like this are designed to find out a child's reasons for action rather than the causes of his behaviour. They show that the speaker regards the child as someone whose behaviour is intentional and who acts usually because he has some aim in the future.

The implications of these different kinds of question and explanation are various: any given view of man will affect one's view of education. Causal explanations of man's behaviour give an impression of a rather passive, machine-like creature, who is at the mercy of all sorts of forces pushing him along, just as a leaf is blown about by a gust of wind. Perhaps this is an extreme analogy and however much man's behaviour is determined by outside forces, he still retains some autonomy. But causal explanations belong really to the realm of the physical or natural sciences. When we heat a bar of metal and find that it expands, we can control the situation so carefully that we can say with confidence that the heat has caused it to expand (without here going into detail about the effects of heat on the atomic structure of the metal bar). But we cannot speak with the same confidence about human behaviour which is far more complex, since man, unlike the metal bar, has intentions and is responsible for his own actions up to a point. There are of course cases where he is not responsible and where it would be appropriate to talk of causes: if a man is pushed off the pavement in front of an oncoming car we can explain his behaviour in none other than causal terms; somebody pushed him and he could not resist, he himself had no aim or purpose in falling in front of the car. So perhaps causal explanations are appropriate for human behaviour as long as we are speaking purely within a physical framework where an external physical force is stronger than man's own.

Teachers frequently talk of causes of backwardness implying that, given a certain set of conditions, such as a large family, cramped living conditions, lack of parental interest in his school progress, supposedly low intelligence, a child will inevitably be backward in school. But these family characteristics, frequently included among causes of backwardness do not affect all children: many coming from such homes would never be called backward. Fortunately then there is no such inevitability linking a child's background and school progress. Since many children, however, who do come from families of such a nature are retarded in school work it would be more appropriate to talk of factors associated with backwardness.

Although it would be pessimistic to try to explain all human behaviour as if it were determined by antecedent causes, it would be unwise to reject this kind of explanation altogether. The rich history of personality and motivation studies adopting this perspective must clearly not be discarded altogether, otherwise much of our behaviour would remain only partially explained.

Behaviourist theories of personality and motivation conceived of man as a mechanical system whose actions were to be understood and explained largely in terms of various forms of external stimulation and the responses made by an individual to these. Stimulus-response theories attempted to account for personality changes and abnormalities in terms of the acquisition of new forms of behaviour that appeared as a result of experience. Since this was the frame of reference within which certain theorists, predominantly Hull, followed by Miller and Dollard, chose to study personality, the main emphasis falls not unnaturally on the learning process.

Hull, whose main theoretical assumption was the principle of reward/reinforcement, set out to develop a general theory of human behaviour, although he relied heavily on experimental work in the laboratory with lower animals. Drawing upon Hullian theory, which itself always remained theory and never reached the stage of being applied to situations outside the laboratory, Miller and Dollard offer their view of the learning in the following terms: 'the learner must be driven to make the response and rewarded for having responded in the presence of the cue. This may be expressed in a more homely way by saying that in order to learn one must want something, notice something, do something, get something. Stated more exactly these factors are drive, cue, response, reward.' (Miller and Dollard, 1941)[2]. Although they did not offer this model of learning specifically for learning in the classroom, it was intended to apply to learning in general. We see how highly mechanistic and devoid of any notion of choice, intention, interest or understanding it is. If we try to apply it to a classroom situation, the picture emerges something like this: in order to learn a child must want something (drive) - teachers' approval; he must notice something (cue) - that the teacher looks pleased when he puts his hand up but displeased when he calls out; he must do something (response) - put his hand up; and get something (reward) - the teacher nods approvingly and asks him to answer her question. What has he learnt then? That to get her approval he must put up his hand in class.

This may be unobjectionable so far as a way of getting children to learn to take their turn in a class teaching situation; it is a simple form of social learning. But how far does this model of learning apply? Suppose a child is learning some Maths or Geography, what does he want? To find out something more about what he is engaged upon or to get a good mark for his homework? What is he to notice? Is there a cue or a stimulus that can make him respond in a certain way? And how is this response to be rewarded? Is the good mark he is given by the teacher sufficient reward or would the information he discovers in the course of his work count? And what happens if the drive is not there in the first place - if the child does not want anything, in Miller and Dollard's homely terms? S-R psychologists do not go as far as suggesting that we should create drives in children by depriving them of basic requirements like food (as is done with animals in the laboratory). To talk of a drive leading to a reward would be similar to trying to solve the problem of motivation by an appeal to needs. However, to an S-R psychologist all motivation is assumed to derive from organic drives or basic emotions which the individual can do nothing to resist. Motivation is defined as the urge to act, resulting from a stimulus; since they see all behaviour as stimulus-directed, they do not accept the notion of purpose of any kind. According to an S-R theory of motivation, a child does not have to want to learn History say, in order to learn it (though he does have to want the reward for learning it). He does though have to be persuaded to study it and to repeat the appropriate verbal responses, which, when reinforced or rewarded in some way, become permanent - or are learnt. As Bigge and Hunt[3] point out, 'an associationist is not taught much about such things as psychological involvement or helping students to see the point of learning. Instead he engages them in activity and assumes that activity with reinforcement automatically produces learning'.

Skinner is the greatest advocate of S-R techniques in learning; he comments

(1959)[4] on the highly inefficient practices in schools that waste useful learning time, mainly because the procedures of reinforcement are clumsy. Teachers in a class of children are poor reinforcers since they cannot supply immediate reward to each child for each correct response. In Skinner's view then, the teacher's principle task is 'to bring behaviour under many sorts of stimulus control . . . teachers at the moment spend far too much time in redesigning curricula in a desperate attempt to provide a liberal education and steadfastly refuse to employ available engineering techniques which would efficiently build the interests and instil the knowledge which are the goals of education.'

It will be interesting to look at some reinforcement techniques which have been examined or adopted in the areas of cognitive and social learning. Skinner himself advocated the use of programmed learning in schools as a highly efficient way of ensuring that each correct response a child makes is reinforced, thus using time more economically than in a normal class teaching situation. A typical programme (which may be in textbook form or fed into a teaching machine) consists of factual content which is divided up into such small steps that in answering questions on small pieces of information given, the learner can seldom make a mistake. Skinner rated the efficacy of positive reinforcement for a correct answer higher than negative reinforcement for an incorrect one. Thus there is no room to learn from one's own mistakes in this kind of procedure. Positive reinforcement is given each time the learner makes a correct response; this reinforcement heightens his motivation and encourages him to continue with the task. Using operant conditioning techniques, 'learning a subject like fundamentals of electricity is largely a matter of learning a large number of correct responses to logically related sequences of questions that constitute the subject . . . once a subject has been carefully divided into a series of many small bits of information (steps), a student has only to learn by repetition and reward (rapid and frequent reinforcement) the correct answer to a series of questions about the small bits of information'. (Fitzgerald, 1962).[5]

Skinner claims the following advantages for the use of mechanical teaching devices in school: reinforcement for the correct answer is immediate, and since it is given by the machine or the book, the teacher can supervize the whole class, who are enabled to work at their own rate; thus if any child falls behind either because of a slower working pace or because of absence from school, he still does not suffer by being made to keep up with the rest of the class; similiarly a child who works faster need not be held back, but can be provided with other tasks; the teacher knows exactly what each child has done and so can supplement reinforcement where necessary.

Research has shown that programmed learning, especially with the use of teaching machines, can be highly efficient in terms of retention. But how far could it encourage children to be actively involved in their own learning? Skinner[6] claims that teaching machines encourage children to 'take an active role in the instructional process - they must develop the answers before they are reinforced'. Yet clearly this is a different interpretation of what it means to take an active role than that held by educators talking of children being active agents of their own learning in a child-centred situation. Whereas Skinner's technique forces the child to produce or develop an answer himself rather than sitting waiting for a classmate to do so, advocates of child-centred education hope that children will pursue their own interests and frame their own questions depending on what they are involved in at any one time. The content in Skinner's view is still teacher directed, so that if all a child has to do to learn is to produce correct answers, many educators today would not call this active learning.

Furthermore, there is serious doubt whether understanding of content thus learned is achieved; although Skinner's claim is that 'the machine insists that a given point be thoroughly understood before the student moves on',[7] it is difficult to see how a machine can make sure something is understood when it can only do what is programmed into it; how can any programme be flexible enough to account for all possible misunderstandings, interpretations or misinterpretations a child may make? The very essence of human learning in an educative sense is that it is active, highly individual and therefore unpredictable. Certainly a machine can be programmed in such a way that the learner does not move on until he gives a correct *answer,* but there is no guarantee that a correct answer presupposes understanding. Educators concerned about the rather passive kind of learning that goes on in many secondary schools, among them Barnes *et al.* (1969)[8] and Holt (1964),[9] show how children can get by in class by giving correct answers to teachers' questions, by learning what cues are the important ones, whether of gesture, intonation or verbal. Children can thus learn to give correct answers fairly easily but answers are responses to specific questions. Even if they are based on understanding, a series of correct answers would surely be a very fragmented kind of learning. The value of programmed learning is perhaps not to be challenged once an individual has decided he wants to master a body of knowledge which he has chosen for himself and has come to understand. As an efficient technique for helping a student consolidate what he has already learned, programmed methods would be unobjectionable.

In programmed learning Skinner is interpreting reinforcement as knowledge of results for each answer given and since the material is so carefully structured it is usually positive in nature. But reinforcement or reward can take many forms: teacher's approval, smiling and nodding, good marks, stars.

Some evidence for the beneficial effects of rewards on classroom learning has been gathered in controlled situations. Carpenter (1954) for instance, found that in a concept learning task, different groups of children were (1) rewarded for each correct response (2) for every second response (3) for every fourth response. His results suggested that the more rewards children were given, the more efficiently they learnt. But this cannot be taken as a general rule: questions must be asked about the relationship between the child and the teacher; about the nature of the reward; and about how informative the reward is, if at all. Page (1958)[10] found that of three groups of schoolchildren receiving (1) grades (2) grades with general comments (3) grades with a stereotyped comment, group (2) showed most improvement on the next piece of work. Clearly the comments were more useful than simply grades or grades with a fixed comment, since they said more about individual pieces of work, rather than just placing them in a category; they conveyed too more personal interest on the part of the teacher. If the term reward is being used in the latter sense it is far more than just a payment (just deserts) for doing something the teacher approves of.

Most S-R theorists do not seem to use the term in this way: a few examples of how psychologists have used the term will illustrate the point. For Hull, a reward is rewarding because it reduces the drive tension in the organism; for Tolman, because it emphasizes the correct response; for Olds and Milner, because it stimulates specific areas of the brain. None of these attempts at definition is very helpful in an educational situation. Premack (1965)[11] proposed a notion of reward that he thought useful in school situations; it is simply this: 'a reward is anything someone likes doing.' In Premack's view, the only condition is that the rewarding activity must be preferred to the activity being learnt *for which it is offered as a reward.* But surely this places a very dubious value on what is to be learnt; it denigrates the value of the task being performed. And suppose a child actually prefers doing some Maths, designing a toy or reading a story to any reward that could be offered for doing it? Rewarding the desired activity then becomes not only useless but nonsensical.

If we consider some of the experimental work done, using rewards, in the field of social learning, we shall encounter some very odd situations. Homme *et al.* (1963) demonstrated the use of reward in gaining control over social behaviour of nursery school children. By first observing the normal behaviour of the children, the experimenters noted that their preferred activities were running around, shouting and pushing furniture about (undesirable behaviour from the adults' point of view, but supposedly desirable from the children's). Using Premack's principle, the children were rewarded for sitting quietly for a period of time, by being allowed to indulge in shouting etc. At a later stage children could earn tokens for sitting quietly; they could then buy permission to indulge in shouting and screaming. The experimenters report almost perfect control of behaviour after a few days of this procedure. Certainly this is a good example of how to *control* children, if that is what adults think desirable, but what kind of learning is it?

Such examples of reward being used as a motivator, whether in the learning of some body of facts or in social learning show the learner under the control of some force he cannot resist. If this is what learning means then reward can be said to be effective in bringing it about. However learning clearly entails more than giving correct responses which might be sufficient for habit training. Two important educational questions must be raised: firstly whether any valuable learning can be said to have taken place if children have not understood or seen the point of what they have learnt; and secondly whether such means of bringing about 'learning' are morally acceptable even if they are motivationally effective.

Discussion so far has centred around rewards and incentives in the form of a tangible object or approval deliberately offered as a means of extrinsic encouragement. Other *conditions* however can also act as incentives. Lewin *et al.* [12] developed a technique of investigating the goal-setting behaviour of adult subjects during the performance of simple tasks in experimental situations. After one performance, subjects were asked to say what they hoped or expected to achieve next time, thus setting themselves a goal or level of aspiration. Results of work on level of aspiration suggest generally that successful performance leads to the setting of higher goals and vice versa. Whether a high level of aspiration leads to better performance is not clearly established, but what does follow is that success increases motivation and failure decreases it. This is a commonsense view that perhaps does not appear to require empirical confirmation; yet what is manifestly important is the value children learn to place on success and their reasons for learning to value it. Further research on social motives shows that some individuals are anxious to succeed mainly in order to surpass others (individuals or groups). Early work suggested a positive effect of social facilitation; individuals worked better when performing a task alongside others even when no interaction or cooperation took place.

McClelland [13] introduced the notion of achievement motivation in which ambition is a key concept. He suggests that human beings all have some sort of ambition or aspiration either to do well enough to surpass others or to achieve a certain standard of excellence to satisfy themselves. However some kind of social motive seems always to be involved: studies have shown a high correlation between the wish to achieve a standard for its own sake and to achieve other people's esteem by so doing. Children may thus strive to achieve mastery in a chosen field and at the same time feel greater satisfaction (leading to increased effort in future) because a teacher whose esteem they value shows pleasure in their achievement. It could be argued that the teacher's approval is rewarding, but this kind of reward effect is manifestly very different from S-R learning where the reward seems to be the main thing the child comes to value.

Not everybody has an equally high degree of achievement motivation which is usually found to be associated with independence training in early childhood. McClelland's hypothesis (1951) that children who are encouraged to be independent and self-reliant at an early age, who are treated warmly by their parents and given a high degree of freedom develop high achievement motivation later on, was confirmed by Winterbottom (1958)[14] in his study of independence training. Children who have rejecting or over-protective parents tend to develop low achievement motivation and instead of aiming for mastery, tend to seek social approval. Such findings might explain different degrees of motivation in children in school: it follows that an emphasis on teacher-directed learning where a child is encouraged to take little initiative, will not help to encourage those who are less ambitious initially, whereas guidance towards independence and responsibility may well help to persuade the under-confident child that he can succeed and that it is worth trying.

One precondition of wishing to achieve mastery is to feel some enthusiasm; every teacher however is familiar with the sight of a child who seems to be almost totally lacking in interest or enthusiasm, for whatever the reason. Whether we can make a child interested is very doubtful, but one way possibly of teaching him the interest of a topic is to show our own enthusiasm for it. Common sense tells us that enthusiasm is very often infectious: children then want to know what makes their teacher so excited about a given topic and catch some of his fervour for themselves. There is little empirical evidence so far to support this view, yet the work of Bandura and Walters (1970)[15] suggests that modelling might be an effective social motivator. They have succeeded in showing how powerful a model an adult can be in evoking similar behaviour in children, yet so far have investigated mainly aggression and fear - largely the kind of behaviour we should want to discourage in children in school. However from everyday observation we know that too much enthusiasm can work in the opposite direction and become anti-motivational. Enthusiasts are sometimes regarded as cranks, (especially perhaps by suspecting adolescents) and as such are avoided.

The concept of achievement motivation has been used not only to show why some children have an individual urge towards mastery and others not; it has also been drawn upon by sociologists working within the structural-

functionalist tradition, investigating school failure associated with social
class. In a commentary on family background, values and achievement,
Banks (1968)[16] notes that the consistent tendency of working class children
to perform less well in school and to leave school earlier than middle class
children, even when ability is matched, needs explanation. Clearly this is
true, but as we shall see, the kinds of explanation offered by sociologists
working within this framework have been causal in nature, because of the
kinds of question that have been asked. Kluckholn and Strodtbeck for
example (1961)[17] have attempted to trace a relationship between value
orientation and achievement orientation which might eventually explain the
link between social class and achievement in school. For instance, Kluckholn
sees the dominant (American) middle class value-orientation as one where
man can control nature, where the future is stressed rather than the past,
where there is an emphasis on activity and where individual efforts are
considered more important and effective than those of the group or
community. Such an outlook is believed to encourage the development
of ambition since it emphasizes the power of the individual and his
orientation towards the future. Some studies such as the Harvard mobility
project have attempted to examine how different patterns of value relate to
achievement: Kahl (1965)[18] found that from 24 boys all from a lower
middle class background chosen for interview, two distinct groups emerged
according to their expressed aspirations. The majority of the 12 boys
interviewed in the college preparatory class came from families characterized
by what Kluckholn might describe as future orientation: the parents looked
to the future and believed in getting ahead. They were aware of their own
relative lack of success and as a result encouraged their sons to regard school
as a means of getting on in life - a means of getting to college and aspiring to
a better occupation than that of their fathers. Parents of the other group
comparable in ability and socio-economic status who were not in the college
preparatory class tended to accept their own status and were oriented to the
present rather than looking to the future for something better. These
findings are similar to those of Swift (1966)[19] in this country who found
that more sons of working class fathers who were dissatisfied with their own
position tended to gain 11+ successes than those of fathers who accepted
their lot. Although there is no confirmed or clear cut relationship between
achievement motivation and achievement values, they do, as Rosen (1956)[20]
suggests, both belong to a complex achievement syndrome. Attempts have
been made to relate different patterns of child rearing process to achievement. Bronfenbrenner (1961)[21] summarizing the findings of several of these
studies, comments that high achievement motivation appears to flourish in a
family atmosphere of 'cold democracy' where initial high levels of maternal

involvement are followed by pressures towards independence and accomplishment.

There is however no clearly defined causal relationship between parental attitudes, social class and achievement. Banks (1968) comments that this is possibly to be attributed either to methodological weaknesses in the studies or to insufficient empirical evidence. But to expect to find a causal relationship in human behaviour surely is to adopt an inappropriate model. However refined the survey design or analysis of data become man's behaviour can never be measured or controlled as finely as this kind of model requires because by its very nature it omits reference to man's personal interpretations of the situation in which he finds himself, the meanings he attaches to it and his own intentions. Human beings, as we saw earlier, do not just let things happen to them as if they had no power to control their own environment or their own actions. Just because a child happens to be born into a certain kind of family, to have parents with certain kinds of attitude and aspiration, it does not mean that he will be so influenced by them that his future is predictable. This in fact would be a highly pessimistic view of man, a sort of social determinism, whereby a child's birth circumstances determined or dictated what he achieved at school and what kind of occupation he was likely to enjoy. The model is very similar to the behaviourist one considered earlier in the discussion of S-R learning: it strips the child of his very characteristics as a human being, that is, of his own understanding, interpretation and intentions. Perhaps this has been the dominant paradigm in the sociology of education until recently, but with the change of perspective developing in the theory and practice of education generally we shall see a new paradigm emerging.

The argument pursued so far has attempted to show how the kinds of question we ask about human behaviour can determine our view of the child in school, the kinds of motivational control that can be adopted to get him to learn and the sort of explanation we offer for his success and failure. Questions about causes of behaviour lead us to take a view of children as passive beings whose behaviour or learning can be modified by reinforcement or reward and whose life chances are patterned by social factors beyond their control. Rewards, incentives and social motivators are generally referred to as types of extrinsic motivation. But the concept of achievement motivation, seen from the individual's point of view, with its emphasis on standards of excellence as well as other kinds of social stimulus that may be caught from a lively teacher, acts as a bridge from the view of the child as one whose behaviour can be moulded or controlled to one who can develop goals, intentions, aims for himself, an active agent rather than a puppet. Most current views of education held by teachers and educators in this country lay emphasis on children as active agents of their own learning; this of course implies that we need to consider not only causes of behaviour but also reasons for action and ask why children choose to act as they do, learn what they learn and how they interpret their experience.

If we view children as beings capable of purpose and intention, we imply that they are able to choose their own course of action instead of having it determined for them. But real choice implies understanding what there is to choose from; and to do this children have to learn for themselves the significance of their past and present experiences. Since one of the main purposes of this chapter is to raise questions about motivation in school, we must consider the way children interpret their experience in school, since although they may share common experiences there, they do not necessarily see the same meaning in them because of the variety of different latent cultures they bring with them from outside. Nor is their interpretation of school experience the same as that of their teacher. Unless the teacher understands, at any rate to some degree, how a child experiences his world, he will not understand how to help him to choose what interests to pursue (the content of his education) or how to help him to pursue them (his method of learning).

From a theoretical point of view then we need a different model of human behaviour from the behaviouristic one considered earlier in this chapter. Drawing upon the work of Berger and Luckman (1971)[22] who attempt to establish a different perspective within sociology, one which regards the individual as an 'active agent making sense of and coming to terms with the world in which he lives', Esland[23] uses this perspective against which to view children's learning in school. Thus learning is not simply repeating what the teacher has just been saying but consists of trying to make sense of it, in terms of one's own previous experience, by engaging in conversation or discussion with the teacher and other pupils. Esland refers to this process of trying to make sense of what is being said as an example of negotiation in a learning situation: pupils attempt to question, comment, find similarities with their previous knowledge, thus in some sense directing the nature of classroom interaction. Barnes (1969)[24] gives some interesting examples of such discussions recorded in secondary school. classrooms, where pupils are attempting to work out meanings for themselves, yet where the teacher is anxious to keep his own control over the pace and content of the lesson, as he has prepared it. It is interesting to note how the situation could be differently interpreted: one teacher might interpret the children's behaviour as disruptive, a deliberate intention 'play up', while another might see it from the child's point of view - an active attempt to understand what the teacher is trying to convey. Both explanations may be appropriate, but in any case, the kind of verbal interaction that goes on in school suggests that learning is inevitably a social process where each individual concerned is striving to incorporate new meanings into his own frame of reference. One of the teacher's tasks then is to create appropriate opportunities for children to do this; by providing situations where an exchange of experience is possible through language and other kinds of activity, he is facilitating the process of interaction which is all-important in a real learning situation. This is far from the mechanistic view discussed earlier, one where learning is seen as an individual matter and where the stamping in of a correct response by reward is seen to count as learning. In the view currently under discussion learning is seen not as a change of response but as a development of understanding and meaning. Children are motivated to learn not by rewards offered for correct responses; their learning is not teacher-controlled; they learn through social interaction in a situation which they can control to some extent themselves.

A similar view of man as an active agent striving after meaning is found in George Kelly's work on the psychology of personal constructs; he sees man trying to make sense of his world as a scientist does: that is in order to explain his experience he sets up hypotheses which he then revises and reformulates according to his interpretation of his experience. Although Kelly (1955)[25] attempted to apply this theory to many fields of human experience - personality development, abnormal behaviour, psychotherapy - education was not one of them, so in practical terms he has nothing directly to contribute to a discussion of school learning. Nevertheless, his view of man is worthy of mention, since it adds support to a perspective in which man is seen as an active interpreter of his own experiences - a view which deserves attention as a theoretical framework within which to view the school context.

If in trying to show how the individual child is helped to pursue learning, to develop concepts and to structure his own world, we first of all look at some important psychological processes involved, we shall discern interesting connections with the structural/developmental view of intelligence discussed in the previous chapter. When the child becomes aware of illogicalities in his own thinking he is enabled to go on to the next stage in logical thought (p.41-2); cognitive conflict, two conflicting pieces of evidence confronting the young thinker challenge him to solve the problem by pursuing it further: it thus has a motivating effect. But to use cognitive conflict in the classroom as a practical procedure for getting children to solve problems for themselves involves careful planning and structuring of appropriate problem situations. It is not easy for children to recognize conflicting evidence until they know enough about the content involved; they cannot recognize what is irregular or incongruous until they know what is regularly the case. Attention towards cognitive conflict may be aroused by novelty which in turn stimulates curiosity; curiosity impels the child to find out more about what he is doing and thus to discover how for example a toy is fixed together; whether all objects float; what will happen to seeds grown under different conditions. Just as intelligence does not merely develop by maturation but is a result of interaction with the environment, so children do not interact with their environment by recognizing and solving problems unless they are given some guidance. But before we consider what part the teacher can play, let us examine the concepts of curiosity, novelty, incongruity and cognitive conflict in relation to their importance in motivation.

Intrinisic motivation may be distinguished from extrinsic motivation in that whereas the latter depends upon reward extraneous to the learning process, a reward often satisfying some need condition, the former depends upon factors hinging on harmonious or dissonant relations within the learning process, for example the notion of perceptual conflict or cognitive imbalance. Reward in this system is closely related to the thought processes involved: satisfaction in solving a problem or resolving a conflict is rewarding to the learner. Berlyne (1960, 1963)[26] in a discussion of intrinsic motivation introduces the term 'epistemic curiosity' to refer to knowledge-seeking behaviour including questioning, observation, problem-solving. Epistemic curiosity then is concerned with pursuing knowledge for its own sake rather than for any reward extraneous to it. Closely associated with this notion, in Berlyne's schema, is conceptual conflict including perplexity, doubt, contradiction and conceptual incongruity. He suggests that conflict in this sense is related to the notion of uncertainty which is aroused by novel, surprising or puzzling situations. Epistemic or exploratory behaviour consists in collecting information to reduce uncertainty - thus the learner is motivated to discover new information for himself.

This is an interesting and plausible concept of motivation: it sees the child as an active, exploring agent who purposefully seeks knowledge for its own sake. What he learns is not devalued by the extraneous reward offered on the S-R pattern. Moreover he is not learning responses to somebody else's (the teacher's) questions or problems, but is recognizing problems for himself and solving them for the satisfaction of getting to know more and making more sense out of his accumulated experiences.

Various sources of evidence, some experimental, some from general educational experience, suggest that this kind of intrinsic motivation is not only a plausible concept but is also effective in school learning and can help children to understand and remember new material, and encourage them to search actively for new information, to attempt to solve problems for themselves as well as to recognize problems when they occur. But since children need constant help and guidance, teachers employ various devices to stimulate and maintain curiosity. The introduction of what is surprising or novel is for example frequently used in the teaching and learning of science. Thus children have to accommodate to and explain the surprising fact that although whales live and swim in water they are not fish but mammals. Before this is surprising to them however they have to have some familiarity with the biological concepts of fish and mammal since at any stage of development knowledge of the familiar must precede recognition of the unfamiliar or novel. Once a child, even a very young one, begins to show an interest in the novel, he ventures into areas of greater complexity both in terms of perception and action. McV. Hunt (1971)[27] in a discussion of intrinsic motivation in young children, attaches great importance to complexity in relation to children's interest and curiosity. In his view, a bored child is one for whom there is too little complexity in his environment. Just as a young baby will cease to pay attention to a very familiar pattern and become habituated to it, so an older child will cease to show interest in a skill he has learnt unless it increases in complexity. For instance, a beginner learning to play the piano will gain more pleasure and interest and will thus persist more if the music he is given to cope with is more complex than that which he has already mastered. Children will feel more challenged by greater complexity in dealing with number concepts than being required to practise the same skills repeatedly in which they are already competent. In planning work for children it follows that what is surprising or complex for one child will not necessarily evoke the same response in another; if surprise is to work as a motivational device, each individual child's stage of conceptual development must be considered. The planning of work must be largely on an individual or small group basis. It is interesting to note as McV. Hunt suggests that some children in the class may act as 'complexity models' for others. The fact that children see and take an interest in others performing tasks which are more complex than those they themselves can do adds support to the case for vertical grouping where younger children may be motivated to imitate the complexity model of an older peer; the same advantage may be derived from a system of mixed ability grouping in the junior and secondary school where again more able children performing more complex skills may provide their less advanced classmates with a model to follow.

Conceptual incongruity or ambiguity - or to use McV. Hunt's term, mismatch - are further devices the teacher may use to stimulate curiosity. Faced with information that does not tally or match, the child is invited to resolve the resulting conflict. Indeed this is the very situation that children find themselves confronted with in some of the Piagetian type situations, designed to show how they are helped to pass on to the next conceptual stage. In Piaget's original experiment on the conservation of liquids children were asked to say whether the amount of liquid was the same when it was poured from a short wide beaker into a tall thin one. Many of the younger children who had not yet grasped the concept of conservation - that is, that the amount of liquid must remain the same, regardless of what it *looks* like - said that there was more water in the tall thin beaker because it reached higher up the vessel. Frank (1964)[28] used a screening device in the usual conservation experiment to show that when children are confronted with an illogicality or ambiguity in their own thinking, they readily adopt a new thinking strategy provided that the ambiguity does not create such a large gap as to be nonsensical. Frank carried out the experiment in the way just described, noting the non-conservers. She then repeated it, this time placing a card across the front of the second beaker, so that children seeing the water being poured in, could not see how high it came. Several of those who had previously thought the tall thin beaker contained more water now gave a different answer: they judged it to be the same ' because it was the same water'. They had not been influenced by the appearance of the water and were now confronted with their own contradictory replies which they had to make sense of. Programmes of science education currently used in schools, such as the various Nuffield projects, aim at providing children with practical experience in science, giving them the opportunity to spot apparent incongruities or contradictions in what they observe: they are, it is hoped, thus challenged to pursue more information to create a total schema in which these apparent ambiguities are resolved. But such learning by discovery cannot be efficient without guidance and help in checking discoveries on the part of the teacher. A child frustrated by ambiguities he cannot explain without help is not likely to be stimulated to further curiosity. Thus the advice that 'we (teachers) need to get out of their way while they go about the business of learning' (McV. Hunt, 1971)[29] is really a vain hope. Teachers certainly need to structure the environment where all children can be guided towards the learning opportunities appropriate for each one; but they cannot then step aside. Their task is one of constant vigilance if the initial interest they have helped to create is to be maintained.

Implicit in the argument for intrinsic motivation is the assumption that there is greater value in seeking knowledge or pursuing interests for their own sake rather than for any extraneous reward, whether it be an immediate one like teacher approval or good marks or a more distant one such as examination success leading to wider occupational choice. But we must not overlook the fact that children may pursue interests and activities for their own sake which are regarded as trivial, valueless or even harmful. Interest as such does not solve all motivational problems since to pursue interests which are not educative is not what teachers would want to motivate children to do. Some selection of those interests which are worthwhile and of value must be made. There is no easy way of setting up criteria for what counts as worthwhile, since this must be a question of personal values and priorities. As such the problem will be discussed in Chapter VI. What concerns us here, once teacher and pupils have decided what is educationally worthwhile, is how to help children to care enough about what they are doing for them to be curious enough to continue without extrinsic reward. Psychological insight into intrinsic motivational processes has offered some help but it must be emphasized that an attitude of caring about what one is doing is nurtured in an atmosphere where adults, particularly teachers, show the same kind of involvement themselves. For a teacher to remark to a class in a secondary school that he's just as bored with the topic as the pupils, but since it is on the syllabus, they must get it over, is not only to devalue what they are supposed to be learning; it is also bound to destroy any interest and kill any motivation the class may have had. It betrays an attitude of non-commitment on the part of the teacher which will never engender enthusiasm in his pupils. Enthusiasm in the sense of being deeply committed to an interest, frequently an unusual one, is often discouraged and condemned as crankiness as we suggested earlier. We must all be familiar with examples of children who have accumulated masses of information and have really come to understand a topic they personally are concerned with: windmills, rare fungi, trains or even, like Cready, in Lacey's[30] study, stocks and shares. Knowlegeable enthusiasts, whether children or adults, are those who have become committed to an interest for its own sake and, once committed, there is an even stronger tendency to remain involved. One problem frequently facing teachers of older children in secondary schools is pupils' lack of interest in school work or indeed in school at all. Many teachers would in fact claim that it is easier to motivate young children by arousing their curiosity than it is to motivate adolescents whose curiosity is often difficult to arouse and impossible to maintain.

It is appropriate here to consider the relative merits of extrinsic and intrinsic motivation before going on to discuss social factors which affect children in school. To use extraneous rewards as a means of getting children to learn is, as we have said, morally dubious. Rewards can control a person's behaviour just as if he had no choice or autonomy of his own. If we are educating children and not just training them then a reliance on extrinsic motivation is highly questionable, since we do not want to turn children into passive automata producing correct responses. Offering children rewards can both devalue what they are supposed to be learning and act merely as a bribe. This is not to deny completely the value of rewards in learning; from one point of view the rewards are just as essential to the moral aspects of education as is punishment. They serve to point out to the learner where he is on the right path; they provide encouragement and they show that the teacher is interested in what children are doing and approves of it. But to make extraneous rewards the main attraction in a learning situation is to draw attention from what is being learnt on to something irrelevant to the content. Intrinsic motivation does not deny the notion of reward, but by definition it lies in the learning process itself: epistemic curiosity is satisfied by discovering something - the reward comes from the activity rather than being offered by another person.

Learning solely in terms of correct responses being stamped in by a process of reinforcement is also doubtful from the point of view of efficacy. Is this kind of learning long lasting or is it forgotten when rewards are no longer given? Does the motivation cease with the withdrawal of reward, as the S-R paradigm suggests? And this leads us to ask what we mean by learning: if we mean no more than producing correct responses (right answers to the teacher's questions) then reinforcement is a highly efficient process. However learning in an educative sense is much more than this: it involves understanding the point of what is being learnt as well as the reasons for learning it. It includes accommodating new experience to what has previously been assimilated, thus extending existing concepts and forming new ones. In order to do this the learner needs to be in a far less restricted situation than response learning allows him to be, since he needs to question, interpret, or even reject what he has learnt. There are times however when extrinsic rewards can be useful and are acceptable, but if relied upon all the time they lead to highly mechanistic learning. Perhaps extrinsic motivation - attracting children to learning by some outside incentive - is a way of leading them into an interest in learning for its own sake, if this has not already begun.

As we saw earlier, learning is never a purely individual matter, nor is becoming involved or motivated in an activity. Becker (1953)[31], writing within a sociological framework, offers us several useful conceptual tools with which to analyze the problem of motivation in a social situation which may be particularly useful for those dealing with adolescents. In his investigation of the way in which marijuana users come to derive pleasure from smoking he sets out to show how the motive to learn or to involve oneself does not always have to be present before the activity is begun; he suggests that people develop a disposition or motivation by engaging in an activity, rather than having the motive to do so at the outset. The argument runs then that it is possible to learn to enjoy certain kinds of activity by doing them; that it is only through doing them that one can learn the interest of them. School learning is a far cry from learning to smoke pot, but it is nevertheless interesting and possibly helpful to ask whether there is a case for persuading pupils to engage in activities towards which they initially have no inclination in the hope that they will gradually see the point and come to understand what the activities hold for them. It is a common experience that interest grows with increasing knowledge; the more we know about a topic, the more our attention is drawn to features we either already recognize or others we wish to know more about. It is worth remembering Bruner's[32] advice that we do not discover nearly so much as when we are already fairly well informed. 'Discovery, like surprise favours the well prepared mind'. Becker's notion of learning motives by engaging in an activity is reminiscent of Allport's[33] concept of functional autonomy where an individual begins an activity for purely instrumental purposes but then persists in the activity for its own sake. He argues that while many activities may originally have served some other motive, their persistence suggests that they have gained drive value of their own - that is, they are now independent of the original motives. Thus it seems plausible that if a pupil works hard at his History say, in order to pass his examination, he will gain an interest in historical knowledge and investigation for its own sake.

However one problem in secondary schools, especially with the older age group is that they do not get as far as being interested in specific subject areas because they are totally uncommitted to the school. School values and all that the school offers seem alien to them so that they do not give themselves the chance of involvement. It is important to realize how the school structure itself can create alternative careers in school which are disapproved of and discouraged by the teachers. Schools that are rigidly streamed create academic opportunities for the able children who can succeed in this area and thus follow a path through school that is officially encouraged. At the same time pupils in lower streams are automatically debarred from following an academic career. By being labelled 'non-academic' or D streamers they have been designated as academic failures. It is not surprising then that many pupils in this situation create other kinds of school careers for themselves; they form anti-school or delinquescent subcultures, to use Hargreaves' term. Hargreaves' study (1967)[34], as we saw in Chapter I, examines the effect of streaming on fourth year boys in a secondary modern school in which he worked both as teacher and researcher. He describes the constant hostility between the A stream boys who accept school values and the D stream pupils who reject all the school has to offer. Their growing dissatisfaction with school has led them to seek status and satisfaction elsewhere; their rejection of the pupil role is manifested in the premature adult roles they adopt - flagrantly smoking and drinking on school premises for example. Similarly, as we discussed earlier, Lacey's study (1966)[35] of a streamed grammar school shows how pupils become differentiated very early on, at the beginning of their second year, when they are streamed by ability. Early in their second year, the bottom stream pupils are considered difficult to teach and lacking interest in school learning and other school activities. These studies both suggest that pupils in low streams lack motivation, but we clearly need to ask how this lack of motivation originated. Lacey's findings give a clear indication that it can be created by the school; thus motivation becomes an organizational matter rather than purely an individual one. Once pupils see themselves failing in what the school approves of they are apt to form anti-school groups and by a process of situational adjustment their attitudes become even more consistently hostile to school values. Becker (1964)[36] uses the notion of situational adjustment to explain how individuals easily turn themselves into the sort of person a given situation requires if they wish to become and remain part of it. Thus for example, if an academically unsuccessful pupil finds satisfaction in being a member of an anti-school group he adopts the habits and attitudes of members of that group so that he is accepted by them and is part of that situation, no longer an outsider. Similarly a pupil who wishes to be successful in school and to adopt its values adjusts to the situation by behaving well in class, doing his homework on time, wearing correct uniform, and participating in extra-curricular activities. But the school structure makes it very difficult for him to do this, if, in streaming its pupils, it places those who want to adopt school values in streams where the situation is hostile; thus such pupils very often find themselves adjusting to a situation they originally found unsympathetic.

Once this process of adjustment (and therefore attitude change) has taken place, it can be difficult to escape because the individual finds himself committed by other social factors. Again we use Becker's concept of commitment to explain this. He considers that a person is committed when we observe him pursuing a consistent line of activity in varied situations, for example consistently rejecting school values. Commitment is maintained by fruitful rewards acquired in the situation, by relationships formed with others, by high status within the group etc. - all of which Becker[37] refers to as side-bets. Although however, as we have seen, the structure of the school can lead to little but failure for those pupils who are placed in low streams, we cannot feel assured that in an unstreamed situation these pupils would be any more committed to school. Adolescents' commitments outside it are likely to be strong in any case; the attraction offered by pop-cultures, presented to them most successfully via the mass media, require less effort than the intellectual challenges provided by the school.

This chapter has, it is hoped, shown that motivation is not only an individual process but is also influenced by social and organizational factors as well. The school organization creates the situation in which social processes operate. It is important to consider the overall organization of the school in terms of streaming, setting, all of which will be discussed later. Classroom organization too can create structures where pupils are labelled and come to see themselves as successes or failures, sometimes very early in their school experience, as the studies of Rist (1970)[38] and Goodacre (1968)[39] show. Situations can be created within the school or classroom which engender a particular kind of attitude towards the school's aims and thus influence motivation on a gross level. Within each social situation pupil interaction, situational adjustment, commitment help to influence the nature of motivation, so that when the teacher comes to consider how he personally can interest children, arouse their curiosity and whet their appetite for learning, he is not beginning in a vacuum. The school structure, the pupils' out-of-school experience as well as the subculture to which they belong in school are all forces the teacher has to consider. He may not be able to exert much influence over some of the strong forces, but his task will be easier if he learns to recognize them and understand their nature.

REFERENCES

1. D.H. Stott, 'Commentary on "The genetic determination of differences in intelligence: a study of monozygotic twins reared together and apart', Sir Cyril Burt', *British Journal of Psychology*, Vol.57, 1966
2. N.E. Miller and J. Dollard, *Social Learning and Imitation*, Yale Univeristy Press, 1941
3. M.L. Bigge and M.P. Hunt, *Psychological Foundations of Education*, Harper & Row, 1962, p.316
4. B.F. Skinner, *Cumulative Record*, Appleton-Century-Crofts, 1959
5. Fitzgerald, *School Review*, 1962
6. B.F. Skinner, *op.cit.*
7. B.F. Skinner, *op.cit.*
8. D. Barnes, J. Britfon and H. Rosen, *Language, the Learner and the School*, Penguin, 1969
9. J. Holt, *How Children Fail*, Penguin, 1964
10. E.B. Page, 'Teacher comments and student performance', *Journal of Educational Psychology*, 1958
11. D. Premack, 'Reinforcement theory' in D. Levine (ed.), *Nebraska Symposium in Motivation*, University of Nebraska Press, 1965
12. K. Lewin *et al*, 'Level of Aspiration' in J. McV. Hunt (ed.), *Personality and the Behaviour Disorders*, Ronald Press, 1944

13. D.C. McClelland *et al. The Achievement Motive,* Appleton-Century-Crofts, 1953
14. M.R. Winterbottom, 'The relation of the need for achievement to learning experiences in independence and mastery' in J.W. Atkinson (ed.), *Motives in Fantasy, Action and Society,* Van Nostrand, 1958
15. A. Bandura and R.H. Walters, *Social Learning and Personality Development,* Holt, Rinehart & Winston, 1970
16. O. Banks, *The Sociology of Education,* Batsford, 1968
17. F.R. Kluckholn and F.L. Strodtbeck, *Variations in Value Orientations,* Row Peterson, 1961
18. J. Kahl, 'Some measurements of achievement orientation', *American Journal of Sociology,* 1965
19. D.F. Swift, 'Social class and achievement motivation', *Educational Research,* Vol.8, No.2, 1966
20. B.C. Rosen, 'The achievement syndrome: a psychocultural dimension of social stratification', *American Sociological Review,* 1956
21. U. Bronfenbrenner, 'The changing American child', *Journal of Social Issues,* Vol.17, 1961
22. P.L. Berger and T. Luckman, *The Social Construction of Reality; Treatise in the Sociology of Knowledge,* Penguin, 1971
23. G.M. Esland, 'Teaching and learning as the organization of knowledge' in M.F.D. Young (ed.), *Knowledge and Control,* Collier-Macmillan, 1971
24. D. Barnes, *op.cit.*
25. G.A. Kelly, *The Psychology of Personal Constructs,* Norton, 1955
26. D.E. Berlyne, *Conflict, Arousal and Curiosity,* McGraw-Hill, 1960
27. J. McV. Hunt, 'Using intrinsic motivation to teach young children', *Educational Technology,* Vol.2, 1971. Reprinted in A. Cashdan and J. Whitehead, *Personality Growth and Learning,* Longman with Open University Press, 1971
28. F. Frank, 1964, referred to by J. Bruner in *Studies in Cognitive Growth,* Wiley, 1966. p.193-202
29. J. McV. Hunt, *op.cit.*
30. C. Lacey, *Hightown Grammar: School as a Social System,* Manchester University Press, 1970
31. H.S. Becker, 'Becoming a marijuana user', *American Journal of Sociology,* Vol.59, 1953. Reprinted in B. Cosin (ed.), *School and Society,* Routledge & Kegan Paul with Open University Press, 1971
32. J. Bruner, 'The act of discovery', *Harvard Educational Review,* 1961, vol.31
33. G.W. Allport, *Personality: a Psychological Interpretation,* Holt, Rinehart & Winston, 1937. Referred to in C.N. Cofer and M.H. Appley, *Motivation Theory and Research,* Wiley, 1968, p. 572
34. D.H. Hargreaves, *Social Relations in a Secondary School,* Routledge & Kegan Paul, 1967
35. C. Lacey, *op.cit.*
36. H.S. Becker, 'Personal change in adult life', *Sociometry,* 1964, Vol.27, Reprinted in *School and Society, op.cit.*
37. *Ibid.*
38. R.C. Rist, 'Student social class and teacher expectations: the self fulfilling prophecy in ghetto education', *Harvard Educational Review,* Vol.40, 1970
39. E.J. Goodacre, *Teachers and their pupils' home background,* NFER, 1968

IV Language and Learning

To write an introductory book on language learning would be a highly
difficult task because of the very wide range of issues that arise and the vast
quantities of empirical work that are available; to write one chapter on
language in an introduction to the Theory and Practice of Education is almost
an impossible undertaking. In order therefore to make any sense such a
chapter must inevitably be limited and can only outline to its readers some
of the main problems that they will want to pursue in their teaching; the
recommended reading can then be followed to fill in this outline according
to individuals' interests.

The main issues with which this chapter will deal are the nature and
function of language; language thought and concept learning; language and
social relationships; the learning of specialist language related to certain areas
of the curriculum and finally language and its relation to school progress and
achievement. And within our framework, each discussion will be centred
around practical classroom issues.

Because we all use language we tend to take its nature and functions for
granted; but without going into the highly complex philosophical problems
raised by the nature of language, it must be recognized that there are
difficulties in talking about its nature without reference to its functions.
Sapir (1949)[1] for example, tried to define language as 'a purely human, non-
instinctive method of communicating ideas, emotions and desires by means of
a system of voluntarily produced symbols'; similarly Wittgenstein[2], writing
of meaning, says 'the meaning of a word is its use in the language'. It is
however useful from a practical point of view to bear in mind the distinction
between *language* as a public system of symbols, agreed upon by common
usage, and *speech* which refers to individual utterances, that is an individual's
use of language. In the classroom context it will be mainly the latter which is
our concern though the distinction in terminology will not always be
observed. The language an individual uses has many functions and any one
utterance may have more than one. For example, a child may be seeking to
establish his relationship with his teacher or peers, while at the same time
conveying information. It would be a mistake to think of language in the
classroom merely as a means of presenting information as perhaps many
teachers in the past tended to do, influenced by the emphasis upon
propositional knowledge or curriculum content. The communication of

knowledge or information is only one of the important functions of language: others include the learning and precise use of concepts (where language is initially used as a recognizing device) and the expression of thought. Language serves as a means of exploring, understanding and gaining control of one's world, establishing relationships with others, developing and exploring aesthetic and moral sensibility.

Before these functions can be discussed in the light of their importance for learning in school it is essential to have some understanding of how children learn language. A cursory glance at some of the psychological literature dealing with language learning suggests that investigators have been predominantly concerned with the acquisition of language in the pre-school years. This emphasis has to a certain degree been misleading for teachers, many of whom tend to make assumptions about language learning that can set considerable limitations upon their own teaching: firstly, that language acquisition is the concern mainly of teachers of young children; secondly, that by the time children reach junior and certainly secondary school they should already have acquired sufficient linguistic competence to cope with the demands of school and that if they have not, then the fault lies in the home and there is little that they, the teachers, can do about it; thirdly that language is merely the medium for learning a certain body of knowledge. These assumptions ignore the fact that language learning is a continuous process, one that never ceases since we all constantly extend our use and understanding of language as our experience widens; they allow teachers to overlook the fact that children need to be helped to learn language at every stage and that language learning is important in its own right and is not just a subsidiary to learning something else.

Rather than take early language learning for granted it is salutary to remember how rapidly a young child learns such a complex rule system in so short a time. By the age of about four most children have acquired all the basic rules of syntax inherent in their native language. It is with this period of early language learning that much recent research is concerned, partly because of different theoretical viewpoints adopted to attempt to explain how children learn and partly because the very rapidity of the learning makes it such a baffling process to explain and understand.

One theoretical explanation of language - readily adopted by the layman because it appears to be common sense - is in terms of reinforcement and imitation. Within this framework learning is explained in terms of rewarding the child when he makes a correct or desired utterance and either ignoring him when he is wrong or correcting him in the hope that he will be able to imitate the right utterance. For instance if a young child says 'I goed' instead of 'I went' he is corrected; and when he eventually does get it right, he is praised. This kind of explanation, of which Skinner[3] and Mowrer[4] are proponents, belongs to a behaviourist tradition which sees the major part of any learning process in terms of rewarding correct responses. But while reward and imitation are useful explanations of some kind of language learning - the learning of vocabulary or learning how to name objects - they fail to explain the far more active nature of language learning. If reward and imitation were the sole mechanisms at work, how could we explain how children come to utter sentences they have never heard before?

McNeill's study of language acquisition in a two-year-old shows how the child's language is creative and innovative: he uses phrases that convey meaning, but because they are syntactically unique he could not have imitated them from anybody else. McNeill (1966)[5] shows how a young child builds up a limited store of words which he then uses to create novel utterances within his own simple but already structured linguistic system. From original phrases like 'the chocolate's all gone' or 'more milk' the child creates his own simple meaningful units by using the same pivot words in a different context: 'all gone outside' was his phrase to indicate the door being closed, while 'more page' meant that his mother was to go on reading to him. Such phrases are quite unlikely to have been imitated from others and suggest the child's ability at an early age to generate his own patterns of speech rather than merely imitating other people's.

The point of this example is not merely to illustrate the limitations of one theoretical explanation (since our context does not allow us to go into this kind of detail) but to show the force of the child's active learning where language is concerned. To accept that importance of the active learning and use of language is an important step for the teacher to take if he is to help to promote language development at any stage. Early utterances of this kind suggest that the child is not only imitating some of what he hears but is formulating his own rules and incorporating what he has learned from others into his own speech structure.

Further evidence to support this hypothesis stems from work on early syntactic structures. By the age of four most children have acquired the basic rules of morphology, that is the formation of plurals, past tenses and so on. (See for example Berko, 1958;[6] Fraser, Bellugi and Brown 1963[7]). Because of the surprising accuracy and rapidity with which children learn syntax, Chomsky (1959)[8] has suggested that there must be some innate mechanism which is exclusively a human characteristic, enabling human beings to learn language. McNeill calls this a 'language acquisition device' (LAD). It enables us not only to learn the syntax of our own language quickly but also helps us to recognize sentences as grammatically correct independently of their meaning. Chomsky's example of a nonsense sentence 'Colourless green ideas sleep furiously' is nevertheless recognizable as an English sentence and illustrates this point. Such an LAD would explain why adults' attempts to accelerate children's learning of syntax by expanding their utterances from a telegraphic form to a grammatically complete one (Rover garden - Rover is in the garden) do not meet with success until the child is capable of using such structures spontaneously. Brown and Bellugi (1964)[9] showed that a three-year-old will repeat the essential content of what an adult asks him to imitate but will contract it to his own type of reduced syntactic pattern. It seems that there is a strong developmental factor at work here, reminiscent of some kind of readiness device. Students concerned with young children will find it rewarding to pursue some of the current experimental work in this area for themselves, but since all teachers, whatever the age of their pupils, should recognize the importance of the active use and generation of language, the early stages should not be ignored.

If there is in fact some kind of LAD guiding children's ability to learn language (Cazden, 1968)[10] we may well ask why such emphasis is laid on the nature of the home environment by those concerned about children whose language learning seems to have been deficient. The explanation is partly a motivational one: children will cease to talk unless someone not only talks to them but also listens to them; for a child to increase his use of language and to expand his vocabulary, he needs to have something to talk about and somebody to talk to. In this way early experience is important, particularly sensory experience. Joan Tough (1973)[11] gives lively contrasting accounts of how children in different home and school environments have a good or limited opportunity to learn to expand their use of language, depending on the skill and interest of the mother or teacher. Some of Tough's classroom examples suggest the urgent need for teachers to learn to listen to what children have to say far more than many of them do at the moment. Children are frequently misunderstood, and valuable teaching opportunities are overlooked because teachers consider their pupils deficient in language learning, and as we have seen in our discussion of judgements of children, regard them as less able and possibly already doomed to failure at an early stage. Such teachers despair of children who cannot understand them, when clearly it would be more appropriate (and much easier) for teachers, with their far greater experience, to learn to understand children even if they do speak some kind of non-standard English, syntactically unique and lexically rich in a different way from that familiar to the teacher.

The learning of basic syntax is accomplished by the time children begin school, but language learning, with all its diverse ramifications, is far from complete, as James Britton[12] emphasizes. The classroom is a highly important context for language learning and should provide children with the opportunity to learn and use language in many different ways - its functions are manifold, as we saw earlier. Gone are the days when the classroom was always a place for silent concentration on individual tasks and children went in fear of breaking the rule of silence. Admittedly, there are some times when quiet is appropriate, but if we acknowledge the importance of continuous language learning in school we must admit that children only learn to use language by practising it; they do not learn to use it by listening to the teacher practising it, as this is entirely a one way process. As Rosen and Barnes (1969)[13] both comment, in a teacher-dominated classroom it is only the teacher who ever has the opportunity of practising language, whereas it is the children who need to.

We shall see later what functions are fulfilled by language in the classroom; for the moment some examples will be given of observations made of children using language in school. Children come to school using an everyday language of their own and much of their talk at the early stages consists in telling the teacher about their possessions, their family, their activities. A skilful teacher can enter into conversation at this level to promote further use of language, but as Joan Tough (1973) shows, must be sensitive to a child's readiness to be drawn into further conversation. Further questioning by the teacher when a child does not feel secure enough to be drawn will merely deter him from further spontaneous speech. Her discussions and illustrations of teachers and young children talking offer students excellent practical guidance on how to tackle the situation. If children are to benefit from talk in the classroom - or discussion as we tend to call it with older pupils - teachers must have some idea of how to exploit their comments in a systematic way.

Barnes (1969)[14], drawing upon observations of specialist teachers and children in their first year at secondary school, shows how it is possible to overlook or devalue what children have to say, by insisting on the use of language deemed appropriate to specialist teaching. A good example of this is his extract from a Chemistry lesson where children's contributions to a discussion of the suspension of solids in a liquid become anecdotal when they start talking of milk turning to cheese and smelling like cheese; the teacher, fearing children's everyday anecdotal knowledge and language, abruptly terminates the discussion by saying, 'Anyway, can we get on?' more intent on the content of his planned lesson than on what children offer spontaneously. By contrast an extract from a Geography lesson shows how children can be encouraged to explore specialist concepts (in this case, sand dunes) by trying to describe what they look like in their own terms, before they finally come upon the word 'crescent' that the teacher intended them to learn. Many of the first year class discussions cited by Barnes show how teachers who are successful encourage children to participate and introduce specialist subject matter to them by allowing them to discuss it in their own terms before introducing specialist terminology. In this way, they are encouraged to think aloud and are not merely required to recall or search for a one word right answer that the teacher has in mind.

One of the barriers to language learning at secondary level is, in Barnes' view, the practice adopted by many teachers of using mainly closed questions where one answer is expected, as opposed to open questions which allow children to explore ideas by suggesting their own possible solutions. Rosen describes this practice as nothing more than getting the pupils to tell the teacher what they know he already knows; it surely would be motivationally more effective for them, at least for part of the time, to tell him something new, using their own language, rather than stereotyped phrases.

We must not lose sight of the fact that children begin to learn to talk by generating their own speech patterns (McNeill, 1966);[15] if language is to continue to be a creative activity, then they must be encouraged to go on doing this. Barnes criticizes what he calls 'the language of secondary education', a register that many specialist teachers tend to adopt that resembles the language of textbooks or official impersonal publications. Illustrations of such impersonal language are found in a first year History lesson: 'these (city) states were complete in themselves because the terrain between cities was so difficult that it was hard for them to communicate . . .'. It is not the use of particular words that makes this kind of comment difficult for young pupils to understand, but the general impersonal tenor of the whole sentence; the language being used is far removed from what children themselves would say. If teachers take it for granted that children can understand this kind of language, this could be the beginning of a gulf between teachers and pupils created by teachers' failure to realize what children do not understand and by children's failure to question what they do not understand.

Britton (1969)[16] gives several substantial extracts between older pupils (in their third and fourth year of secondary schooling) in various contexts, sometimes with and sometimes without a teacher. These conversations show on the one hand how pupils explore social concepts (the family, quarrelling parents' authority and so on) and personal relationships, and, on the other, how a teacher can learn to develop pupils' language by talking with them but without assuming a dominant role in the discussion.

The studies referred to so far illustrate how children can learn through talking. It is equally important to consider how they might learn through writing. Britton has explored this field in his work with the Schools' Council Writing Research Unit in London.[17] In his examination of the written language of eleven to eighteen-year-olds he has shown that the style of writing varies according to the audience for whom it is intended. Britton sets up the following categories, which vary from the personal or intimate to the more impersonal or public, as a useful scale on which to analyze pupils' written language: writing for oneself; for the teacher as a trusted adult; for the teacher with whom the child has either a special or a general relationship; for the teacher as examiner; for a wider known audience; for an unknown audience. Just as the spoken language a child chooses is affected by the person he is talking to so also is the written language affected by the supposed audience for whom he is writing. The difficulty in trying to encourage children to write for different groups of readers ('pretend you are explaining to a visitor from outer space that . . .') is that the child knows that the teacher, in most circumstances, is the only one who will read his writing and since very often the work is assessed and graded, the child will be writing for the 'teacher as examiner' category.

We must not forget too that language learning does not end once children have left school or completed their formal education. As adults we acquire new interests and gather new experiences; as we do so we inevitably extend our knowledge of specialist areas with their own particular language without which it is difficult to pursue an interest in depth in a committed fashion. An interest in architecture, medieval music or industrial archaeology is inevitably accompanied by the learning of new concepts which require language perhaps hitherto unfamiliar. As adults we too begin by using our own everyday language to explore new fields but soon find the need to develop the more precise language skills appropriate to the area of interest.

For most practical purposes we are concerned with thought as it is conveyed to others rather than thought which is never communicated. Teachers can only know what and how children are thinking if they can express their thoughts and, although some thought may operate at a level of signs rather than symbols, intelligible thought must involve symbols of some kind, usually language. If teachers wish to know how to develop children's understanding and thinking they must begin with what children offer them, with the words and speech structures that children use. This means that they must analyze what children do with words, that is, analyze their *function*. It is only when they understand what kind of language games children are already playing that they can go on to initiate them into further language games appropriate to other forms of thought and understanding. More will be said on this issue later but first we shall consider some of the work on the origins of thought and language.

Language is so obviously and inextricably linked with thought that in order to be able to appreciate their mutual dependence teachers should have some understanding of the theoretical background within which observations of their relationship have been made. To consider the origins of thought and language we turn to the work of Vigotsky and Piaget to examine two different theoretical explanations of the interrelationship. In Vigotsky's[18] view 'thought development is determined by language . . . the child's intellectual growth is contingent on his mastering the social means of thought, that is, language'. Drawing on comparative data (the sounds produced by animals and human infants, together with their attempts at problem solving), Vigotsky recognized that speech and thought initially develop along different lines, independently of each other; speech at this stage is pre-intellectual and is largely emotional in nature, for example babbling, calling or crying. Similarly there is a pre-linguistic phase in the development of thought when the infant will perform simple actions, solve simple problems and clearly has some simple concept based mainly on recognition of the familiar, but has to accomplish all this without any attempt at speech.

In the human infant these two lines cross, according to Vigotsky, during the child's second year when he begins to learn to speak and to use his rudimentary language to help his problem solving activities. Speech is beginning to become rational rather than just emotional and 'thought' becomes verbal. This stage is marked by a sudden increase in the child's vocabulary and attempts to use language and also a certain curiosity about words. The child's activities are now almost invariably accompanied by speech; his actions appear to be guided by his own autonomous speech which at first is overt but later on appears to die away. Everyone familiar with young children at play knows how they talk to themselves, giving a running commentary on what they are doing, regardless of whether there is anybody present. Vigotsky suggests that even when children cease to talk aloud when playing this now inner or silent speech still plays an important function in regulating and directing activities. If the child's activities are frustrated or he encounters problems he cannot surmount in play, speech reappears at a remarkable rate, apparently to help him solve the problem.

The notion of language acting as a regulator mechanism receives support from Luria's work. In his clinical study (1956)[19] of five-year-old twins, retarded in all aspects of intellectual growth, he showed that when better opportunities were provided to promote language development, their behaviour generally showed signs of catching up with that of their age group. Play, which previously had been random, non-productive and non-directive became far more advanced with the use of language, in that the boys could now plan activities and follow them through without abandoning whatever they had been doing after only a few minutes. Further experimental work conducted by Luria (1959,[20] 1961[21]) supported the view that one important function of language is to guide and regulate behaviour which otherwise becomes random and inconsequential. On this view then language is seen to be a necessary condition of thought and of the development of intelligence.

Piaget's[22] emphasis is rather different; although ready to admit that language is necessary for thought to develop he does not regard it as a sufficient condition; rational or intelligent activities he sees as rooted in *action*. Action is considered important at three stages of development: the early sensory-motor stage when the infant is learning about his world through direct sensory experience (mainly touching, tasting, smelling); at the early stages of concrete logical operations when he begins to be able to classify and form categories - which he can best do manually before working it out by the use of language; and finally at the stage of logical thinking, when action, according to Piaget, is at the roots even of propositional logic. In these three areas Piaget suggests that language alone is not enough to explain thought because operations that characterize it nevertheless must be rooted in action. Without language however operations would necessarily remain at the stage of successive actions; they could be performed only one after the other and not simultaneously. This in fact is what language allows us to do: namely to be released from the here and now world of action to a level where future, past and present can be combined and where the purely hypothetical is possible.

The views of Piaget and Vigotsky differ in emphasis rather than in nature. But for our practical purposes two conclusions are of utmost importance: that children's intellectual development will be impeded without the use of language and that language development itself will be impeded without opportunities for activity. Although empirical evidence has cast doubt on the hypothesis that language development can be accelerated by adult expansion (Bellugi and Brown, 1964),[23] that concept development can be accelerated by practice in using specific linguistic structures (Sinclair de Zwart and Inhelder, 1969)[24] or by practice at specific activities before the child has reached an appropriate stage in development, we are still fairly sure that once this stage has been reached, constant use of language in an active environment is a necessary condition for continued development. Children do not talk, as we remarked earlier, unless they have something to talk about, hence the importance of a varied environment in the classroom, a rich programme of experiences outside it and opportunities provided to talk about activities and experiences. A child's environment may be rich in opportunities, but he has to learn to recognize them and to learn the interest of his surroundings; thus a vague idea of letting children loose to discover what is interesting for themselves usually makes nonsense. For most children, if not most adults, learning to find the interesting features of one's surroundings or experiences is a social activity; it has to be shared by a teacher who knows how to further the interest and by peers who participate in it.

Having considered the origins and interrelationship of language and thought in a general way, we now turn to a consideration of the part played by language in concept learning. Basically, to learn a concept means to recognize an object or event as belonging to a category or to recognize something already familiar. Early concepts then clearly do not depend upon the use of language; a baby learns to recognize his mother as the one who feeds and protects him long before the concept 'mother' is learned; animals too can be said to have acquired a concept when they distinguish between different objects; in food seeking experiments rats can learn to distinguish between different shapes; chicks have been shown to learn a relationship concept when they seek food from the brighter of two squares (black or grey; dark or light grey; grey or white). But clearly an adult human being develops far more sophisticated concepts than these and it is useful for us to examine what kinds of concept adults do use in order to understand how they are developed in children.

Dearden[25] offers a useful but simple account of the main kinds of concept we use: he distinguishes three important categories, though, as noted, this is a simplified scheme and not all concepts fit neatly into one of the categories, while some categories can be further subdivided. *Perceptual* concepts include physical objects such as cat, flower, earth, blue, straight, that is concepts which share certain manifest characteristics with other members of the same category. This group of concepts begins to be acquired by infants before they have a grasp of language, during the normal course of their random exploration of the environment. *Practical* concepts in Dearden's classification are those which are best understood by reference to their function, such as chair, post-office, book, door. *Theoretical* concepts include the far more abstract ones such as wisdom, truth, freedom, mass, weight. When we come to examine how these various types of concept are learned we shall see the rather different function of language and the implications for the ways in which teachers might help children to learn concepts of different kinds.

Children explore practical concepts by direct experience - looking at the objects, tasting them, touching and feeling them. There is no doubt that some sort of recognition goes on, but it is difficult to know whether the concept they 'discover' is the same as the one an adult has when he uses the publicly accepted symbol - its name - to denote it. If an adult points to an animal, telling the child it is a cat, how can the child know what is being pointed to unless he already has a concept of what a cat is and already understands the social convention of pointing? As far as he is concerned pointing could mean the finger used, the animal's fur, its colour, its tail and so on. This explanation of how children learn the names of objects is clearly not very satisfactory any more than is the abstractionist model whereby a child is supposed to abstract the attributes common to the class of objects denoted by a specific label (attributes such as fur, four legs, tail) and to understand that the label denotes a cat. Simple though it may seem, the early stages of language which involve no more than learning the names of objects are highly complex to explain theoretically. Wittgenstein suggests that children learn to use language by participating in 'language games' and learning the rules by playing these games. And before a child starts using words himself, he has had plenty of language preparation; he has handled objects, heard an adult refer to them by name, can recognize them. It is only when a child uses language to denote objects in the same way as adults that we can even suspect that he shares the same concepts. Yet to use words correctly as labels does not necessarily mean that the child fully understands the underlying concepts. Jahoda (1963)[27] shows how six-year-olds use geographical terms like 'town', 'city', 'capital' correctly in some contexts (for example 'London is the capital of England'), but in other contexts reveal incomplete understanding.

Learning to play language games is then a continuous process; moreover it is a social process. To make themselves intelligible children must learn the public rules governing the use of words. Without these rules (which are of course not explicitly taught) there would be no common understanding and no language as we know it. This notion of public rules governing the use of language is clearly applicable to the learning of practical concepts: children learn the uses and functions of concepts not only by observing adults using them but by talking about them themselves; language has gone beyond the mere labelling stage. They might learn the use of a spoon by observation, but it would be difficult to learn the use of a post-office or a bank merely by observing what people are doing in them. Without language none of the activities that go on in these places would make any sense at all, so that the concepts could never evolve.

Theoretical concepts, those we aim to introduce children to in school in various forms of knowledge and understanding would be quite impossible without using language in its widest sense. Labelling would be far too limited. How could the label 'truth' tell us anything about the concept behind it? Even when specific theoretical concepts are labelled by the same word (fish, mammal, bird - Natadze, 1963),[28] real understanding develops only by reference to theoretical insight gained by symbolic means - the use of publicly shared language.

What has been said here about the learning of concepts through language should serve to cast doubt on the validity of pure discovery learning in school. Children cannot possibly discover for themselves what they have no inkling of; they would not even recognize what they had discovered without constant checking, discussion and guidance from their teachers. This is absolutely essential as concepts are learned, differentiated and extended. Continuous reference to examples and dialogue between teacher and pupil are needed if pupils are to learn concepts precisely enough to make real sense of them. Group work is helpful especially when children have grasped certain concepts but unguided group discussion can be just as fruitless as the unguided discovery a child might pursue on his own.

Since language is manifestly important in acquiring any but the simplest of perceptual concepts, how do those children come to understand their world who cannot use language? Work up to the early 1960s had suggested that deaf children, because of poor linguistic powers are likely to be retarded in concept formation. Oléron (1953)[29] reports a study of deaf five to seven-year-olds showing that even though deaf children achieved increasing success with age on a transposition task, they are unlikely to reach the standard of hearing children. Chulliat and Oléron (1955)[30] had similarly found that the deaf were impeded in their ability to transpose experience to new tasks by the paucity of their language which prevented them from organizing schemes of past experience satisfactorily; Vincent (1957)[31] found that deaf children, when required to classify things by more than one criterion, were unable to do so because of the rigidity of their mental structure. Ewing (1957),[32] summarizing the literature to date on concept learning in deaf children, comments that 'There are indications that subnormal linguistic experience causes a lack of intellectual flexibility' and hence inability to form concepts at the level reached by normal children.

This in fact seems a very plausible explanation of the retardation of the deaf, in view of the important function of language that we have been discussing. But Furth more recently (1966)[33] has questioned this long held assumption. Observing that mature deaf adults seem to differ only minimally from similar hearing adults although they do show certain differences in thinking, he posed certain questions. Are these differences in thinking to be attributed to deafness itself and thus to reduced linguistic competence or might they be due to the fact that deaf people are ill-informed on many things that a hearing person picks up casually in the course of ordinary social intercourse? Are deaf people socially restricted because of their handicap? To what extent are their personality and thinking shaped by the emotional effects of their handicap and the years spent in the restricted environment of a boarding school for the deaf?

Such considerations prompted Furth to launch a highly ambitious programme of experiments to attempt to discover the precise nature of deaf children's thinking in order to establish whether they need necessarily remain

retarded or different throughout life. His finding led him to the tentative
conclusion that although the deaf are retarded in certain areas of concept
learning (for example, in the discovery of a concept but not in its use; in
shifting from one principle to another in categorization, because of rigidity
of thought) this is a result of their limited social experience rather than a
direct or necessary consequence of linguistic deficiency. He suggests that we
should look for a relationship between *social* environment and intellectual
development rather than between linguistic deficiency and intellectual
deficiency. The restricted nature of a deaf child's early environment does not
motivate him to ask questions, to pick up information casually or to be
offered random information in a variety of situations in the same way as a
normal child does. The fact that deaf people seem unable to look for reasons
or principles but are not unable to reason is to be attributed to the nature of
their early training and education, Furth suggests. Parents of deaf children
are not encouraged to convey information to them by pointing, gesture,
pictures; they therefore not only grow up ill-informed, but are not
encouraged to examine facts or display any intellectual (epistemic) curiosity.
Once they have grasped a principle it seems that they are taught to use it
repetitively and therefore rigidly; the kind of thinking considered retarded,
then, seems to be actively encouraged by their early upbringing, possibly
because those caring for them are relieved to find some kind of thinking going
on, but certainly because they lack the skills and techniques to use non-
linguistic means of stimulating curiosity. Furth makes suggestions for some
kind of enrichment programme employing non-verbal techniques.

An interesting suggestion for experimentation, but one fraught with
difficulties, as we shall see later, is to compare normal deaf subjects with
hearing people whose experience has been restricted. Furth[34] says 'It would
simply consist of obtaining a sample of persons who could be assumed to be
culturally deprived and comparing the performance of these persons with
that of the deaf on some critical tasks'. It is certainly of interest and value to
question the assumption that the thinking difficulties of the deaf are always
due to linguistic incompetence but to regard it as a simple matter to assume
that others are culturally deprived is dangerous and bound to create more
problems than it would hope to solve.

To the category of theoretical concepts belong those in which specialist
areas of knowedge and forms of understanding are couched. It is only in
school that children have access to new kinds of specialist knowledge each of
which is embodied in its own specialist sublanguage with its own particular
concepts. The more deeply a person comes to understand an area, the further
the language is away from that of everyday life. In fact, in order to gain a full
understanding of a specialist area, its language must be mastered so that the

appropriate observation and description, generalization and abstraction can be made. It is indeed difficult to argue precisely or to speculate at a hypothetical level if one is restricted to everyday speech which is imprecise and personal in nature. The important but difficult step children have to be helped to make is the transition from their everyday language in which they will first explore their own new experiences, say in Science or History, to the language appropriate to such thinking. This is difficult, as Rosen (1967)[35] reminds us, since if children are passionately interested in an area they will be personally involved, and yet are required to eliminate the personal element from their talking and especially from their writing. The only way they can make the transition is to be encouraged to use their own language initially, gradually adopting specialist terms and stylistic conventions which they become familiar with through active discussion with their teacher. Britton gives an example of how a successful teacher manages to do this in his report of a Nuffield Science Project with first year secondary school pupils (Barnes, 1969).[36]

If a teacher becomes over-concerned with the terminology of his subject, pupils will be baffled; it will seem too arid, distant and difficult for them to participate in and their learning is likely to deteriorate into meaningless note-taking and rote learning. An example quoted by Barnes (1969) of a Chemistry lesson well illustrates the case in point (Barnes *et al.*).[37] Science in particular requires an impersonal register which has been evolved to meet the needs of scientific method and enquiry. It is the language of the educated adult, and as such has a certain excitement for children provided that they learn to use it effectively; to do this they need considerable linguistic preparation - just as Wittgenstein suggests in the initial learning of simple concepts in one's mother tongue. If teachers emphasize the content of their subject and assume either that language will come of its own accord for the more able pupils, or that some of the others will never be able to learn it, then they are doing an injustice not only to their pupils but also to their own subject. The teacher's own use of language in class is clearly of prime importance; if he devotes most of his teaching time to posing closed questions or formulating notes for his pupils, they will probably never gain a glimpse of the real excitement and interest his specialist subject holds.

Scientific language, as we have seen, is essentially impersonal, to match the nature of the objectivity of science; in talking or writing about science children learn not to express personal feelings, opinions and so on. But other areas of experience we hope to introduce pupils to in school do not demand the same attitude; that of aesthetic awareness, for example, requires a personal response. Most children are given at least a limited opportunity for aesthetic experience, be it in painting, music, design, literature. However it is a sad reflection of the kind of aesthetic education most people have, to note how limited their expressive powers are in this field. Those whose comments on a work of art consist of little more than terms like 'nice', 'lovely', 'beautiful' surely do not derive as much appreciation as if they knew more precisely what they found appealing about it. Knowing what is pleasing involves having the appropriate language in which to express one's own appreciation and response. The language of aesthetics is by no means easy, but children can be helped towards this form of awareness firstly by enjoying aesthetic experiences, secondly by knowing something about them, thirdly by being made sensitive towards the different interpretations of some of the very general terms that tend to be used. What could be understood by a 'good' work of art? What reasons can be given for liking a sculpture, for saying a piece of music is great, that a picture is beautiful?

Yet another important area where appropriate linguistic understanding and use is of prime importance is that of morality - not a specialist area, as Science, Mathematics, History might be said to be, since morality permeates all of social life and therefore all school activities, but it is certainly an area that has its own language and concepts. Moral terms such as good/bad, right/ wrong are used by adults to very young children. As part of their moral education children have to learn to distinguish between the descriptive and evaluative use of such terms in order to be able to understand the nature of moral values and what these imply for their own behaviour. There is nothing evaluative in talking of a 'bad apple' or 'going the wrong way' where the terms 'bad' and 'wrong' are used literally and not figuratively or metaphor- ically, whereas to tell a child it is 'wrong' to tell lies implies a moral judge- ment. Unless children are helped gradually to understand the subtleties of the moral language they encounter, they are far more likely to be morally trained or even indoctrinated than morally educated.

From what has been said so far about the importance of using language appropriate to certain areas of discourse it will have emerged that the choice of language is regulated to some extent by the context in which it is used. This notion will be explored in two ways: we shall examine first of all how language may be affected by the context or culture in which it develops in order to explore ways in which children's experience of their world is shaped by the language they learn. Then we shall go on to consider how we learn to choose language appropriately according to the nature of the social situation in which we find ourselves.

An interesting theoretical viewpoint to consider is that of the cultural anthropologists, Whorf and Sapir, as they deny that man possesses a biological predisposition for language acquisition (contrary to the views of Chomsky and McNeill). Sapir believed that our perception of the world is largely shaped by language and that therefore 'the worlds in which different societies live are distinct worlds' (1949).[38] Similarly Whorf[39] who formulated the hypothesis of linguistic relativity (1956) believed that our world, initially nothing more than a flux of impressions, has to be organized largely by the linguistic system of the culture in which we happen to be born. He comments that 'no individual is free to describe nature with absolute impartiality but is constrained to certain modes of communication even while he thinks himself free'.

Whorf was particularly interested in vocabulary constraints and suggested that the words available in our native language determine the concepts we can acquire. One of the most frequently quoted instances of this is the vast range of specific words in the Eskimo language to denote various kinds of snow and icė. Similarly the language spoken in the Brazilian jungle is abundantly rich in words for palm trees and parrots - all instances where English, by comparison, has only one or two specific words, and where differences, where required, have to be expressed in phrases, for example 'tightly packed snow'. Whorf's hypothesis was that we perceive what we have words for, implying that the language available to us serves to shape our world. Similar claims were made for the influence of structural differences in language upon human experience: a Hopi (Red Indian) language has no verb system as we know it, but expresses duration of time by a complex series of nouns.

It would appear from these hypotheses that language is causally related to cognitive structure - and of course if this were so it would have important implications for subcultural differences in relation to language and learning in school. But the direction of causality cannot be determined: it is not possible to be sure whether we form only those concepts for which there is appropriate language already available or whether we develop new language because we need to express those concepts we have. Probably the availability or frequency of usage of concepts is in question. In English we have no specific words for certain kinship relationships probably because we do not single them out for separate consideration. We have to talk of a paternal or maternal grandfather rather than having separate terms; similarly aunts and uncles are so labelled regardless of whether they stem from our mother's or father's side of the family or whether they belong by marriage or by blood. These differences are not important to our kinship structure, whereas certain cultures where such differences are important have an abundance of terms to make the necessary distinctions.

Apart from the interest of such speculations, the cultural relativist position has been briefly introduced here because it was on this view that Bernstein based his early work on language codes which he considered to vary according to subculture or class. The implications of this view will be examined later in the context of school learning.

But let us first consider a rather different effect of context upon language. The cultural relativity hypothesis suggests that the language an individual has at his disposal is one shaped by a broad context, the culture into which he is born, and that he therefore contributes little to his own linguistic and perceptual development. Even if this view has been disputed, it does highlight the importance of context for language and here we shall consider context in a narrower sense and ask how the situation an individual finds himself in helps to influence the language he chooses to use. Here the speaker is by no means completely constrained but it will become clear that a child learns to distinguish between language deemed appropriate or inappropriate by adults according to the nature of the child's relationship towards those with whom he is speaking.

Like other areas of human action discussed in this book, language is not something static but is a dynamic process. Language can control an individual by helping to shape his perception, concept learning and thought processes, yet in the social sphere it can also be used by him to control others. The study of language can in fact reveal much about the nature and network of social relationships in any community. Language can serve as an index of social interaction, since it both unifies and divides in the sense that people sharing a common language or dialect regard themselves as belonging together; newcomers to the group have to learn to use the appropriate language before they are fully accepted, yet if they venture to use it before members are prepared to accept them their behaviour may be regarded as offensive. For example for an outsider to use familiar or pet names for members of a group is usually unacceptable. It follows then that to use a different language from the majority marks one out as being different. Language can be said to be a symbol of group and individual identity. An individual's right to use language in certain ways and in particular contexts is usually controlled by what is socially acceptable, permitted or prohibited. Just as dress, eating habits and other social conventions are regulated by the rules established in a given community so language and speech are to some extent governed by similar rules. For example, children in most schools are not permitted to address their teachers by their first names, though this is a rule which may be relaxed in institutions which regard themselves as particularly progressive. It is still considered inappropriate for teachers to use anything but surnames in addressing boys in some grammar and public schools and a teacher who flaunts this rule is regarded as somewhat odd. In fact a deliberate breach of such speech rules and conventions often represents a rejection of the role others expect him to play, thus disrupting the social order in his immediate community and causing a way of life hitherto taken for granted to be questioned. An unintentional breach of such rules on the other hand is regarded as social ineptitude.

Values are attached to different kinds of language whereby some kinds are regarded as of higher status than others: standard or BBC English tends in this country to have a higher status than a Liverpool or Glasgow dialect. High status language is deliberately chosen by those who have the choice to give some indication of their own status. Certain groups of individuals can exercise power over others socially by means of the language they use: it is fairly common for example for members of the medical or legal profession to be seen by their patients or clients as more powerful than themselves, partly because of the specialist, manifestly learned terminology they employ. Furthermore accent too can be regarded as an indication of social power or high status. Giles (1971)[40] showed that speakers of received pronunciation (RP), that is, BBC English, were rated as more prestigious, competent, intelligent than speakers with South Welsh or Somerset accents, but less favourably on social traits. Regional speakers were considered to have greater personal integrity, social attractiveness and sense of humour. We saw in our discussion of making judgements of children how easily first impressions can be formed on the basis of appearance, dress and so on. The language a child uses or the accent he has acquired may equally serve as a cue for forming a judgement. If Giles' finding is general then the 'well-spoken' child with a standard southern English accent is going to be at an unfair advantage when judgements are made.

The school is clearly one of the contexts where such rules and conventions about the use of speech and language operate. When children come to school they have to learn rules governing forms of address to the teacher, appropriate vocabulary, grammatical structure and pronunciation that are acceptable. By subtle means they learn the role expected of them as pupils, one of its important characteristics being a greater social distance between pupil and teacher than the young child has previously experienced in his relationships with adults. He frequently has to learn to respond to verbal cues he has never yet encountered but which his teacher expects him to act upon. Joan Tough (1973)[41] shows how a four-year-old boy fails to respond to an indirect request such as 'Would you pick the towel up for me before someone treads on it?' 'What do we do with a towel Jimmy?', 'Would you like to hang it up?' and only does as requested when a direct instruction is given. Such phrases as 'would you like to . . .', 'would you mind . . .' are indirect ways used by adults to make a request or command seem more polite, but their implication is lost with young children who have always been ordered to do things in direct command form at home. A child used to a different set of verbal cues may easily assume that if he is not being told directly what to do he need pay no attention to what his teacher says. He therefore appears to be deliberately disobedient, but in fact has failed to understand what is required of him.

Adolescents are more likely deliberately to flaunt rules of linguistic convention in an attempt to reject the pupil role imposed upon them. Countless examples come to mind of fourteen and fifteen-year-olds failing to use what the teacher considers an appropriate mode of address, suitable choice of vocabulary and so on. Social differentiation in school is recognized by pupils using non-standard English who receive their teachers' disapproval. As we saw earlier, children's everyday language is frequently rejected by teachers who want to force pupils to use standard English; but this can become colourless and lose vitality if the pupils regard it as something not their own. Barnes' observations show how teachers exert subtle control in the classroom by the use of the language of secondary education, to use his term.

Poor linguistic competence, including the use of non-standard English has, at least since the 1950s when differences in educability caught everybody's attention, been put forward to explain the apparent disadvantage of lower working class children over their middle class peers. After the 1944 Education Act when equality of opportunity was interpreted as the right of all children, regardless of family circumstances, to have the chance to obtain a place in a selective school, it was found that still a far greater proportion of middle class children succeeded in gaining grammar school places, mainly on the basis of intelligence tests used for selection purposes. Subsequent research revealed that lower working class children were less successful than middle class ones not only at the stage of the 11+ transfer but right from the time they entered school up to sixth form level. Fewer working class children were placed in higher streams within the school or higher groups within the class; more are labelled as incipient failures by their teachers at the infant stage (Fuchs, 1968;[42] Goodacre, 1968[43]). Once at secondary school more are placed in lower streams and leave early, and subsequently fail to take advantage of further education (Little and Westergaard, 1964).[44] We have already seen how teachers help to shape these disadvantages, but little has been said so far about basic differences in learning which might depend on the ability to understand and use language. Joan Tough (1973)[45] showed how nursery school children may fail to understand a teacher's linguistic cues if her style of speaking differs from that which a child has learned to interpret at home. Even at this very early stage then differences in language ability or competence lead to differences in understanding, responding to the teacher and social learning.

Clearly children do come to school with different degrees of linguistic competence and it would be interesting first of all to consider various kinds of learning to see how far they depend on language and thus where the children at a linguistic disadvantage are inevitably going to be hampered in their learning. Are some of the most important types of school learning such as the acquisition of skills, the learning of concepts, the development of logical reasoning, the growth of moral understanding impeded because of a poor grasp of language? Simple skills, such as walking, climbing, running are acquired by autogenous practice before children can use or understand language, but as Luria (1956)[46] has shown, language serves to regulate even behaviour of this kind so that it becomes better planned and more coordinated. However, more complex skills such as athletic skills, the use of tools and machinery, the use of instruments and apparatus could not simply be picked up (or if they were, would be learnt clumsily and with errors) but require instruction and explanation as well as demonstration if they are to be fully understood. The learning of concepts has already been discussed at some length; a reminder here will suffice. Perceptual concepts and some practical ones can be learned without language, but abstract, logical, relational concepts inevitably rely on the use of language. How for instance could a child learn the significance of 'either/or', 'neither/nor', 'although' and so on without participating in language games with others more experienced than he? Logical reasoning, although it has its roots in action, as Piaget shows, cannot develop adequately without the use of language which frees the thinker from the here and now, enabling him to deal with simultaneous mental operations and not to be confined to consecutive ones. Hypothetical thinking, the basis of scientific and mathematical reasoning, involving conditional propositions would clearly suffer. Furthermore, the kind of social and moral learning that would be possible without language would be akin to training; a child or even an animal can be trained by conditioning techniques to adhere to certain social conventions and even to appear to behave morally. He learns to do what he knows adults want for fear of punishment and disapproval or to obtain reward or favour. But moral understanding to a point where one is able to work out one's own values must develop as a result of understanding reasons for actions and being able to justify one's moral stance. Such understanding relies heavily on linguistic means. If all these basic kinds of learning, let alone the learning of different forms of understanding embodied in different areas of the curriculum, rely on language, then it is of major concern to teachers if some children begin with an initial linguistic disadvantage. Since so much formal school learning depends on the use of language, the problem for teachers is to identify the source of linguistic disadvantage.

Bernstein (1958)[47] was one of the first to tackle the problem of differences in spoken language. Set within a sociological framework, his theory attempted to explain speech differences in terms of early social relationships the young child forms within the family. In his early papers he tried to trace the relationship between social class, language and learning.

Social class, always a problematic term, was seen for his purposes as two broad subgroups: the working class where neither parent has had a selective secondary education or any skilled training and the middle class where both parents have had a selective secondary education and hold non-manual jobs. There is too a transitional or upwardly mobile working class group, some of whom have had some experience of selective secondary education or have been trained in a specific skill. The marked differences in language, social relationships and control that Bernstein discusses refer mainly to the two extremes of these subgroups - *lower* working class and middle class. Scant justice can be done here to the evolution of Bernstein's theory and students should certainly pursue some of the summaries of his theory to help them to tackle his original papers if his ideas are not to be misinterpreted, as sadly they have been, by those who are only superficially familiar with them. Working on the hypothesis that lower working class children will be less linguistically competent than their middle class peers because of the greater stress laid by middle class parents on language, he established that on a verbal test of intelligence (Mill Hill Vocabulary Test) working class adolescent boys scored significantly lower than a comparable middle class sample, while on a non-verbal test (Raven's Progressive Matrices) the discrepancy in performance was not significant. He went on to argue from these findings, albeit from a very small sample of subjects, that a great deal of potential ability is being lost in that working class subjects may have failed to reach grammar school because of their poor performance on the selection tests which are mainly verbal.

Differences in the kind of speech system or language code that children develop are part of the process of socialization, Bernstein suggests. Families from different social backgrounds have different attitudes towards child rearing and thus different kinds of relationship are formed between parents and children; these relationships in turn affect the use of language. Several general conclusions emerge from empirical studies carried out by Bernstein and his co-workers, indicating where these early differences originate. From an analysis of replies given by 50 working class and 50 middle class mothers, all randomly selected, Bernstein and Henderson (1969)[48] drew conclusions about the ways in which the different types of social interaction that develop duly affect the child's dependence on and use of language to express his needs. Clearly there will be exceptions: not all apparently working class or middle class mothers will conform to a general stereotype, so it is important to remember that what follows indicates a general tendency. Middle class mothers are less likely to use coercive means of controlling their children (including smacking or unelaborated commands) but will tend to explain to their children why they regard their behaviour as undesirable, they are more likely to enter into and encourage conversation with their children and will attempt to answer difficult questions rather than evade them as many working class mothers do. Jean Jones (1966),[49] again using a questionnaire technique, drawing from a sample of 360 mothers found that middle class mothers tend to prepare their five-year-olds for a more active role in school than do working class mothers, by reading to them, encouraging them to join a library, talking about school and showing their children similarities between home and school, recognizing the educational significance of toys and play. In terms of language development, this active role adopted early by middle class infants will make them more ready to talk to their teacher, wanting to find out things by asking rather than simply waiting to be told. Bernstein and Henderson's evidence supports this view: they suggest that middle class children are encouraged to learn the principles of skills, whereas working class children assume a passive learning role in that they are told by their mothers how things work and not expected to work it out for themselves, thus failing to gain autonomy or to engage actively in their own learning. Robinson and Rackstraw (1967)[50] dealing with the way mothers cope with children's questions, found that working class mothers are less likely to reply accurately to children's questions or even to answer them at all; less likely to explain or give elaborate answers; more likely to appeal to tradition in getting children to conform or obey. What emerges then from these various studies is that children are socialized differently according to the family subculture and that the emphasis put upon speech and language during the socialization process differs according to social class.

What then are the educational implications of such differences in early socialization and its effect on the use of language? Bernstein[51] suggests the possibility of two different language codes. The restricted code is characterized by short sentences, frequently unfinished and with poor syntactical structure; frequent use of short commands and questions; a limited use of adjectives and adverbs; avoidance of impersonal and passive forms; use of clichés and idiomatic phrases without variation according to context. The restricted code speaker does not make himself explicit through language but relies heavily on gesture, intonation, and appeals to the listener in terms of 'You know what I mean?', 'See?' and so on. The elaborated code because of its greater structural complexity is one in which the speaker does make himself explicit without having to rely on non-verbal cues or the shared sympathy of the listener. Because of fewer clichés and well-worn phrases, the speech used by elaborated code speakers is at once more personal and less predictable. From this brief description of the codes it can be seen that a restricted code is more likely to be used when people share common experiences and are well enough acquainted with one another for meanings and intentions not to have to be made explicit. It would normally be used by any speaker within his own family or with close friends for example.

Bernstein suggested in his early work that most working class speakers, as a result of the way in which they have experienced socialization in the early years, are confined to a restricted code, while middle class speakers have access to both. Since formal school learning requires children to make themselves explicit through language, those who can do so - middle class children - are at an educational advantage. One way in which working class children fail to make themselves explicit in words is that meaning for them tends to be implicit, context bound or particularistic, whereas the middle class child can operate in a context independent situation.

The work of Hawkins (1969)[52] with five-year-olds who were asked to tell the story depicted in a series of pictures shows these differences: working class children tend to use pronouns instead of nouns so that unless the listener knows the context in which they are operating (in this case, unless he himself is looking at the pictures) he will not be at all clear about what the children are describing. The middle class five-year-olds are able to make clear to a listener what the pictures contain: their speech is universalistic or context independent. If such linguistic differences are apparent so early and in the case of working class children do limit their opportunity to benefit from school experiences, then it is quite possible that by the time they reach secondary school the gulf between middle and working class children is considerable. We shall see in another context that there are gross social class differences in educational performance: differences in the use of language may well be one important contributory factor.

Bernstein's work has been stringently criticized on methodological grounds (see especially Coulthard, 1969);[53] no doubt much of this criticism is justified, but anybody who pursues the *development* of such a theory as Bernstein's (amply documented over the past sixteen years) must acknowledge that the investigator is bound to stumble and make modifications in groping his way towards further understanding. Research methods indeed would not develop at all if errors did not give rise to modification and eventually to improvement. But of greater concern here in the context of language in education are the implications Bernstein's work has had for educational practice, many of them unfortunately based on a misunderstanding of his basic tenets. His early papers, published towards the end of the 1950s, came at a time when teachers had been made aware of gross inequalities in educational opportunity in this country. The idea that working class children were failing because of their linguistic disadvantage was seized upon eagerly by teachers to explain why such children, in spite of the teachers' efforts, were not succeeding in school.

However it was unfortunate that Bernstein's notion of a restricted code gradually came to be regarded as an inferior kind of speech, as some sort of non-standard, second-rate language which made school learning difficult and impeded logical thinking. In spite of Bernstein's comments (though perhaps not pointed or forceful enough in the early papers) that a restricted code was not to be regarded as second-rate, and that one code is not *better* than another, since 'each possesses its own aesthetic, its own possibilities' (Bernstein, 1964),[54] the implication seen by his critics (for example Labov, (1969)[55] and, more important for practice, by teachers, many of whom became half-familiar with his theories, was one of linguistic disadvantage or even deprivation. And the idea of linguistic deprivation as one aspect of cultural deprivation was not without support in educational circles, particularly in the USA where compensatory educational programmes have been in operation from 1960 onwards. One of the assumptions upon which compensatory programmes were based was that certain disadvantaged children have difficulty in school because of poor language development and that educational methods can remedy these difficulties. The hampering effects of children's early impoverished home environment were thought to be reversible by the use of certain remedial or enrichment techniques.

The emphasis placed on language in American compensatory programmes must be attributed partly to the assumed interdependence between thought and language, though as we saw earlier, the nature of this relationship is by no means clear. Nevertheless great emphasis was placed upon language in the American pre-school intervention programmes, such as the Bereiter and Engelmann language development programme.[56] The basic aim of this programme is to develop in pre-school children sufficient understanding of language for them to grasp 'identity statements' and their negative counter-parts ('this is a cat'; 'this is not a dog'), to accelerate their concept learning and enable them to understand from their teacher when they are right or wrong. Four-year-old children work with one teacher in groups of five for twenty minute periods a day. Effort is concentrated on helping them to classify objects by showing them pictures and bombarding them with questions to which they are taught to respond in chorus. It is thus a programme based on drill in sentence structure and use of words and as such has been used to teach standard English to negro children and other non-standard English speakers. Other programmes, such as that of Blank and Solomon (1968)[57] give individual language tuition to children where the teacher works upon the child's responses and draws him into conversation about his activities while he is playing - in some ways reminiscent of the methods used by Joan Tough (1973)[58] in the ordinary classroom. These programmes have had varying degrees of success but naturally enough have

not escaped criticism, particularly on the grounds of teaching methods
employed. Language programmes as such have been far less widespread in
this country, though we may note the Gahagans' 'Talk Reform' programme
(1970)[59] begun in 1964 in infant schools in East London and carried out in
normal school conditions. Schools selected had large immigrant populations
and otherwise consisted mainly of working class pupils. This programme
included activities for improving auditory discrimination and attention (using
a battery operated telephone), activities for improving speech and for
developing sentence structure and vocabulary.

Clearly there are many children who come to school less linguistically
competent than others and who therefore need help in this area. But what
has come under severe criticism in recent years is the notion that such
children are linguistically deprived or even non-verbal. One of the most
virulent critics of the notion of linguistic deprivation was Labov who,
working within a linguistic rather than a sociological or psychological framework, wrote an impassioned argument declaiming verbal deprivation as a
myth (1970).[60] He is defending the non-standard English spoken by negro
ghetto children, but some of his comments might well be applied to other
non-standard English speakers. The myth in Labov's view has arisen partly
because speech data gathered from different social groups have been collected
in very artificial situations. It is not surprising if a child, sitting in a strange
room with an unfamiliar adult at the other side of a desk fails to reply to his
questions, thus appearing non-verbal. Labov's methods instead were to use
negro investigators who entered into conversation with negro children in a
relaxed situation: he describes the interviewer sitting on the floor, sharing a
packet of crisps with an eight-year-old boy who has brought a friend along
with him. This more natural context is conducive to conversation in a way
that a more conventional interview technique fails to be. Labov's article is
based on studies carried out with negro boys of ten to seventeen during the
period 1965-7. Apart from suggested improvements in methodology, he
examines the grammatical structure of negro non-standard English to see
whether it does in fact have rules of its own or is merely randomly inaccurate
as is frequently claimed, and to consider whether it does impede logical
thinking. His findings were that *negro* non-standard English does not differ
basically in syntax from standard English, having its own consistent rules and
that it does not prevent logical thinking. Samples of speech such as that of
Larry, a fifteen-year-old school failure, talking about the nature of God, do
show logical clarity but are clothed in a speech form which many teachers
would reject and which most would have difficulty in understanding. In
Labov's view then, no child is non-verbal or verbally deprived: his vernacular
may be different from standard English but this in itself would not impede

logical thinking or retard him in school learning. It is rather teachers' refusal to accept this vernacular and reluctance to learn to understand it that does make school learning problematic and unpalatable and eventually leads to school rejection.

While it is important to remember that Labov is dealing with *negro* non-standard English which has its own marked characteristics we may ask whether the same applies to other variants of English - non-standard forms such as Cockney or local dialects for example, all falling into the category of a restricted code.

Attention may be drawn here to Ewing's argument that the deaf are in experience similar to 'culturally deprived' children. If the vernacular spoken by groups previously so-labelled is as rich as Labov, Rosen[61] and others suggest, surely there is no case for using them as a comparison to deaf children whose linguistic problems are of quite a different order.

Although the concept of linguistic deprivation has not met such stringent criticism in this country - probably because the term itself never became so powerful as in the USA - Rosen (1972)[62] writes strongly against the idea of working class speech being second-rate and inappropriate for school learning. He too questions the methods used in attempts to elicit speech from children in artificial situations and hotly criticizes Bernstein's attempts to defend the value of working class speech. Such remarks as 'A restricted code gives access to a vast potential of meanings, of delicacy, subtlety and diversity of cultural forms, to a unique aesthetic',[63] are considered purely parenthetic and therefore of limited conviction since Bernstein never goes on to examine working class speech in detail or to investigate what a restricted code cannot do. This in Rosen's view is one of the large gaps in our knowledge of language: no one has hitherto examined in detail the strengths, richness and potential of working class language; and few attempts have been made to investigate how language is used in schools. This deficit is beginning to be made good however by the work of Barnes, Britton and others, as we have already seen.

At this point we return to the earlier part of the discussion where emphasis was laid upon the classroom as a context for language learning. We may conclude from a teaching point of view that it is important to work with the language a child brings to school, whatever his age and stage of formal education; and that from a research point of view (in which teachers are beginning to participate) it is essential to explore characteristics of language that is actually used in school by teachers and pupils. To say that school learning is based on a middle class elaborated code is a vacuous generality unless we have hard evidence that this *is* actually the language used by teachers and pupils.

The aim of this chapter was to introduce readers to some of the main areas of interest in the field of language and education and to indicate some of the important problems where all teachers will benefit from a deeper theoretical understanding of the issues involved. Whatever a teacher's main concern is, whether with very young children or with a specialist subject in the secondary school, it is important for him to remember that language is not only a medium for learning what the school offers in terms of content. It is an essential part of the curriculum in its own right and as such should always be deliberately incorporated into any teacher's programme. And if teachers work on the much advocated principle that learning begins with what the child already knows and has to offer, then language learning too will achieve the importance it deserves.

REFERENCES

1. E. Sapir in D.G. Mandelbaum (ed.), *Selected Writings of E. Sapir,* University of California Press, 1949
2. L. Wittgenstein, *Philosophical Investigations,* Blackwell, 1953, vol.1, p.43
3. B.F. Skinner, *Verbal Behavior,* Appleton-Century-Crofts, 1957
4. O.H. Mowrer, *Learning Theory and the Symbolic Processes,* Wiley, 1960
5. D. McNeill, 'The creation of language', *Discovery,* 1966. Reprinted in A. Cashdan (ed.), *Language in Education,* Routledge and Kegan Paul with Open University Press, 1972
6. J. Berko, 'The child's learning of English morphology', *Word,* Vol.14, 1958. Reprinted in S. Saporta (ed.), *Psycholinguistics,* Holt, Rinehart & Winston, 1963
7. C. Fraser, U. Bellugi and R. Brown, 'Control of grammar in imitation, comprehension and production', *Journal of Verbal Learning and Verbal Behavior,* 1963. Reprinted in R.C. Oldfield and J.C. Marshall (eds.), *Language,* Penguin, 1968
8. N. Chomsky, 'Review of Skinner's "Verbal Behavior" ', *Language,* 1959
9. R. Brown and U. Bellugi, 'Three processes in the child's acquisition of syntax', *Harvard Education Review,* 1964. Reprinted in A. Cashdan (ed.), *op. cit.*
10. C.B. Cazden, 'Environmental assistance to the child's acquisition of grammar', quoted by D.I. Slobin, 'Imitation and grammatical development in children' in N.S. Endler, L.R. Boulte, H. Osser (eds.), *Contemporary Issues in Developmental Psychology,* Holt, Rinehart & Winston, 1968
11. J. Tough, *Focus on Meaning,* Allen & Unwin, 1973
12. J. Britton, *Language and Learning,* Penguin, 1970
13. D. Barnes, J. Britton, H. Rosen (eds.), *Language, the Learner and the School,* Penguin, 1969
14. D. Barnes *et al., op.cit.*
15. D. McNeill, *op.cit.*
16. J. Britton, 'Talking to learn' in D. Barnes *et al., op.cit.*
17. J. Britton, Schools Council Writing Research Unit
18. L. Vigotsky, *Thought and Language,* MIT Press, 1962
19. A.R. Luria, *Speech and the Development of Mental Processes in the Child,* (USSR, 1956), Staples, 1959
20. A.R. Luria, 'The directive function of speech in development and dissolution', *Word,* 1959. Reprinted in A. Cashdan (ed.), *op.cit.*

21. A.R. Luria, *The Role of Speech in the Regulation of Normal and Abnormal Behaviour,* Pergamon, 1961
22. J. Piaget, *The Language and Thought of the Child,* Penguin, 1959, and J. Piaget, *Comments on Vigotsky's Critical Remarks,* MIT Press, 1962
23. R. Brown and U. Bellugi, *op.cit.*
24. H. Sinclair de Swart, 'Developmental psycholinguistics' in D. Elkind and J. Flavell (eds.), *Studies in Cognitive Development,* Oxford University Press, 1969
25. R.F. Dearden, *Philosophy of Primary Education,* Routledge & Kegan Paul, 1968
26. L. Wittgenstein, *op.cit.,* Vol.1, p.7 and p.23
27. G.Jahoda, 'The development of children's ideas about country and nationality', *British Journal of Educational Psychology,* 1963
28. R.G. Natadze, 'The mastery of scientific concepts in school' in B. and J. Simon, *Educational Psychology in the USSR,* Routledge & Kegan Paul, 1963
29. P. Oléron, 'Conceptual thinking of the deaf,' *American Annals of the Deaf,* 1953. Reprinted in P. Adams (ed.), *Language in Thinking,* Penguin, 1972
30. R. Chulliat and P. Oléron, 'The role of language in transposition tasks', 1955. Referred to in D. Lawton, *Social Class, Language and Education,* Routledge & Kegan Paul, 1968
31. M. Vincent, 'The performance of deaf and hearing children on a classifying task'. Referred to in D. Lawton, *op.cit.*
32. A.W.C. Ewing (ed.), *Educational Guidance and the Deaf Child,* Manchester University Press, 1957
33. A Furth, *Thinking Without Language,* Collier-Macmillan, 1966
34. A. Furth, *op.cit.,* pp. 154-5
35. H. Rosen, 'The language of text-books' in J. Britton (ed.), *Talking and Writing,* Methuen, 1967
36. D. Barnes *et al., op.cit.*
37. D. Barnes *et al., op.cit.*
38. E. Sapir, 1949, *op.cit.*
39. B.L. Whorf, 'Science and linguistics', *Technology Review,* 1940. Reprinted in E.E. Maccobey *et al.* (eds.), *Reading in Social Psychology,* Methuen, 1959
40. H. Giles, 'Our reactions to accent', *New Society,* 1971
41. J. Tough, *op.cit.*
42. E. Fuchs, 'How teachers learn to help children fail', *Transactions,* 1968
43. E. Goodacre, 'Teachers and the pupils' home background', NFER, 1968
44. A. Little and J. Westergaard, 'The trend of class differentials in educational opportunity in England and Wales', *British Journal of Sociology,* 1964
45. J. Tough, *op.cit.*
46. A.R. Luria, 1956, *op.cit.*
47. B. Bernstein, 'Some sociological determinants of perception', *British Journal of Sociology,* 1958
48. B. Bernstein and D. Henderson, 'Social class differences in the relevance of language to socialization', *Sociology,* 1969
49. J. Jones, 'Social class and the under 5s', *New Society,* 1966
50. W.P. Robinson and S.J. Rackstraw, 'Variations in mothers' answers to children's questions as a function of social class, verbal intelligence test scores and sex', *Sociology,* 1967
51. B. Bernstein, 'Social structure, language and learning', *Educational Research,* 1961
52. P.R. Hawkins, 'Social class, the nominal group and reference', *Language and Speech,* 1969

102 *Theory and Practice of Education*

53. M. Coulthard, 'A discussion of restricted and elaborated codes', *Educational Review,* 1969
54. B. Bernstein, 'Elaborated and restricted codes: their social origins and some consequences', *American Anthropologist:* "Ethnography in Communication", 1964
55. W. Labov, 'The logic of non-standard English', *Georgetown Monographs in Language and Linguistics,* 1969. Reprinted in A. Cashdan (ed.), *op.cit.*
56. C. Vereiter and S. Engelmann, *Teaching Disadvantaged Children in the Pre-school* Prentice-Hall, *1966*
57. M. Blank and F. Solomon, 'A tutorial language programme to develop abstract thinking in socially disadvantaged pre-school children', *Child Development,* 1968
58. J. Tough, *op.cit.*
59. D.M. Gahagan and G.A. Gahagan, *Talk Reform,* Routledge & Kegan Paul, 1970
60. W. Labov, *op.cit.*
61. H. Rosen, *Language and Class: a Critical Look at the Theories of Basil Bernstein,* Falling Wall Press, 1972
62. *Ibid.*
63. B. Bernstein, *Class, Codes and Control,* Vol.1, Routledge and Kegan Paul, 1971

V Authority

The progress that children make at school will depend not only on the views that teachers hold about such things as intelligence, motivation and language and the judgements that they are thus led to make of their pupils. That progress, and indeed those judgements themselves, will depend equally, if not more conclusively, on the kinds of relationship the teacher develops with his pupils, the approach he takes to classroom control and the kind of atmosphere that is generated by the view he takes of the competing demands of freedom and authority. It is to this question of the teacher's authority, therefore, that we must next turn our attention.

Questions about authority cause teachers concern at the levels of both theory and practice. Whether they will in fact have the authority to control their pupils is a question that worries all trainee teachers and new entrants to the profession and it is a question that continues to concern most teachers throughout their careers. Nowadays, however, many teachers are also uncertain about whether they should be exercising authority over their pupils at all or at least to what extent such control can be justified. There is a feeling abroad, strengthened by developments such as the 'free school' and increased demands for participation by pupils in decision making of all kinds, that any exercise of authority is an infringement of the freedom and rights of the child so that a certain uneasiness results for those teachers who regard these things as important yet find themselves required by the exigencies of the school situation to place restraints on children's behaviour in many different contexts. Nor again are the practical and theoretical aspects of the problem readily separable, since to a large degree the extent to which one is able to exercise authority will depend on how clear one is about the justification of it, since confidence is needed here perhaps more than anywhere else in education and confidence can only come from a conviction that what one is doing is right. Conversely, much that can only be described as arrant nonsense has been said and written about the freedom of children by those whose view of the issues involved has not been tempered by experience of the realities of the teaching situation. Again, therefore, theory and practice need to be interwoven if we are to achieve a view of the place of authority in education that is both clear and constructive. Again too we must begin by attempting to sort out the different issues that are involved.

In doing this we must consider two main kinds of question, firstly that concerning the justification of the exercise of any kind of authority by teachers and, secondly, a number of related questions concerning the nature of authority, the ways in which teachers can and do come to exercise it and the repercussions that different approaches to control in the school and in the classroom may have on the development of pupils. These two kinds of question are not, of course, entirely independent of each other, since any discussion of the ways in which a teacher can acquire authority, and especially of the kind of authority that is appropriate to education, must presuppose and, indeed, depend for its substance on some view about its justification, but it will be in the interests of clarity to discuss the two issues separately and most useful to begin with the problem of justification.

Freedom and Authority

We must begin our discussion in this field once again by attempting to clarify the concepts we are concerned with and, in particular, by trying to achieve some clarity over the notion of 'freedom' and the use of the adjective 'free'.

In its purely descriptive uses, the word 'free' denotes the absence of some hindrance or restraint. Thus to describe a piece of mechanism as 'free' is to suggest that it has been jammed or blocked in some way, while to describe a man as 'free' is to imply that he has been under some kind of restraint, in prison, for example, or with a full engagement book or even merely married.[1] In its most common use too, the word indicates the absence of a fee or charge that might act as a hindrance to the acquisition or possession of some object, commodity or service. Furthermore, in all of these uses of 'free' there seems to be the added implication that the hindrance or restraint that is absent is an undesirable hindrance or restraint. As evidence of this, it is interesting to note and compare the use of the suffixes '-free' and '-less'. In most, if not all, cases the use of '-free' suggests 'good riddance' and the use of '-less' expresses regret at what is missing. What is meat-free to the vegetarian is meat-less to the carnivore and the same can be seen in the contrasting notions of carefree and careless driving (Ryan, 1965).[2] Even in its largely descriptive sense, therefore, and in politically neutral contexts freedom is generally regarded as something worth having.

However, all of this does point to the need for some qualification to be made, for some specification of the hindrance that has been removed or that might have been there. In many contexts it is, of course, possible to understand or to supply the appropriate qualification. If an AA patrolman tells me the engine of my car is now free, I can assume that he has found it to be clogged up with some kind of foreign substance which he has been able to remove, but if he tells me that he himself is now free, I will need to know something of his history to be able to find some clues on the basis of which I can supply the necessary qualification to understand what he is talking about. It is this consideration that has given rise to a distinction that has been made between the two kinds of freedom, between the negative and positive views of freedom, between 'freedom from' and 'freedom to', but it is surely the case that in all contexts both of these elements are present and we emphasize that aspect that seems the more significant. It is only meaningful to speak of the freedom to do something if we are conscious that we are free from a restraint that has or might have denied us that freedom or to speak of freedom from something if we are conscious of that thing as having prevented us from being free to achieve some desirable goal or activity (Ryan, 1965).[3]

Freedom, therefore, implies the absence of a restraint that has acted or might have acted as a hindrance to action of some kind.

Often, however, the emotive implications of the term come to the fore and we find it is being used prescriptively, not to describe a state of freedom so much as to demand that such a state be created. This is the kind of meaning the term usually has in social contexts. When Rousseau began *The Social Contract* with the words, 'Man is born free; but everywhere he is in chains', he was not describing men as he might have been if he had said, 'Man is born naked; but everywhere he is in clothes'; he was in fact prescribing or demanding that men should be treated in certain ways and similar demands have been made in much the same form in many other contexts. It is not always entirely clear, however, what such demands amount to. Again some kind of qualification brings clarification so that discussion of freedom of speech or freedom of opinion or freedom of association or freedom of worship will be more meaningful than discussion of freedom in an unqualified sense. To speak of freedom in this kind of unqualified way cannot be to demand the removal of all restraints. To demand this would be to demand licence rather than freedom, a distinction which is very important since it suggests that the existence of some restraints is not incompatible with the notion of social freedom. It is, therefore, a demand not that all restraints be removed but that their existence in all cases be justified.

If this is a correct analysis of the notion of freedom, then, it provides us with a negative point that will contribute towards the justification of the exercise of authority, namely that the idea of an authority used to apply justifiable restraints is not incompatible with the notion of freedom. Further-more, we must note that every human society must have rules and those rules must be enforced by someone if they are to have any meaning at all,[4] so that we have a further, if again negative, point that authority is a necessary part of any rule-governed society. Neither of these points, of course, offers us any positive clues as to what particular restraints can be justified. It is, however, no small thing to have established that some justification is possible in view of the doubts about this that often exist in people's minds. We must, however, turn to a consideration of more positive arguments for the exercise of authority and in particular those that may indicate the kinds of situation in which it might be argued to be appropriate.

The classical argument for social freedom is undoubtedly that set out in J.S. Mill's essay, 'On Liberty'. The position Mill takes here is uncompromising. 'All restraint *qua* restraint is an evil'.[5] But he suggests one fundamental justification, 'one very simple principle',[6] for the existence of restraints. 'That principle is, that the sole end for which mankind are warranted, individually or collectively, in interfering with the liberty of action of any of their number, is self-protection'. A man may be restrained from interfering with or causing harm to others. Authority exercised to apply restraint in such situations is justified. It is not justified if it is used to restrian him from doing those things which affect him only, those actions that can be called 'self-regarding' actions.

The argument here, then, is that freedom can only be reasonably demanded by anyone up to the point at which the behaviour of one individual or group in a society begins to act as a limitation on the freedom of other individuals or groups. As a judge once said to an Irishman before him on a charge of assault and battery, 'Everyone's freedom is bounded by the position of the other man's nose.' Too much freedom for some people will lead to too little for others and it is at the point where this begins to happen that the exercise of authority can be justified to ensure that freedom can be enjoyed by all rather than licence by some.

If we apply this to education, we will find that there is beginning to emerge a case at least for one type of school rule, for the exercise of authority by the teacher at least in the context of general behaviour and the maintenance of order. Where the enjoyment of 'freedom' by one pupil or group of pupils is resulting in a limitation of the freedom of others, through over-use of some facility, for example, the making of excessive noise, running in the corridors or any other behaviour which is likely to endanger the safety of others or to create an atmosphere in which the ability of others to profit from the educational opportunities offered by the school is impaired, then the teacher must exercise his or her authority to apply restraints in order to promote a proper level of freedom for all. In the sphere of behaviour, then, a good case can be made for the teacher's authority. Schools, like all other rule-governed societies, must have rules that are framed for the protection of all members from each other's excesses and, provided that these rules do not go beyond what that consideration seems to justify, a good case can be made out for them.

No argument that we have adduced so far, however, justifies the use of authority to compel children to join this rule-governed society in the first place. For the law to require that children attend school between the ages of five and sixteen and for us as teachers to demand of them not only certain kinds of behaviour but also certain kinds of learning while they are there requires a different and more positive justification than we have given so far. This proved a difficult problem for Mill too since it goes well beyond what can be justified in the name of self-protection, yet Mill was strongly committed to the value of education and the qualitative superiority of certain kinds of intellectual activity of the kind that he felt schools ought to promote.[7] The justification of the exercise of authority by teachers in the area of the curriculum, then, is a much more difficult problem than that in the sphere of behaviour, although we must not lose sight of the fact that even in the realm of rules of conduct, learning of a moral and social kind will go on, so that the distinction between behavioural and curricular problems cannot be pressed too far.

A more positive justification for the use of authority to require children's attendance at school and to direct their activities while they are there must be sought in the notion of education itself or ideas one has about the purposes of the school and the educational enterprise generally. However we will see in the chapter on the curriculum how difficult it is to define education in terms that will be generally acceptable or to reach agreement on what the purposes of the schools should be or what kinds of learning we should be using our authority to require pupils to engage in. Many different views are held and, although they all need some kind of justification in themselves, each will give rise to a justification for the use of authority in the school in different areas. The view that schools should be concerned primarily to promote the development of the rational mind will result in different demands to be made of pupils, for example, from those that will be justified by the view that they should be more concerned with the social welfare of their pupils. Indeed, some views of education, such as those that have advocated non-interference and the current views of some sociologists about the dangers of imposing values on children, are such as to provide no justification for any exercise of authority at all in this area. Once some kind of overall justification for education itself seems to have been established, however, we will have a basis for the exercise of authority in particular situations. Once we are committed to the value of a particular subject, for example, the 'discipline' of that subject will take over and provide us with our cues as to when authority can be justifiably exercised. The absence of any kind of consensus in this area, however, makes this kind of justification highly subjective and, as a result, less satisfactory a basis than perhaps we would wish to have for requiring a great deal of children and applying real and extensive restraints to their behaviour.

There is, however, one kind of argument that may reveal to us something like a lowest common denominator here, something that will offer some justification at a fundamental level for the exercise of authority in education. Whatever view one takes of the kind or selection of knowledge that should be presented to or even imposed upon children, it would be difficult to maintain that that knowledge should not be characterized by being true. In short, whether one believes that children should be introduced to Physics or French, Byron or the 'Beano', Beethoven or the Beatles, the one common feature of the 'knowledge' to be presented to them that all would agree to would be that it should manifest a respect for truth. We can say, then, that there is a conceptual connection between the notion of 'education' and that of 'truth'. Some justification for the exercise of authority by teachers may be found, therefore, in an appeal to this connection and a demonstration that in particular cases authority is being exercised in the cause of promoting truth, by insisting, for example, that children explore all sides of an argument before reaching an opinion, rather than adhering to a prejudice acquired from their parents or elsewhere. If education is connected in this way, then, with the pursuit of truth, the exercise of authority by educators can be shown to be justified if it has the purpose of assisting this process.

Paradoxically, however, this argument constitutes an equally strong if not a more compelling case for the promotion of freedom. This concern with truth necessitates academic freedom and academic autonomy, 'freedom of opinion' as it is more usually called. The classic arguments in support of this are again those of J.S. Mill's essay 'On Liberty' and we must briefly note them here.

Mill[8] argues that truth cannot be pursued nor can human knowledge develop without freedom of opinion for those who seek after it. He gives several cogent reasons for this claim. Firstly, we cannot assume infallibility so that we must concede that any opinion may be true and, therefore, ought not to be suppressed. If anything, this is an argument that has more force today when it is perhaps clearer than it was in the nineteenth century just how hypothetical and consequently open to modification all our knowledge is. Secondly, Mill argues, even if a silenced opinion is wrong, it may contain some truth and, since the prevailing opinion on any issue is rarely wholly true, we need the clash of contrary opinions to help us towards the whole truth, a point supported by many philosophers who have seen the development of knowledge as an unending of triadic dialectical process of thesis, antithesis and synthesis. Thirdly, even if the opinion that is accepted and allowed is the whole truth and nothing but the truth, it can only be held as such by those who have been able to weigh it against contrary opinion. Without that it will be 'held in the manner of prejudice, with little comprehension or feeling of its rational grounds'. It will be dogma rather than real conviction and, as a result of this, truth will lose its essence.

This, then, for Mill is one aspect of that liberty which is essential to human progress. Liberty is necessary for 'the free development of individuality'[9] and also without liberty 'there is wanting one of the principle ingredients of human happiness, and quite the chief ingredient of individual and social progress'. Unless there is freedom of opinion, unless people are free to disagree, human knowledge will not develop. These are the classic arguments for academic freedom and they lead us to recognize not only the hypothetical and evolving nature of human knowledge, which we have had reason to note elsewhere, but also that if there are conceptual connections between education and knowledge and education and truth, there must also be such a connection between education and autonomy.

However, they would seem equally to constitute an argument for the exercise of authority in the interests of the promotion of knowledge, truth and autonomy, or, to put it differently and somewhat paradoxically, the exercise of authority to promote freedom, either by enhancing the range and scope of the choices open to the individual or by developing in him the ability to make choices by means other than either 'plumping' for something or acting according to prejudices, wherever and however acquired. We have noted elsewhere in this book (see Chapters III and VI) how working from children's interests requires us also to give them opportunities to acquire interests and how 'discovery methods' are only effective if linked to careful preparatory work, if employed, as Bruner[10] suggests, by the well-prepared mind. We now have a theoretical justification for this apparent infringement of freedom in so far as its main purpose can be to enhance freedom and to promote autonomy since, as Bruner also tells us, the freedom of the child is increased by approaches such as discovery learning. In this connection, it is also interesting to note that those psychologists, such as Piaget (1932) and Kohlberg, (1966)[11] who in considering the stages of the child's moral development have posited the existence of an autonomous stage at the end of the process, have not wanted to suggest that this stage is automatically reached by all children as a result of a purely developmental or maturational process; they believe that the attainment of autonomy can only be the result of education. This, then, is a task for the teacher which he can only accomplish by the exercise of authority.

If there is any substance to these arguments we have tried to set out, certain implications follow for the practice of education. In the first place, it becomes clear that the teacher must take whatever action he judges necessary to promote the progress of his pupils towards autonomy, to enhance their freedom and their opportunities to use it, to create the conditions necessary for these developments to take place and, more controversially, as we will see when we consider the problems of curriculum content in Chapter VI, to introduce and extend those studies that he feels are justified on other grounds, whether for vocational reasons, because of the choices of the pupils themselves or because of a conviction the teacher himself has that they are 'intrinsically worthwhile activities'. There are perhaps no hard and fast answers to be given in practice to questions about when the exercise of authority by the teacher is justified in these areas but these are the kinds of justification to be sought.

Secondly, some negative conclusions at least emerge from these arguments For they imply that the exercise of authority by teachers cannot be justified in areas that cannot be shown to be connected in some way with the promotion of the qualities we have just discussed. It is difficult, for example, to justify its being exercised to ensure that all pupils travel to and from school with caps on their heads, unless it can be shown that a warm head will mean a warm brain and that a warm brain will reach its educational goals faster. Nor can we, without stretching our notion of education to breaking point, find a justification in it for any requirement that relates more to fashion than to education. Fashions are too ephemeral to constitute a basis for any learning of a permanent kind. One has only to look at those head-masters of today whose hair is of a length that they would not have permitted to their pupils five or six years ago to realize how shifting this ground is. The spectacle of one headteacher forbidding entry to school to a child who insists on wearing blue rather than white socks and another sending a child home for precisely the opposite reason merely trivializes in the public eye the work of the schools and retards rather than advances the progress towards anything that can really be characterized as education.

Thirdly, we must note that if the justification of the teacher's authority is to be found in his obligation to promote the freedom and ultimately the autonomy of his pupils, it must follow that his authority is merely provisional provisional, since if he is successful it will be progressively eroded until it disappears altogether. Certainly, university teachers have to get used to seeing their pupils draw level with and sometimes forge ahead of them, and, to some extent, this should be the experience of all successful teachers. If we are right, then the oddest thing about the teacher's authority is that it must contain within it the seeds of its own destruction, what the melodramas call a self-destruct mechanism.

This, then, is the kind of justification that can be found for the teacher's authority. In general, it leads us to the conclusion that the important question for the teacher is not one of authority and freedom, but of authority and authoritarianism, the use and the abuse of authority. The teacher's central concern in planning the work of his pupils should be not the rather naive question of whether he should direct their work or leave them to their own devices, but the rather more subtle issue of the kinds of authoritative action he is justified in taking. It is the abuse of authority not the attempt to exercise it properly that leads to resentment and progressive indiscipline in schools. Teachers often comment on the 'sense of fairness' of their pupils, especially in secondary schools; this phenomenon is no more and no less than their ability to recognize, intuitively and therefore sometimes more quickly than the theoreticians, when authority is being exercised properly over them and when it is being abused.

As every teacher knows only too well, however, it is one thing to be able to demonstrate the differences between the uses and the abuses of authority; it is quite another matter to ensure that in practice one has any kind of authority in the classroom. An understanding of its justification will be of some help, of course, but in addition to this it is necessary to have some understanding of its nature and its origins, of how we come to be able to exercise it, as this will indicate to us some of the ways in which we can work to improve it. It is to this aspect of authority that we must now turn.

Patterns of Authority

There have been many discussions of the question of what authority is, whether, for example, it is the same as power or force, and it would not be appropriate or helpful for us to get ourselves too caught up in such debate here. It must be stressed, however, that authority is very difficult to define precisely. It is an ability that some people seem to have to get other people to obey them without recourse to the use of force or even sometimes to the giving of reasons. It is the quality of the well-known centurion of the New Testament who described his authority by saying, 'I say to this man "Go!" and he goeth'. At a more mundane level, it is that which makes us accept, often quite unquestioningly, the advice of anyone we regard as an authority on something, like, say, second-hand cars or coastal navigation. We do what such people instruct or advise without compulsion or compunction. If this is what authority is or if this is what it means for someone to have authority, then it is certainly not force, even though the threat of force may sometimes be there in the background. In fact, we tend to say, when we see people, teachers or parents, for example, having to use force, that they have lost their authority or that their authority has broken down. Authority, then, is this kind of ability to get things done without recourse to force or other methods of persuasion.

It is important to understand this, because it has crucial implications for the way in which we must tackle what is probably the most vital question in this area for the teacher, namely that of where he can get authority from or how he can be sure that he will have authority in the classroom. If we realize what a nebulous quality it is, we will immediately appreciate that it is not something 'given' and, therefore, not something we can look to someone else to provide. Many people in any society have authority besides teachers - policemen, referees, umpires, mayors, kings and so on - but it clearly does not make sense to ask where they get their authority from in the way in which one might ask where they get their helmets, whistles or blackboards from, even though in some cases visible trappings such as badges, white coats, academic gowns, chains of office, orbs, sceptres and the like may be worn to symbolize the possession of authority.[12] Nor does it even make sense to claim that authority, at least as we have defined it, has been conferred on them by the MCC, the FA, the DES, the Archbishop of Canterbury or any other person or body. Such persons or bodies cannot confer authority on anyone, since they cannot ensure that people will do what such a person tells them to do without question. It is not as simple as that, as many a teacher and foot-ball referee knows to his cost. The most that a body of this kind can do is to promise to step in when one's authority has been challenged, questioned or even defied, in other words when it is lost. Furthermore, if we ask where these bodies get their authority from, we see that we have only pushed the question back a stage. The real question, therefore, is not 'Where does authority come from?' but 'How do people come to exercise authority?'. Once we put it that way, we begin to see both how to set about seeking an answer to it and that there may be several kinds of answer to be found. We can also see that from the teacher's point of view this kind of approach is likely to be more helpful because it should indicate some of the ways in which he can work at developing his authority.

A number of different categories have been used in attempts to delineate the possible sources of authority and it will be worthwhile to look at these briefly. One major distinction that has been drawn is that between authority exercised *de jure* and that exercised *de facto*. If a man has authority *de jure*, that authority derives from a right to issue commands that goes with a position that he holds and stems from certain rules, a legal system of some kind, which authorizes him to issue commands and will back him or step in if those commands are challenged. Such a man is our referee and in the same way teachers may have some authority conferred upon them by the position they hold. On the other hand, to say that a man exercises authority *de facto* is not to say he holds any position or has any backing for his authority: it is to say merely that people do in fact obey him. The classic example of this is the ordinary member of the audience who takes charge when there is a fire at a theatre or a cinema and organizes an orderly exit. He is able to exercise authority perhaps because of certain personal qualities he has or a superior knowledge and experience that he is thought to possess, but not from any position or status that he holds.

This latter point brings us to a second distinction that has been emphasized, that between being *in* authority and being *an* authority, between positional and expert authority. Sometimes, as we have just seen, *de facto* authority will derive from the fact that someone is regarded as *an* authority in a particular area, that he has a relevant expertise. His injunctions are accepted because of this expertise, even though he does not hold a position that confers on him the right to issue commands. We have already referred to those people whose word on certain matters, the internal mysteries of the motor-car, for example, are regarded as 'law'. It will be clear that if a man who is *in* authority is also accepted as *an* authority, his position will be considerably strengthened by the possession of such expertise.

A further distinction was made by Max Weber,[13] when he suggested that there might be three possible answers to the question of how people come to exercise authority, three different sources from which their ability to issue commands and have them accepted as legitimate might derive. Firstly, he suggests that the authority of some people may derive in part from *traditional* sources. Some people are obeyed because they are seen as representatives of a traditional and accepted system. A father in a family, when he exercises authority, does so largely for this kind of reason. In some situations too, perhaps especially in schools for younger children the authority of the teacher will derive in part from this source. A second source of authority that Weber posits is what he calls the *legal/rational* source. An increasing number of people in modern societies exercise authority because they have been elevated to it under a system of rules the legality and rationality of which are accepted by those over whom the authority is being wielded. They have *de jure* authority within an accepted rule-governed situation like that of the football field, the cricket pitch or the classroom. Thirdly, Weber draws our attention to the *charismatic* type of authority exercised by some people because of their personal characteristics and outstanding qualities. He himself had in mind here outstanding historical figures like Christ and Napoleon, but the notion has relevance at less elevated levels too. We might perhaps, in the case of teachers in particular, distinguish two aspects of this concept, that of being *an* authority which we have already considered and that of the kind of personal flair or brilliance which can lead us to obey certain individuals without evidence of either their expertise or their legal right to issue commands.[14] In other words, this concept offers us a distinction between two kinds of *de facto* authority.

The Authority of the Teacher

With these categories in mind, let us now turn to a more detailed examination of the authority of the teacher and the factors that will affect both its nature and its extent. The most important thing to be stressed at the outset of this discussion is that our analysis so far indicates that it is something which can and should be worked at by teachers. The following discussion may indicate some of the ways in which teachers can work at the development of their authority but it will also reveal some of the external factors that will come into play and which must be taken into account by them. There are two main kinds of factor that we must note, those deriving from the school itself, its organizational structure, its goals and the kinds of pupil it contains, and those deriving from the personal characteristics and qualities of the individual teacher. The kind of authority each teacher can exercise and the kind of authority he will in practice exercise will be a resultant of the interaction of these two forces.

We saw earlier that authority is an essential part of any rule-governed society. The kind of authority that is appropriate will depend on the kind of rule-governed society in question. Clearly a society that is tightly structured, highly cohesive and has a clear view of its goals and purposes will require and will give rise to a different kind of authority structure from one which is much looser, more diffuse and less clear-cut in its view of its essential purposes. No society of course is completely bureaucratic but obviously there are different levels of bureaucracy and each will give rise to a different pattern of authority. Schools must inevitably be less clear-cut in their goals and purposes than many other institutions, and there will be great variations between schools themselves. At one extreme we might picture a school which is based on a relatively fixed view of child nature and of knowledge, which regards children's abilities as readily measurable and consequently streams its pupils according to their ability, which has a view of knowledge as something external to be acquired by pupils and as a result places its emphasis on class-teaching methods, on subject boundaries, on encouraging the kinds of stock response to questions we discussed in Chapter IV, and perhaps on regular examinations and tests, seeing its role in terms purely of the intellectual advancement of its pupils. In such a school, the relationships between teacher and pupil will tend to be distant and impersonal and the authority structure will tend to be relatively clear-cut, hierarchical and for the most part positional, the emphasis being on the teacher as set in authority; where his expertise is relevant, it will be an expertise in a particular subject area. Tradition will also be of significance to the teacher in his attempts to establish his own individual authority in such a school.[15]

At the other end of the spectrum, we may imagine a school which sees children as having many facets to their development and their abilities as too diffuse to be readily measurable, which as a consequence does not stream them by general ability, which has a broader view of knowledge and perhaps not too much regard for the sanctity of subject boundaries and which as a result will often abandon class-teaching in favour of other methods of the kind we discuss in Chapter VI, designed in one way or another to involve the children themselves more fully in their own education, in short, a school which takes a looser view of its own role and of the nature and purposes of education. In such a school the authority patterns will be very different. Teachers will be less distant from their pupils so that the relationships will be more interpersonal. The extent of their authority will depend far more on their expertise not only in a subject area or areas but in a wide range of pedagogical abilities. Position and tradition will be of relatively little help to teachers in such a school; the onus will be much more on personal qualities of a number of kinds.

Clearly, no real situation is quite as clear-cut as these we have described but perhaps the caricatures we have drawn will serve to indicate the extent to which the type of authority a teacher can exercise will be affected by the kind of school he is in, by both the content of what he is teaching and the method or pedagogy he is using.[16] Any occupational role is governed to some extent by the institutional structure within which it is practised and this structure in turn will be subject to pressures from the headteacher, the local authority, the governing body and all other outside agencies that wield authority over the teacher himself. But this is only one kind of factor that will determine the kind of authority the teacher will be able to exercise. The nearer a school comes to the second of the types we have just pictured, the more onus there will be on the personal qualities of the individual teacher. We must remember too that while the organization of the school will determine to a large extent the kind of authority a teacher may exercise and will make it easy or difficult for him to achieve a proper control of his classes, no kind of school can confer authority on him or ensure that his authority is accepted by his pupils. In all situations, this will depend on his own qualities and abilities.

What sorts of quality are important here? Obviously, the most important single factor is the individual teacher's expertise. Where a teacher cannot rely on tradition or position, on being *in* authority, to ensure that he is obeyed, he must depend on his skill and knowledge, on being *an* authority. It is important to remember, as we hinted just now, that there are two aspects to this. One of these is clearly his expertise in his subject, his ability to answer children's questions and provide them with knowledge in a given area of the curriculum. The other important aspect of this expertise, and one that becomes crucial as we move towards a looser and more open view of schools, of the curriculum and of education, is his pedagogical skill, his ability to organize pupils' work, to advise them on many aspects of it, to ensure that they are stretched while steering them away from work of a level that would be likely to defeat them, to develop the kinds of interpersonal relationship that will both forward their learning and establish his right to direct it. The more interpersonal these relationships become the more onus will fall on the teacher's ability to develop them.

This ability will in turn depend on a number of factors, such as the age and the sex of both teacher and pupils, the view he takes of knowledge and of the purposes of education, and the extent to which he is in sympathy with the ethos of the school. It will also depend on those wider personal qualities sometimes subsumed under the single title, 'personality'. There is no doubt that the personality of the teacher will affect his ability to develop relationships and, therefore, to establish his authority with his pupils. The significance of this should not be overstated, however. Many teachers are too ready to exaggerate the importance of personality and to take the view that you have either got it or you have not. There are two dangers in this. The first is that it leads to a defeatism on the part of those teachers who feel, rightly or wrongly, that their personal qualities are not strong and a resultant failure to appreciate that there are ways, such as those we have tried to show, in which one's authority can be developed. Secondly, it can lead to too great a dependence by some teachers on a charismatic type of authority, which, while it may have certain short-term advantages, cannot in the long term lead to effective education, since it is based not on reason but on emotion and largely blind admiration. We all know what Napoleon did. As John Wilson once remarked in a similar context,[17] that it is when the individual loves Big Brother that he really loses his freedom. 'Personality' is important in the development of relationships and of one's authority in the classroom, but it is not crucial and it can even be inimical to education if one comes to depend upon it to the exclusion of other, more important aspects of one's teaching.

We must finally note the changes that are taking place in the nature of the authority wielded in many areas of society and no less in our schools. These changes are due to changing attitudes in society as a whole, a growing unwillingness to be 'dictated to' and increasing demands that reasons should be given for any infringement of our liberties, a justification and a demonstration that what is being required is 'fair' and 'equal'. In this respect, it is worth remembering that Weber's main point was to stress the trend in society towards an increased bureaucratization and away from the traditional, unquestioned sources of authority towards those with some legal/rational basis. The development of the 'open society' is paralleled by that of the 'open school',[18] that school which has the looser organizational structure we were discussing just now. The more schools move towards unstreaming, integrated curricula, greater pupil involvement, freedom and even participation in management, the more, as we have seen, the teacher's role becomes 'achieved' rather than 'ascribed' and the basis of his authority moves from the positional to the expert. Tradition and status are bent reeds now, as the current experience of many teachers and schools reveals, and increasingly the onus is on the teacher to establish his authority rather than to expect it to be conferred on him in some way by the job itself. The developments we have been considering make increasing demands on that authority that stems from the teacher's understanding of and skill in handling the many facets of present-day educational practices. These are the ways in which teachers can and should work at improving the nature and the extent of the authority they wield and these are the ways in which the trainers of teachers must help them.

The fact is, however, that while few teachers will want to quarrel with the desirability of the kind of rational basis for authority we have been recommending, all will know that in practice such an ideal is seldom to be attained. In fact, although we have singled out for the purposes of our discussion these different types of authority, the authority any individual teacher wields will be an amalgam of all of them and will vary from age-group to age-group, from class to class, even from day to day. All teachers will have to have recourse on occasion to blatant use of charismatic power, to punishment and the threat of punishment or perhaps sheer bluff. In this connection it is perhaps worth noting another useful distinction that sociologists have made between different bases of social control. They have suggested that our methods of getting people to obey us must be normative, calculative or coercive (Etzioni, 1961).[19] In other words, we can get people to do as we tell them either by persuading them that it is worth doing, that our norms are to be accepted, or by offering them incentives or inducements, or by resorting to force, whether overt or other-wise. In practice, teachers will find themselves using all of these measures or some mixture of all three, but all teachers and schools would probably be aiming at some kind of normative order and endeavouring to avoid as far as possible the need for coercion. Such an attitude would be based on three considerations. The first and most straightforward of these is that based on the relative ease with which this kind of order once achieved can be maintained. There is no doubt that life is easier and far more pleasant when one is working with pupils who want to learn than with those who have to be driven and threatened if they are even to remain in the room and behave themselves. In fact, it is sometimes suggested that some of the changes currently taking place in schools are prompted by an awareness that it is increasingly difficult to coerce pupils, especially older pupils, that calculative methods will not work with pupils who can see nothing for them in school work, and that if the establishment of a normative order necessitates changing the norms in a way that will make them more acceptable to such pupils, then this must be done. If you cannot beat them your only solution lies in joining them. The second reason for preferring a normative order is more complex but absolutely crucial. A system of control that has this kind of basis is the only kind of system that is conducive to education in the full sense. We have seen often enough that to be educated is to have come to value what one has been engaged in for its own sake. If this is not achieved, education has not taken place. Furthermore, in discussing the relation of authority to freedom at the beginning of this chapter, we noted the arguments for freedom and autonomy in education and saw that the concept of education itself requries that our authority be progressively eroded in favour of the autonomy of the pupil. Again the only basis for this is a normative social order. The third reason for preferring this kind of order derives from a consideration of the possible effects on pupils of different kinds of authority and methods of control. There are a number of facets to this and we must turn to a detailed examination of them.

The Effects of Authority and Freedom

We might first note how little is known about the effects on teachers of different patterns of authority and freedom in the classroom. Little research has been done in this area but it would seem to be a fruitful one since there are many things that one would like to know here. There is evidence that teachers achieve more success when they are in tune with or enthusiastic about the particular schemes they are engaged in. Teachers who believe in unstreaming, for example, have more success in teaching mixed ability classes than those who are opposed to it (Barker-Lunn, 1970)[20] and it also emerged in a study of the teaching of French in primary schools that more success was achieved by teachers who were enthusiastic

about the experiment and pleased to be involved in it (Burstall, 1967).[21]
One would, of course, expect the teacher who is thus in harmony with
what he is doing to be more successful and, indeed, to gain more satisfaction from his work. This would suggest in turn that teachers should be
given the kind of flexibility that will enable each of them to develop his
own pattern of working and of authority. As we have seen, however, there
are factors which set limits on the extent of the variety that is possible.
What does seem a more reasonable conclusion is that teachers should
choose their schools and schools their teachers with the need for this kind
of 'match' in mind. It is not clear how important this factor is, as against
considerations of such things as salary, location and general convenience,
when teachers are looking for a post. It is also apparent that a greater level
of job satisfaction and success is achieved in schools where there is freedom
for teachers to experiment with new curricula and new methods and where
they are involving in planning and policy making, but again this is probably
true only in the case of those teachers who want such freedom and involvement. Those who do not want it will not only fail to take advantage of it
and will thus be less efficient; they have also been known to sabotage the
efforts of more enthusiastic colleagues. We need to know a lot more than
we do about the effects of different kinds of structure on different teacher
personality types and the effects of the teachers on the structures. There
is more evidence, however, of the effects of different patterns of organization on the pupils and to this we must turn.

   The first thing we must note here is the difficulties that can arise for all
children, although for some more than others, from an excess of freedom
given to them too soon. The work of Erich Fromm[22] has indicated the
dangers that can arise from man's 'fear of freedom' and this is an important
consideration for teachers. Fromm was appalled at the limitations to the
freedom of the individual that were part of the regime of Nazi Germany
from which he had fled to the USA, but he was also struck by the inability
of people to cope with freedom and their readiness to accept even extreme
forms of authoritarianism. In looking at children in the USA, he draws our
attention to the fact that they are gaining more and more freedom but that
this entails emancipation from a world that offered them security, so that
they experience a conflict between the freedom that they want and the
fear of losing the security that reliance on authoritarian figures can
provide. The same phenomenon forms a major feature of the existentialist
philosophy of Jean Paul Sartre[23] who sees it as obligatory for every human
being to choose for himself and to make his own decisions, but recognizes
the constant temptation that besets everyone to abrogate this responsibility
and to slip into a role which will make decisions for him. Others have

noticed the same tendencies in children. Some children reveal a real reluctance to take responsibility for their own work, for example,[24] and this has been noted also in Higher Education students who have asked for lectures to be made compulsory rather than attendance at them left to their own discretion (Dunham, 1965).[25] In the realm of moral education too, it is apparent that many children prefer to be told 'what is right and what is wrong' rather than being left to reach their own conclusions on these matters (McPhail *et al.*, 1972).[26] An awareness of this is vital to the teacher. For if he does not take charge in such cases, often a leader will emerge from among the pupils themselves. Some guidance from him is needed and he must realize that the development of autonomy and the ability to cope with freedom is a gradual process; children must have time to learn to welcome and to use their freedom. They are only potentially free and, as we saw earlier, it is the teacher's job to lead them to freedom rather than to hand it to them straightaway.

It must also be kept in mind that children will react in different ways to the demands of freedom. The most influential factor in deciding how they will react will be their own backgrounds, the ways in which they have themselves been handled both at home and at school. In this connection, it is particularly important to note what psychologists have told us about the 'authoritarian personality' (Adorno, 1960).[27] Such a person tends to value obedience highly; he obeys rules for their own sake or from fear of punishment rather than from a concern with the reasons behind them; he may resent authority but he will readily succumb to it and he himself likes to wield power over others he regards as his inferiors; he tends to be conformist rather than original and is consequently suspicious of change or of anything new; in his relationships with others he is concerned more with status than with personality characteristics and tends, as we saw in Chapter II, to hold stereotyped views of them; as a parent his affection for his children will be conditional on their good behaviour and obedience.

Children brought up against this kind of background by parents who reveal such traits or, to a lesser extent, by teachers of this kind, tend to acquire the same characteristics themselves quite early in their development. They will as a result prefer a fairly rigid system both at home and at school; they will prefer direction and control to any freer, more suggestive or cooperative approach to education; they will have more respect for the *de jure* or legal authority of the teacher than to that based on any expertise or personality characteristics he might show. This kind of background and the resultant personality development, therefore, will be crucial in determining the reaction of pupils to the authority patterns of the school and the degree of freedom they allow. However, it will equally be a product of certain kinds of authority pattern and we must now turn to a consideration of the effects on pupils of different kinds of school and classroom organization.

Quite the best known and most quoted research in this area is that of Lippitt and White[28] in examining the effects of three types of leadership style which they dubbed as autocratic, democratic and *laissez-faire*. The results of this experiment have been questioned on the grounds that it took place in a voluntary youth club rather than a school and we must also remember that the reaction of the children was not uniform in each situation, as one would expect in view of their differing backgrounds, but most people have nevertheless seen some significance in these findings.

A number of tasks was set to each group and the role of the leader in each was clearly defined. The autocratic leader was to initiate and guide all the activities of his group; he was not to reveal to them the overall programme but rather to dictate each stage of the work for each individual member. In the *laissez-faire* group, members were to have complete freedom to decide what to do and how to do it; the leader was involved only when asked for information, advice or materials by the group. The leader of the democratic group was to generate group discussion for the formulation of policy, to ensure that all members had an overview of the programme and that each shared responsibility for the work and the final achievement.

The main results of this experiment were than in the autocratic situation children worked well while the leader was present but when he was absent this stopped and was often replaced by misbehaviour of all kinds; little initiative was shown by individuals and no pleasure or satisfaction in what the group produced - in fact, in one case a mask they had made was destroyed. On the social plain, two kinds of reaction were detected, aggression between members of the group or a submissive reaction, involving little hostility between members but a good deal towards out-siders. There was little evidence of friendliness either between the children or towards the leader.

The *laissez-faire* climate resulted in haphazard work from the children which seemed little affected by the absence or presence of the leader. Less consistent application to the work was shown and there was a good deal of time-wasting. No interest at all was shown in the products of their work.

In the democratic group, the work done did not reveal the same level of industry as that displayed by the autocratic group but it went on consistently even when the leader was absent. The children were more personally involved in what they were doing, wanting to discuss it with each other and with the leader and far more friendly behaviour was shown between individual members of the group and towards the leader.

Further evidence of a similar kind comes from the work of Anderson and Brewer[29] who studied two types of teacher behaviour amongst younger children. These types of behaviour they described as 'dominative' or 'authoritarian', where the teacher tended to dominate by issuing orders and instructions, and 'integrative', where the teacher tended to accept children's suggestions and offer suggestions in return rather than giving orders. The effect seemed to be that the dominative behaviour was met with aggression on the part of the children, who showed rebellious and dominative behaviour themselves, while the integrative teachers gained the children's attention more often and the children showed more cooperation with one another and with the teacher and more spontaneity in what they were doing.

This latter point raises the question of the possible effects of different approaches on the kind of thinking that children learn to engage in. A rigid and authoritarian approach would seem to be unlikely to promote original or individual thought. Children who reveal this kind of divergent thinking are those who tend to challenge authority, to question traditional knowledge and the norms of the school and such children are rated fairly low on behaviour and regarded as troublesome by their teachers (Getzels and Jackson, 1962).[30] Convergent thinkers tend to express more authoritarian views than divergent thinkers, to value conformity, to respect rules and to think that obedience is important.[31] There are two aspects of this that seem relevant to teachers. Firstly, one of the problems of promoting 'creativity' in schools, as we saw in Chapter II, is that 'creative' children tend to be less comfortable to work with than those who are more conformist and teachers must learn to live with this if such potential is to be developed. Secondly, it is pertinent to ask how far these characteristics of convergent thinkers are the product of the kind of approach to education and particularly the pattern of authority favoured by the teacher.

The kind of approach adopted by the individual teacher, then, will have considerable implications for the child's attitude to work, the kind of thinking he comes to favour and his attitudes to other people, his social education. Similar effects can be discerned in the organizational structure of the school as a whole. We saw earlier that this will be a major factor in determining the kind of authority that the teacher can and must wield within it. It is clear now that it will also have its effect on the development of the pupils and the effects of the different patterns of authority generated by different kinds of organizational structure are clear, especially from the studies of streaming.[32] The main impact is on the moral and social development of pupils and it is to a consideration of the main features of moral education that we must now turn, both because the significance of organizational factors in moral education is so often over-looked and because this is another area in which the degree and the kind of authority exercised by the teacher is crucial.

Moral Education

Two main kinds of difficulty face the educationist when he tries to unravel the problem of how the school is to fulfil its unavoidable responsibility for the moral education of its pupils. The first of these derives from funda-mental disagreements and uncertainties that exist about what shall be taken to constitute moral knowledge; the second from the fact that moral attitudes are caught rather than taught and that, more than in any other field of education, what one does here is affected by the general ethos of the school. Both of these issues raise questions about the proper role of authority in moral education and we must consider each of them separately.

It is clear that there is no established body of knowledge that can be held to constitute moral knowledge and, therefore, no general agreement over the content of what should be taught under this heading. When it is possible to discern in a society one code of morality to which all or most of the citizens of that society subscribe, as was the case when a Christian code held sway in Britain, then perhaps it can be argued that it is the job of the school to transmit the content of that code, although even then we might have some qualms about encouraging an unquestioning acceptance of such a code. However, when one is living and teaching in a pluralist society, in which many different codes of value can be recognized, the question of which of these codes one should try to hand on becomes impossible to answer. To try to inculcate any one code into one's pupils is to lay oneself open to the charge of indoctrination, a word we also use, now that it seems no longer applicable to ourselves, to describe the induction of children into the code of single-code societies. Such an approach is also of little use in a society in which, as in our own, values are rapidly changing, since it provides no basis on which people can relate the code they have acquired to new problems or can reach and evaluate new solutions to them.

This presents a real dilemma to the moral educator and one that he can only resolve satisfactorily by concentrating on the 'form' of morality rather than its content. In order words, there are certain general features of all moral codes and of all moral behaviour that can be discerned very clearly if one looks carefully enough, and the moral educator can feel that he is in fact an educator and not an indoctrinator if he concentrates on these rather than on any attempt to impose any particular code of values on his pupils. It is plain, for example, that a moral code should be coherent and rational, that it should not be at variance with any known 'facts', that the person adhering to the code should be able to apply it with intelligence and understanding to new and unique situations and that he should have come to accept it from choice rather than from habit or as a result of its imposition on him. In other words, the moral autonomy of the individual becomes crucial, as does the need to ensure that the individual has a sound basis for the exercise of such autonomy. The aim of the moral educator, therefore, has become the development of this kind of moral autonomy in all pupils.

This is well illustrated at the practical level by the work of the Schools Council Humanities Curriculum Project,[33] the object of which is to draw the attention of pupils in secondary schools to a number of major moral issues facing contemporary society, problems like those of relations between the sexes, race relations, war and society and so on, to provide them at the teacher's discretion with evidence of all kinds that might be relevant to a discussion of such problems, cuttings from newspapers, extracts from books, poems, photographs and the like, and to allow them to engage in free but informed discussion under a teacher-chairman who remains wholly neutral so that they can reach their own conclusions on these issues, while at the same time learning how moral issues of this kind should properly be tackled.

The same notion of moral autonomy plays a major part in the views of moral development that have been put forward by psychologists such as Piaget and Kohlberg.[34] Even Freud, who is so often interpreted as denying freedom of choice to the individual, can most intelligibly be seen as offering us more autonomy rather than less, as suggesting that a greater understanding of the effects of unconscious motivation on our behaviour can be reached and that this will give us more control of our actions and, therefore, a greater degree of autonomy.[35] Piaget and Kohlberg both suggest that there are several stages of moral development, a sequence that must be followed on the way to adult or rational morality. In the pre-moral stage children conform to rules to avoid punishment; in the stage of conventional morality they conform in order to gain approval; only if and when they reach the stage of autonomous moral thinking can they act according to moral principles they have understood the reasons for. This is the level of what Kohlberg calls 'self-accepted' moral principles, culminating in a stage of 'orientation not only to actually ordained social rules but to principles of choice involving appeal to logical universality and consistency'.[36]

However, this is not a stage that is reached automatically by a process of maturation. It is something that must be achieved. One factor in its achievement is certainly the kind of formal provision that the school can make such as that recommended by the Humanities Curriculum Project which we have just considered. This kind of provision in itself is not enough, however, since it is clear that moral development is not only a matter of formal teaching. In fact formal teaching would seem to have relatively little impact when compared with the effects of other informal experiences that pupils have (Hartshorne and May, 1930).[37] As we have said, moral attitudes are caught rather than taught and this brings us to the second aspect of this problem.

Moral education, or at least moral development and learning, is as much or more a function of the attitudes displayed by individual teachers in the normal course of their work, of the way in which they handle their pupils and of the general organizational structure of the school and the attitudes inherent in it as of any more formal provision that certain teachers, such as those of Religious Education or even of Moral Education itself, may make. In short, it is the responsibility of every teacher and the collective responsibility of the school as a whole. Every teacher, therefore, needs to be aware of the impact that his own approach and the general approach of the school to the pupils is likely to have here, in order to be able to control and modify it. We have already referred to the effects of the organization of the school on the development of particular kinds of attitude to life and to people. It is particularly important if it is likely to have the additional effect of blocking the route to moral autonomy.

If a highly authoritarian stance is taken by a teacher or by the school in general, where children are constantly ordered about and expected to obey without being given reasons for what is being demanded of them, it is not likely to be easy for them to pass from the early stage of uncritical rule-following to one where they can decide for themselves on what is the right course of action. If they are to learn to act rationally they must be brought to see the relevance of reasons to actions as early in their experience as seems appropriate. Moral autonomy is unlikely to result from consistently authoritarian treatment.

Conversely, of course, the ability to make proper use of moral autonomy to reach informed and rational judgements is unlikely to be attained if autonomous behaviour is expected before the stage of autonomy has been reached. This presents a major problem to the teacher of younger children. One cannot hold back moral education, like Latin, until children have the mental equipment to deal with it in a rational way, since, as we have seen, it is going on all the time from birth onwards. We must, therefore, face up to the fact that some moral 'content' will have to be offered at a stage when the pupils are not equipped to handle such matters critically. Indeed, the preliminary work of the other Schools Council project in this field, the Moral Education Curriculum Project indicated that pupils want their moral education to have a content to it, to be directive, and the approach of that project has reflected this finding even in its work at secondary school level.[38]

The important thing to ensure in this kind of situation is that one's intentions are right and that they are clearly recognized by the pupils. It is possible, as we have seen, that to offer pupils a moral education of this kind is to impose on them; but it is equally possible to do it in such a way as not only to avoid this danger but, even more positively, to lay the foundations for future autonomy. For, if one's intention is that they should ultimately learn to think for themselves on such issues, one can show them, even before they can appreciate the full force of the argument, that reasons are relevant to moral decisions,[39] and one can, as Aristotle suggested, provide them with the kind of habit-training that will give them the moral fibre to stick by their decisions when ultimately they come to be able to make them for themselves. In this way it may be possible to ensure a proper progress from externally imposed discipline to self-discipline. In this process the nature of the externally imposed discipline is crucial.

A major element in a moral education of this kind would seem to be the introduction of what used to be called democracy in education but which is now, with more clarity and directness, more usually called pupil-participation. There would seem to be no better way of training pupils in the ways of making decisions than by allowing them a real say in the decisions that are taken within the school. For this reason and also because of the increasing pressures of the pupils themselves, recent years have seen an extension of this kind of development at all levels of education. There are few universities or colleges of Higher Education in which students are not represented on all committees from the governing bodies downwards; many schools have a council at which staff and pupils can meet to discuss and take decisions on matters of joint concern; and the possibility of pupil representation on the governing bodies of all schools, including the primary schools, is being seriously debated. What we have said so far would suggest that these developments are to be welcomed as likely to contribute in themselves a great deal towards the development of individual autonomy for those who act as representatives on such bodies and the creation of a climate in the school that is likely to be conducive to a similar development for all pupils. This is a very important part of education itself. Two further points, however, emerge equally strongly from what we have said so far and have an important bearing on this issue.

Firstly, we must not lose sight of the fact that the road to autonomy is a long one. We have stressed throughout the dangers of too much freedom too soon and of the need for authority to be exercised in the interests of freedom, to ensure that the road to freedom does not become blocked for any pupil as a result of too early an exposure to it. This would seem to indicate that the degree of participation by pupils in the government of their schools must be carefully graded to suit their ages and the level of that can reasonably be expected of them. The extent of their participation and their share of control must gradually increase as they move nearer to full autonomy and reveal higher degrees of responsibility. The point at which this process should start is difficult to determine, but one would feel that it ought to start as early as seems feasible.

Secondly, what we have said so far would also suggest that in any case a distinction must be made within the affairs of the school between those on which almost a full share of responsibility might be given to pupils and those where the teachers must remain firmly in control. In practice, it may not be so easy to make this distinction, but a broad line can perhaps be drawn between matters relating to the general running of the school on which pupils, as consumers, may even have more relevant experience to bring to bear than many teachers, and academic matters concerning such things as the content of courses or combinations of subjects, on which it must be the case that teachers' views should carry much more weight than those of pupils. The points we made earlier about academic freedom would seem to support this view and this kind of distinction. To give pupils or students at any stage of education a full voice in academic decisions is to suggest that in this area they know as much as or more than their teachers and if that claim has any substance then it would seem that they need no longer be detained in school or college. We have maintained throughout that the teacher's authority is provisional and must eventually disappear; logically, it should only disappear when he has nothing more to offer towards the education of his pupils.

The participation of pupils in the organization of the school, if properly handled, can be a major tool in the hands of teachers as they lead their pupils towards full autonomy and gradually surrender their authority in the interests of the children's freedom. At the point where full autonomy is achieved, their job is done and their authority is no longer either needed or justified. Again what is required is that teachers be sensitive to the changing balance of freedom and authority in the upbringing of each child at each stage and in every context. Education as we defined it in our earlier discussion requires a gradual movement towards the total erosion of authority in the interests of the freedom and autonomy of the individual and all that we have said subsequently would seem to confirm this. It also suggests that where authority is necessary, it should be a rational authority, that our methods of control should be normative as far as possible, and our relationships based on mutual trust and confidence. Only a climate of this kind is likely to be conducive to the attainment of freedom by our pupils.

Such an ideal is not easy to achieve and it is impossible even for the most highly skilled and gifted teacher to maintain this kind of authority all the time. Often, as we have said before, he will be reduced to other measures and sometimes, when authority of any kind deserts him, he will have to have recourse to punishment. We must conclude our discussion of authority in education, then, with an examination of what is involved in the use of punishment by teachers and of the place of punishment in education.

Punishment

We said earlier that rules must be backed by sanctions and it would be a mistake to imagine that we can forever avoid a situation in which these rules will be broken and the sanctions will need to be brought into play. Punishment becomes necessary, then, when a rule is broken and our authority is lost, when we say to this boy 'Go!' and he saith, 'Drop dead! , when the normative and even the calculative orders have broken down, the mere threat of coercion is not enough and the coercive measures themselves become necessary. The point of punishment, then, is to re-establish authority and respect for both the rule and whoever issued it. The aim is to re-establish control.

The first thing we need to get clear about any discussion of punishment is what precisely it is; for we need to be able to distinguish it from other related notions like vengeance, deterrence, discipline and so on. We need to know, if we are beating or beheading someone, how we can be sure we are punishing him rather than working out our spite or indulging our sadistic propensities. It has been suggested that there are five criteria that must be satisfied if we are to use the word punishment appropriately of any act (Flew, 1954).[40] The act must involve an unpleasantness for the victim; it must be related to a supposed offence; it must be the supposed offender who is being punished; it must be the work of personal agencies; and it must be imposed by virtue of some special authority conferred by the system of rules against which the offence has been committed.

It is one thing to say what punishment is; it is a very different matter to justify its use; yet it is to the question of its justification that we must next turn. Two kinds of answer have been offered here. Some philosophers have offered a justification of punishment based entirely on retributive grounds. They look back to the offence and answer the question, 'Why ought we to punish?' with a reason, telling us that it is because an offence has been committed. Others have offered a utilitarian justification, looking to the results, the consequences of the act of punishment and answering the question by reference to the purposes, telling us that we must punish in order to achieve certain goals.

The retributive argument can really be summed up in the words of the Old Testament 'an eye for an eye and a tooth for a tooth' and there is a strange ring to many of the arguments produced in support of it. We are told, for example, that there is a deep-rooted retributive feeling in all of us and that this is a justification for acting retributively towards offenders, but the presence of a feeling, however deep-rooted, can never in itself constitute a justification for giving full rein to the expression of that feeling. Secondly, they claim that a moral imbalance has been created by the offence and that this must be corrected. Apart from the problem of making the punishment fit the crime, the difficulties of which have been well expounded by Gilbert and Sullivan, there is a problem here that derives from the fact that not all rules are moral rules and not all moral rules are backed by sanctions. In other words, punishment is not always a matter of a moral imbalance nor does every such moral imbalance bring punishment on our heads. This does suggest, however, the need to distinguish the use of punishment in moral contexts from other uses of it. Thirdly, retributivists often speak of the offender's right to punishment and, although this is indeed 'an odd sort of right whose holders would strenuously resist its recognition,'[41] it does draw our attention to the difficulties of any view that suggests that we should regard the commission of an offence as an excuse to manipulate someone, to try perhaps to turn him into a different person. These arguments are not entirely convincing, although they are certainly worthy of more elaborate discussion than we have been able to give them here. A number of interesting features do emerge, however, which we will take up in a moment when we come to consider the place of punishment in education.

The utilitarian view of punishment regards it not as retributive, but as preventive, deterrent or reformative. The view is well summed up in the words of Jeremy Bentham.[42] 'All punishment is mischief, all punishment in itself is evil. Upon the principle of utility, if it ought at all to be admitted, it ought only to be admitted in so far as it promises to exclude some greater evil.' In other words, punishment involves pain and pain for the utilitarian is always bad and can only be justified if it can be shown to lead to pleasure, happiness or the avoidance of greater pain in the future. Only the consequences, therefore, can justify punishment.

Again this is a view that merits more detailed consideration than it can be given here. Its main difficulties, however, stem from the fact that while it may offer us useful suggestions as to the most efficient methods of social control, it is not strictly a theory of punishment as we have defined it. For if the only criterion we are to take account of in dealing with offenders is a consideration of the likely consequences of our action, then there will be occasions when we will be led to take action that will involve no unpleasantness for the offender at all, or even action which is taken not against the offender himself but against some other person. Action taken against the mother of a juvenile offender, for example, may be more effective in curbing his behaviour than action taken against the offender himself. If a calculation of likely consequences is all that need concern us then punishment as such will not always necessarily be the best solution.

It is this feature of the utilitarian view that has made it attractive to some educationists, who have felt that deliberate acts of nastiness should be no part of education and that it is better to have the freedom in which to decide what is best for the individual child in each situation. It has been noted that there are similarities between the notion of education and that of 'reform'[43] and that teachers should be concerned to make their pupils 'better' rather than to act as agents of retribution. It is suggested, therefore, that they should 'treat' offenders rather than punish them. When one puts it in these terms, however, the difficulty with this line of reasoning becomes apparent. There is an equally cogent counter-argument which says that the notion of education requires us to respect every individual as a person, as a moral being, to regard him as responsible for his actions and as entitled to punishment if he commits an offence; that we cannot without doing violence to the notion of education justify reforming him, moulding him, shaping him or in any other way treating him like a thing rather than a person; that the only way to lead him to understanding and ultimately to autonomy is to enable him to learn the moral lessons that are implicit in acts of punishment.[44]

Both of these points of view seem to have some merit and some reconciliation may become possible if we make certain distinctions within the kinds of situation in which questions of the rights and wrongs of punishment arise. A distinction might be made, for example, between those offences which are committed against moral rules, where we must be aware of the morally educative dimensions of any action we take, and those where the rule broken has no real moral import, if there are such rules, and where it might as a result be possible to take appropriate action without the same kind of moral compunction. It might be important too to take account of the ages of the pupils concerned. For an act of punishment to have the kind of morally educative effect that is wanted the child must be capable of understanding the reasons for it and appreciating its point; otherwise, it will be in his eyes an act of naked aggression.

This latter point draws our attention to the need to keep in mind the evidence of the possible psychological effects of punishment on children. There seem to be two main aspects of this. Firstly, it seems that in terms of getting pupils to learn effectively what you want them to learn, positive factors, such as encouragement, interest on the part of adults and rewards for successes seem to have more effect than 'negative reinforcements' such as punishment. It seems likely to be better, therefore, to reward good behaviour and success and thus to try to prevent bad behaviour than to wait until the bad behaviour occurs and punish it. Secondly, there is little doubt that if punishment is seen by children as an example of aggressive behaviour on the part of adults, as it will be in the case of children who do not understand its moral purport, the tendency will be for them to imitate it and to meet aggression with aggression. Nor is there any doubt of the adverse effects on the climate of a class or school of the widespread use of punishment, as we saw before when discussing the effects on pupils of authoritarian methods generally. In educational terms, it is likely to be counter-productive not only in the case of those pupils who are the recipients of it, but also in the case of all the others who have to live and work in the kind of atmosphere that is engendered.

Prevention is undoubtedly better than cure here. Punishment is a last resort that no teacher should welcome having recourse to. Rather than looking for a justification of it, whether moral or otherwise, we should be working at devising methods of control that will as far as possible obviate the need for it. There are several factors that should be kept in mind as we do this. We need a clearer view of how the rules of any classroom come to be agreed and of the extent to which they are the result of negotiation with the pupils, even when such negotiation is not made explicit; we need to be aware of the variations of structure and method that pupils will experience from teacher to teacher and from classroom to classroom; we need to remember that the fewer rules we have and the less explicit we are about them the more flexibility and room for manoeuvre we will have in our interpretation of them; in particular, where rules are not explicitly formulated, we can on occasion ignore breaches of them, a line that is sometimes far more effective in achieving the 'extinction' of particular forms of behaviour than the reinforcing process of recognizing the offence and punishing it, provided of course that it is not reinforced by the recognition of the other pupils. We will also find it helpful to distinguish those rules that are readily accepted and agreed by our pupils, those, for example, that relate very clearly to the agreed aims and purposes of the school or lesson, and those where their acceptance is less positive and their acquiescence less certain. Teachers and pupils will each define the goals of education differently and clearly where these definitions agree the authority of the teacher will be more readily accepted.

This brings us back to a point we made early in this chapter, when we said that the exercise of authority by the teacher can only be justified when it can be shown to be conducive to the achievement of the goals of education or the agreed goals of both pupils and teachers. When this is not the case, it becomes authoritarianism, an abuse of authority, and in this day and age this is unacceptable to pupils. It is here more often than not that direct head-on clashes occur of the kind that are always to be avoided, since they act to the ultimate detriment of the pupil, the teacher, the school and education itself. These are the situations in which punishment or restorative action of some kind comes to be required. It is always better to avoid them. Since they cannot always be avoided, however, it is important to be clear about what such action is. It is action taken to restore lost authority. As such its justification is not to be sought in itself, since in itself punishment or any other such action has no merit and is at best a necessary evil. It is to be sought in the aims and purposes of the authority it is being used to support, sustain or re-establish. Only in so far as that authority can be justified, can we justify any reasonable attempts to maintain it.

REFERENCES

1. cf. S.I. Benn and R.S. Peters, *Social Principles and the Democratic State,* Allen & Unwin, 1959, Ch.9
2. A. Ryan, 'Freedom', *Philosophy,* 1965
3. *Ibid.*
4. cf. T. Hobbes, *Leviathan,* Ch.26
5. J.S. Mill, *On Liberty,* Ch.5
6. *Ibid.,* Ch.1
7. cf. E.G. West, 'Liberty and education: John Stuart Mill's dilemma', *Philosophy,* 1965
8. J.S. Mill, *op.cit.,* Ch.2
9. *Ibid.,* Ch.3
10. J. Bruner, 'The act of discovery', *Harvard Education Review,* 1961
11. J. Piaget, *The Moral Judgement of the Child,* Routledge & Kegan Paul, 1932 and L. Kohlberg, 'Moral education in the schools', *School Review,* 1966
12. cf. T.D. Weldon, *The Vocabulary of Politics,* Penguin, 1953, Ch.3
13. M. Weber, *Theory of Social and Economic Organization,* Oxford University Press, 1947, Ch.3
14. cf. R.S. Peters, *Ethics and Education,* Allen & Unwin, 1966, Ch.9
15. D.H. Hargreaves, *Interpersonal Relations and Education,* Routledge & Kegan Paul, 1972

16. cf. B.B. Bernstein 'On the classification and framing of educational knowledge' in M.F.D. Young (ed.), *Knowledge and Control,* Collier-Macmillan, 1971
17. J. Wilson, 'Education and indoctrination' in T.H.B. Hollins (ed.), *Aims in Education,* Manchester University Press, 1964, p.32
18. B.B. Bernstein, 'Open Schools, Open Society?', *New Society,* 1967
19. A. Etzioni, *A Comparative Analysis of Complex Organizations,* Free Press, 1961
20. J.C. Barker-Lunn, *Streaming in the Primary School,* NFER, 1970, Ch.4
21. C. Burstall, 'French in Primary Schools Research Project', *New Research in Education,* 1967
22. E. Fromm, *The Fear of Freedom,* Routledge & Kegan Paul, 1942
23. See, for example, J.-P. Sartre, *Being and Nothingness,* Methuen, 1957
24. cf. F. Musgrove and P.H. Taylor, *Society and the Teacher's Role,* Routledge & Kegan Paul, 1969, Ch.2
25. J. Dunham, 'Appropriate leadership patterns', *Educational Research,* (referring to the work of R. Rice and T. Zinkin)
26. cf. P. McPahil, J.R. Ungoed-Thomas and H. Chapman, *Moral Education in the Secondary School,* Longman, 1972, Ch.1
27. T.W. Adorno, E. Frenkel-Brunswik, D.J. Levinson and R.N. Sandford, *The Authoritarian Personality,* Harper & Row, 1960
28. R.K. White and R. Lippitt, *Autocracy and Democracy: An Experimental Inquiry,* Harper & Row, 1960
29. H.H. Anderson and H.M. Brewer, 'Studies of teachers' classroom personalities', *Applied Psychology Monographs of the American Association for Applied Psychology,* Nos. 6, 8 and 11, Stanford University Press, 1946
30. cf. T.W. Getzels and P.W. Jackson, *Creativity and Intelligence,* Wiley, 1962
31. cf. L. Hudson, *Contrary Imaginations,* Penguin, 1966
32. cf. J.C. Barker-Lunn, *op.cit.,* Ch.9, and D.H. Hargreaves, *op.cit.*
33. *The Humanities Project: An Introduction,* Heinemann, 1970
34. J. Piaget, *op.cit.,* and L. Kohlberg, *op.cit.*
35. cf. R.S. Peters, *Authority, Responsibility and Education,* Allen & Unwin, 1959, Ch.5
36. L. Kohlberg, *op.cit.,* p.7
37. H. Hartshorne and M.A. May, *Studies in the Nature of Character,* Macmillan, 1928-1930
38. P. McPhail *et al., op.cit.*
39. cf. R.M. Hare, 'Adolescents into adults', in T.H.B. Hollins (ed.), *op.cit.*
40. A. Flew, 'The justification of punishment', *Philosophy,* 1954
41. A.M. Quinton, 'On punishment' in P. Laslett (ed.), *Philosophy, Politics and Society,* First Series, Blackwell, 1963, p.85
42. J. Bentham, *Introduction to the Principles of Morals and Legislation,* Ch.13
43. cf. R.S. Peters, *Ethics and Education,* Allen & Unwin, 1966, Ch.10
44. P.S. Wilson, *Interest and Discipline in Education,* Routledge & Kegan Paul, 1971, Ch.4

VI The Curriculum

Curriculum planning is the focus of all discussion of education since all educational decisions, whether they be concerned with the organization of schools, the grouping of pupils within the schools, the education of the teachers who will teach in them, the choice of equipment to be used in them or whatever, must ultimately be taken in the light of what is seen to be the essential 'stuff' of education, the school curriculum itself. To ask questions about the curriculum, then, is to raise all the age-old controversies of educational theory, as we will see in what follows.

Curriculum planning is also a matter that is of direct import to the teacher, since one of the most striking, and indeed most welcome, features of much of the curriculum development that recent years have seen has been the direct and active involvement of teachers in it. Furthermore, many recent developments evince a trend towards a greater individualization of educational provision and depend, therefore, for their success on the wisdom of the on-the-spot decisions of the teacher in the classroom. Any kind of teaching must in the end stand or fall according to the skill and understanding of the individual teacher, but this is particularly crucial where individual work is involved and in the early stages of any new scheme. Indeed, since it might be argued that what is needed now is continuous curriculum development, the ability of the individual teacher to attend to this will continue to be of paramount importance. Many schemes have been discredited not because of any fundamental weakness inherent in them but because of the inept manner in which they have been operated by teachers who were not fully apprised of the principles and purposes underlying them. Every teacher, therefore, needs a full appreciation and understanding of the fundamental issues that are at stake in curriculum planning and development, since at the level of the classroom all teachers must take decisions that can only be taken properly with such understanding. The days when someone else took these decisions and the individual teacher could concentrate largely on problems of method and presentation are almost over, and, if education is to continue to develop, it is right that they should be. No exploration of those aspects of Education Theory that are of direct concern to the teacher would be complete, therefore, without a full discussion of the issues involved in curriculum planning.

If we are to engage in this kind of discussion to any purpose, however, we must begin by being clear about what we mean by the curriculum and what different elements are to be identified in our use of this term. Many different kinds of organized activity are to be seen in any school and, unless we wish to be faced at the very beginning of our discussion with the problem of evaluating these against each other, the most useful definition of the curriculum we can adopt is that it denotes all those activites that pupils are deliberately involved in by the school, 'all the learning which is planned and guided by the school, whether it is carried on in groups or individually, inside or outside the school'.[1] The significance of this definition is that it recognizes that learning is a function not merely of set lessons of whatever kind but of all the experiences a child has, so that all such experiences that teachers plan and organize for their pupils should be seen as contributing to their learning and thus should be considered together with those things that are done in set lessons when we examine or plan a school's 'curriculum'.

However, although we are starting from an all-embracing definition of the curriculum, we must immediately identify several different aspects of it if our examination of the problems associated with curriculum planning is to have real point. We must not assume, for example, that it is the same as a syllabus or even as all the syllabuses of any one school put together, for to do this would be to see it purely in terms of its content and thus to adopt too narrow and constricting a view of our task. Recent discussions have stressed the need to identify at least three elements in curriculum planning, albeit closely interrelated elements - objectives, content or subject matter, and procedures or methods.[2] By objectives is meant such things as the qualities of mind, the skills, the kinds of knowledge that it is intended to develop in our pupils; by content is clearly meant the subject matter by which it is hoped these objectives will be achieved; and by procedures the programme of activities or work that teachers and pupils will be engaged upon to attain these goals. Some would add a fourth element - evaluation.[3] It is clearly important in curriculum planning not to lose sight of the need to be able to evaluate the extent to which success has been achieved both in terms of the curriculum itself and the progress of individual pupils. It is also important that the evaluation procedures we use and the assessment techniques we employ should grow out of the curriculum itself and, certainly, that they should not be allowed to determine its objectives, content or methods, although this has often happened in the past. No discussion of the curriculum would be complete, therefore, without a full examination of the problems of evaluation and, in particular, since this is of most direct concern to teachers of the issues involved in establishing appropriate assessment procedures.

It has been claimed[4] that many of the difficulties associated with previous attempts at curriculum planning, both of a 'traditional' and of a 'progressive' kind, have arisen from a failure to distinguish these elements from each other.

Too often the curriculum has been seen in terms of content only, so that its objectives have been the acquisition of bodies of largely propositional knowledge rather than the development through the acquisition of such knowledge of understanding, judgement or imagination. This has been the major fault of the 'traditional' curriculum. 'Progressive' curricula, on the other hand, it is claimed, have laid too much stress on methods - projects and activities of various kinds, for example - and have not only failed to identify or achieve these complex objectives but have also often failed to lead to significant learning of any kind, since they have been inclined to ignore the bodies of knowledge from which understanding and other such qualities of mind can develop. Both kinds of approach are inadequate because they fail to recognize that a consideration of objectives must logically precede any consideration of content or method.

Curriculum Objectives

If we accept that curriculum planning must start from a consideration of objectives, there are a number of further questions that must be asked. In particular, we need to know what sorts of objective we might have as teachers, how precisely our objectives should be formulated and how we can set about justifying them and distinguishing between them. Each of these questions we must look at in turn.

The question of what sorts of objective teachers might have has been answered for us in great detail by the American educationist B.S. Bloom and several associates.[5] Bloom sets out for us a full range of educational objectives organized into three domains - the cognitive, the affective and the psychomotor. The cognitive domain is defined as comprising 'objectives which emphasize remembering or reproducing something which has presumably been learnt, as well as objectives which involve the solving of some intellective task for which the individual has to determine the essential problem and then reorder given material or combine it with ideas, methods or procedures previously learned.'[6] The affective domain comprises 'objectives which emphasize a feeling tone, an emotion, or a degree of acceptance or rejection'.[7] The psychomotor domain consists of 'objectives which emphasize some muscular or motor skill, some manipulation of material and objects, or some act which requires a neuromuscular coordination.'[8] Bloom has produced two handbooks devoted to detailed examination and specification of objectives in each of the first two domains and has promised a third dealing with psychomotor objectives should such a work be needed. This particular approach has attracted a great deal of attention in recent years. It has, however, been criticized on two main grounds, firstly that it is too precise and specific and, secondly, that, lacking any definition of 'education', it provides no criteria for evaluation between objectives. Since these criticisms raise the next two questions we said earlier needed to be asked about curriculum objectives we will consider each of them in turn.

The argument that this approach fails because it attempts to be too specific has two main facets. In the first place it is possible only at the conceptual level to distinguish objectives with this degree of detail, as indeed Bloom himself is aware. Every activity we involve pupils in will have a range of objectives so that it is not even possible in practice to distinguish the three 'domains'. Some would also question whether the difference can be maintained even at the conceptual level. Most activities will involve 'some intellective task', 'a degree of acceptance or rejection' and possibly 'some manipulation of materials and objects' too at one and the same time. In most craft or design projects, for example, it would be impossible to distinguish the development of a knowledge and understanding of the scope and limitations of the materials, a growing awareness of beauty and form and the practical skills needed to achieve both. All are inextricably interconnected in the one set of activities. More fundamentally, it is claimed that it does not make sense to be concerned with knowledge of any kind without being at the same time concerned with a feeling for those standards of truth which are part of what it means to know.[9] This in itself, of course, does not constitute a serious objection to the objectives approach because it can still be argued that it is worthwhile and helpful to make these distinctions in our thinking about and planning of the curriculum, but it does mean that a lot more attention must be given to a consideration of the interrelatedness of objectives and, in particular, to the nature of the interrelations that exist between them.[10]

The second aspect of this line of criticism, however, is much more fundamental. It takes the form of an argument that is based on a view of education as an open-ended and continuous process to which the allocation of specific terminal objectives is inappropriate. It is argued, for example, by Richard Pring that 'the view of an educational process as adopting means to achieve in others specific behaviour or specific ways of seeing, judging and evaluating things does not take account of the autonomous (even if only partly developed) nature of the recipient'.[11] He goes on to argue that the same point emerges when one looks at the nature of an educational inquiry or activity. These, he says, are 'ongoing events' and 'one's conception of the inquiry or activity is altered in the very pursuit of it', so that to specify outcomes in advance is to lose sight of the nature of what one is engaged in. Charity James makes a similar point when she argues that objectives tend to become constraints on teachers and pupils, who are inclined to accept them as in some sense 'given' and unquestionable, so that both lose the opportunity to be active participants in the educational process.[12] This, as Richard Pring points out, is what John Dewey meant when he told us that education is a lifelong process, that our ends constantly change as we approach them and in fact are never attained. This, he also argues, is what happens in practice even to those teachers who set out their objectives very precisely. His conclusion is that we should be working for agreement on principles of procedure rather than on terminal objectives, that we should be concerned not with particular preconceived goals but with the norms and principles according to which we intend that our pupils shall act within the continuous and lifelong process of education.

If we accept this line of argument, and it would appear to be strong to anyone who sees education as an open-ended, continuous process of developing autonomy for the individual, we must accept the tentative and ever-changing nature of our curriculum objectives and our approach to curriculum planning must be a more open and less rigid one than our original discussion might have suggested. Indeed, it might appear that any effective control over curriculum development is to be abandoned and we may founder on that concern with methods which we attributed earlier to the 'progressive' curriculum. Clearly this is a danger, but in fact, as Pring suggests, it should be possible, even if it is likely to be very difficult, to reach some sort of agreement on principles of procedure for any particular curriculum project, as has been done, for example, in the Schools Council's Humanities Curriculum Project.[13]

This does, however, involve us in decisions about the activities we are to involve our pupils in and, whether we speak of principles of procedure or continue to speak of objectives or even of content itself, choices have to be made among those that are possible on the basis of our view of which are desirable. In short, the value question must be faced at some stage and the basis on which we can look for a solution to problems of this kind must now be considered.

As we said earlier, the second major criticism that has been made of Bloom's taxonomy is that it provides no basis for the evaluation of objectives against each other (Gribble, 1970).[14] His approach makes it necessary for him to avoid all questions of value, all questions concerning the grounds on which we might choose one objective rather than another. His only criterion seems to be that these are objectives one can identify in what is actually to be seen going on in schools or can read in discussions of what should go on in schools. As Gribble says,[15] his taxonomy is deliberately neutral. He has no concept of education so that he cannot make any comparative evaluation of objectives and cannot provide us with any criteria by which we can decide what will count as an *educational* objective. Perhaps more seriously, he also gives no account of the nature of knowledge so that questions must be asked about the validity of the assumptions he makes about this in setting out his taxonomy, assumptions upon which both the distinction between the cognitive and the affective domains is made and other distinctions within the cognitive domain such as those between knowledge and certain other intellectual abilities.[9] Again this results in a failure to make clear what is to count as an educational objective and how we can justify the adoption of certain objectives rather than others in these terms.

The difficulties we have referred to both become clearer when we attempt to establish a concept of education in the light of which distinctions of this kind can be made. For it then becomes apparent not only that such a concept is vital to us in selecting our purposes as teachers, but also that, while we may have many purposes in what we choose to do, those activities that can be called 'educational', as opposed to those that might be described, for example, as 'vocational', are characterized not by being directed at certain specific goals or objectives extrinsic to the activities themselves, but by certain intrinsic features of a kind likely to promote the development of those qualities that we would associate with the notion of an 'educated' person, qualities such as rationality, autonomy, understanding, critical awareness and so on.[16] These are the qualities of mind that an examination of the concept of education itself reveals as the ultimate concerns of education and these are the principles of procedure that 'educational' considerations will give rise to. It is for this reason that, as we saw above, the Schools Council's Humanities Curriculum Project has explicitly eschewed clearly defined objectives and has accepted as a fundamental principle of its practical proposals that, since its central concern is to help pupils to deal with controversial issues, the notion of education requires that this should not be tackled from a point of view of clear objectives as to what the outcomes of involvement with issues of this kind should be, but rather on the basis of broad agreement on principles of procedure such as the desire to encourage autonomous thinking and critical awareness. Teachers' and pupils' perspectives will inevitably change as such work proceeds; only the long-term aims, the principles of procedure, will remain constant. The same must hold good for other areas of the curriculum if we take this kind of view of education as a process of continuous develop- ment of certain qualities of mind in which teacher and pupil should both be active participants. It is difficult to know what else education could be if it is to be something different from such processes as indoctrination or socialization or training.

To say all of this is not, of course, to say that this kind of activity is all that schools should be concerned with. Socialization is an important function of schooling, as is vocational training and preparation. In areas such as these, however, it will be relatively easy to outline not only our objectives but also the content and the methods by which we plan to achieve them. It is because many people feel that there is or should be more to schooling than this and that education is not just socialization or training that the major problems arise for curriculum planners. This is why we must direct our main attention to a consideration of what a concern with education as such entails for curriculum planning. We have seen some of the difficulties it creates in the area of curriculum objectives; we must now turn to a consideration of what it implies for decisions of curriculum content. This brings us to what is the central question of curriculum planning and indeed the central question of all educational theorizing, how we are to justify particular approaches to the curriculum. We must, therefore, devote some time to an examination of some of the answers that have been and are being given to this question.

Curriculum Content

One approach to this question has started from an analysis of the nature of knowledge itself. Traditionally, this was the approach adopted by Plato to decisions about what education is and what it should be concerned with,[17] but similar views have appeared more recently and in more sophisticated forms. Starting from the assumption that education is centrally concerned with the development of the rational mind, Paul Hirst, for example, has tried to show what this entails for education by an analysis of knowledge which he claims reveals that there are several logically distinct forms of understanding and that the development of the rational mind entails initiation into all of these forms, that what it means to be educated is to have been brought to an awareness of these distinct forms of understanding and to have acquired the ability to operate within and between them.[18] Such areas as Mathematics, the Physical Sciences, the Human Sciences and History, Literature and the Fine Arts, Morals, Religion and Philosophy are logically distinct from one another and the central concern of education should be to initiate pupils into all of them. If our concern is with the principles of rationality, autonomy and understanding, as we have just suggested that the notion of education itself suggests it should be, then these are to be attained by involving pupils in all of these forms of knowledge or understanding.

Let us be clear about the logical considerations involved here. It is not differences of subject matter that we are to be concerned with but certain fundamental logical differences by virtue of which we can recognize them as separate *disciplines*. What are these logical differences? Firstly, we are told that each form has 'certain central concepts that are peculiar in character to the form. For example, those of gravity, acceleration, hydrogen and photosynthesis characteristic of the Sciences; number, integral and matrix in Mathematics: God, sin and predestination in Religion; ought, good and wrong in Moral Knowledge'.[19] He does not want to say that these concepts are never used outside that particular form but that when we are building up a rational structure of knowledge, these concepts fall naturally into their appropriate form in such a structure.[20]

Secondly, each form has its own distinctive logical structure. When we build up a systematic body of knowledge, we will find that we are building up networks of relationships through which we can understand experience and that these networks fall into the categories we referred to earlier. A network of mathematical relationships will be of a distinct logical kind from a network of scientific relationships and so on. Again this is not to say that there is never overlap, since, as Hirst tells us, 'certain areas of knowledge presuppose others, parts of the physical sciences, for instance, are plainly unintelligible without a good deal of mathematical knowledge',[21] but the logical differences stand.

Thirdly, each form has its own distinctive truth criteria, its own way of testing and establishing the validity of the assertions that it consists of. Thus the truth of a mathematical assertion is established by reference to whether certain logical requirements are satisfied in its relationship to the agreed axioms of Mathematics, while a scientific assertion is verified by appeal to observable experience and empirical evidence acquired by appropriate experimental procedures.

Lastly, and following from what has already been said, each form has its own distinctive methodology. In each form it is possible to see 'particular techniques and skills for exploring experience'.[22] Each has developed its own unique procedures for extending human knowledge in its own peculiar field, its own methods for extending and categorizing those aspects of human experience that fall within its purview.

This kind of analysis of human knowledge provides a very positive basis for curriculum planning in so far as it offers within its own terms a justification for a whole range of decisions we might make concerning curriculum objectives, content and procedures. If education is concerned with the development of the rational mind and if rationality can be categorized by reference to these several forms of understanding, then many of our difficulties over curriculum planning are solved. It is clear what teachers and schools should be bending their efforts towards. It does not, of course, in itself provide a justification of all traditional school 'subjects' since some, such as Geography, are *fields* of knowledge rather than forms, to be distinguished by their subject matter rather than by any distinctive logical structure, and have emerged as convenient focuses for particular areas of knowledge rather than as distinct logical networks. These will need to be justified on other grounds. On the other hand, it does not rule them out, any more than it rules out other interdisciplinary activities that are to be seen on school curricula,[23] as we shall discover later when we look at the problems of integrated studies, and it does provide a justification for large areas of curriculum planning.

A similar or related view, and one which has been explicitly combined with this notion of forms of understanding in order to provide a justification for certain kinds of curriculum content,[24] is that which begins from an analysis of 'education', of what it means to be educated, and suggests that to be educated is not only to have developed understanding or some kind of cognitive perspective, to have achieved a level of autonomy and to have come to care about what one has been involved in but also to have been initiated into certain worthwhile activites.[25] In short, it is suggested that an analysis of the concept of education reveals that the content of education must be seen as being intrinsically valuable, that it cannot be something whose justification is to be found outside itself, that education cannot be instrumental, a means to something else, that, as Dewey said, 'the only end of education is more education', since, as we saw above, to teach or to learn something with only an extrinsic aim in view is to be engaged in a process that is more properly called 'training' than 'education'. Thus the content of education as such must consist of that which is valued for itself. It has been further argued that one can pick out certain kinds of activity like 'science, history, literary appreciation, philosophy and other such cultural activities'[26] and show that these are worthwhile in a way that other activities are not and that they are, therefore, the very stuff of education since these are the activities we find ourselves engaged in whenever we reflect upon or try to explain any form of human activity. In short, these are the forms of understanding that are essential to any attempt to take a rational view of human life and existence. It is at this point that the connection between these views of the curriculum becomes explicit and we see that both will lead to a justification of the same kind of curriculum content, although one must not forget that this kind of argument is relevant only to the educational objectives of the curriculum and that it is quite reasonable, not to say necessary, for schools to be concerned with much that is not educative on this kind of analysis.

On the face of it, however, this general approach would appear to lead to the justification of a largely traditional form of curriculum so that, at a time when the traditional is not fashionable, it has not escaped criticism. In fact, it could be claimed that at the practical level curriculum development has been following a course which is directly the reverse of that which this approach points to, since the predominant characteristics of curriculum change in recent years have been the development of such things as integrated studies, interdisciplinary enquiry and project work of all kinds based on pupils' interests and calling for a degree of individualization of provision and self-initiation of work by pupils not usually associated with the 'traditional' approach to curriculum planning.

Critics of this approach to the curriculum have expressed their dissatisfactions with it in a number of forms. The most cogent of these are those that derive from some important questions that can be asked about the view of knowledge, of truth, of values, even of mind itself on which this approach is based. It can be argued, for example, that the epistemology of the division of knowledge into logically discrete forms is far from fully worked out. It is one thing to propose the hypothesis that knowledge is divided into several distinct kinds; it is quite another matter to spell out what the differences between these forms are. No satisfactory explanation of any of them other than the logical/mathematical and the empirical/scientific has been given and, while this does not necessarily imply that no such explanation could be given, it certainly does not constitute very satisfactory evidence for the existence of other separate forms. Furthermore, some philosophers have taken a different view of knowledge and have argued, as John Dewey did for example, that all knowledge does fall into one or other of these two categories, that all knowledge which is not of the logical/mathematical form is, like our knowledge of the natural sciences, hypothetical and empirical, so that the truth of an assertion in any of these fields is to be assessed not by whether it satisfies the demands of a peculiar form of logic that cannot be elucidated but by whether as a hypothesis it 'works', whether it is the best and most useful explanation we have yet been able to work out for a particular set of phenomena, whether scientific, aesthetic, moral or even religious.

A further and associated point that has been made in criticism of this approach to curriculum planning is that it leads to what many would regard as an undue emphasis on cognitive achievement. To start from the conviction that education is the development of the rational mind is to be committed to a view that must lead to this kind of emphasis and to a disregard of other aspects of the development of pupils. It is surely true that the concept of education itself requires that the educand must be brought to care about and to value the process he has been involved in, that some sort of affective development must be involved and, if this is so, then any view that ignores this dimension, as a view based entirely on logical and epistemological considerations must, will provide a less than adequate basis for the planning of an educational curriculum.

The attempt to base curriculum planning on an analysis of the concept of education such as that of Richard Peters does have the merit of recognizing the importance for the teacher of this affective aspect of the development of children. It also highlights, as we have seen, several other features that must be present if we are to use the term 'education' properly. It goes too far, however, in the view of many people, when it attempts to argue that as a result of this certain kinds of curriculum content be chosen in preference to certain other kinds, in short, when it presses the idea of education as necessarily concerned with intrinsically worthwhile activities to the point where it asserts that these activities can be objectively identified. For to argue this is to assume a theory of knowledge similar at root to that associated with the view of education as the development of the rational mind. In other words, it assumes an objective status for human knowledge, for truth and for judgements of value, the difficulties of which become apparent as soon as we attempt to decide at the practical level what these intrinsically worthwhile activities are. When we do this, we quickly realize that worthwhileness is not something which inheres in objects, in bodies of knowledge or in activities, but that, like beauty, it is to be sought in the eye of the beholder. It is almost certainly true that the use of the term 'education' implies a conviction on the part of the person using it that the activities he is referring to are to be valued for themselves, but to say that is not to say that everyone does or must view them in the same way. The difficulty of deciding who is to be the cultural weights and measures officer is the reason why this approach cannot resolve the problem of curriculum content for us, since a variety of views are expressed, by teachers, parents and pupils, for example, on what is intrinsically valuable. Logical considerations alone can never constitute a justification for anything. A further criticism of this kind of approach derives from the view that is being put forward currently by a number of sociologists based on what they have called 'the stratification of knowledge' (Young, 1971).[27] Briefly, these sociologists are concerned about the difficulties we have already identified in the view of knowledge as objective and, accepting the subjectivity of knowledge, they see it rather as 'a product of the informal understandings negotiated among members of an organized intellectual collectivity' (Blum, 1970)[28] and the curriculum in consequence as a social system. Socially constructed knowledge is ideology, that is, it is the knowledge of an organized interest group, and the present dispute over curriculum content is seen as a result of competing ideologies, so that any attempt to impose a particular body of knowledge on children is regarded as an attempt to gain control of them by exposing them to the influence of only one such ideology. Whether this is done intentionally or is merely an accidental by-product of the system, the values of the school are imposed on all of its pupils and this is one reason for the demands of people like Illich, Freire and others for a deschooling of society.

Thus a distinction is drawn between educational knowledge or theoretical thought and common sense knowledge, everything that passes for knowledge in a society (Berger and Luckman, 1967),[29] and it is claimed that we must explore the activities of teaching and learning from this point of view (Esland, 1971)[30] and examine the possibilities of basing the content of the curriculum on the common sense knowledge of the pupils rather than the educational knowledge of the teacher, thus avoiding the alienation that results when pupils are presented with knowledge to which they cannot relate and which has no meaning or significance for them in the context of their own experience and existence.[31]

A major difficulty of this view is that it offers no help with the question of how we are to decide what 'common sense' knowledge to promote or how to promote and extend it. It does have the merit, however, not only of drawing our attention again to the difficulties of regarding knowledge as having some kind of status independent of the knower, but also of alerting us to some of the dangers of taking such a view. It reminds us that the school is a part of society and that changes in that society must be reflected in the school curriculum. It is not enough to base our curriculum planning only on a consideration of the nature of knowledge, since it would then be subject only to very limited kinds of change. Nor is it possible to discern elements in our culture which are objectively worthwhile. Any culture is the product of the interaction of the individual members of a society and what the members of that society regard as intrinsically worthwhile will change; indeed, in a pluralist society there will be no general agreement over this kind of issue at any time. Curriculum development must reflect this and the curriculum itself must be open to this kind of influence on its development; it must be sensitive to variations of culture within a society and to the continuous process of change (Lawton, 1973).[32] This view alerts us, therefore, to the need to give full attention to the social dimension of curriculum planning, while adding its weight to the growing argument against the idea of curriculum planning based on a concern with the nature of knowledge alone.

A final point that must be made in listing the main difficulties that some educationists have found in this approach to curriculum planning through a concern with the nature of knowledge is that it leads to no fundamental concern with the psychology of the child. The main preoccupations of the psychological research that has been associated with this kind of view have been the differences between individual pupils or groups of pupils in the rates at which they can assimilate certain bodies of knowledge and questions concerning the most effective ways of presenting material to children and the sequences in which such material can best be organized to facilitate the learning of it.

The general trend away from this view of education which we noted earlier has been a result of all of the difficulties we have listed but in particular it has derived from a concern that more attention should be given to the nature of the child than is required by that sort of approach. This was certainly the starting point for Jean Jacques Rousseau, who has as good a claim as any to be considered the initiator of a new approach to education. If the view we have been considering is sometimes described as 'traditional', it is not only because it has tended to be associated with a curriculum organized in the best traditions of English education, it is also because fundamentally the view of education as the development of rationality through the acquisition of certain kinds of objectively true knowledge goes back at least as far as Plato and it was this Platonic/Christian tradition in educational practice that Rousseau inveighed against in his *Emile*. Rousseau urged us to start from the child in making our educational provision rather than from the subject matter. 'We know nothing of childhood; and with our mistaken notions the further we advance the further we go astray. The wisest writers devote themselves to what a man ought to know, without asking what a child is capable of learning. They are always looking for the man in the child, without considering what he is before he becomes a man.'[33] Thus did Rousseau begin a movement that was taken up by educators like Dewey and Montessori and that has culminated in many of the changes that we can see in our schools today.

This general movement is sometimes characterized as 'progressive education'; sometimes it is called 'child-centred' or 'learner-centred'. At root it is an attempt to plan the curriculum on the basis of the 'needs' or the 'interests' of the child, to seek for a justification for the content of education not in the nature of knowledge nor even in the nature of society but in the nature of the child, the one who is to be educated. We must look now at some of the forms this approach has taken and some of the ways in which this kind of argument for the content of the curriculum has been developed.

Rousseau's own proposals for the practice of education do not help us much here since basically they amount to the advice that, in the early years of childhood at least, we should try to leave the child alone to develop naturally, to grow, and thus protect him from the corrupting influences of society - a primitive version of one aspect of the view currently being put forward by certain sociologists which we looked at just now. However, this points to curriculum abolition rather than curriculum planning and this policy of non-interference cannot provide any kind of basis either for the theory or the practice of education, since it raises both practical and conceptual difficulties. Growth in itself cannot be an adequate or helpful criterion for educational decisions since education is not maturation[34] and

teachers, if they are to have any *raison d'être,* must have a positive role
to fulfil.

Attempts have been made, however, to reconcile this view of the
desirability of promoting the natural development of children with an
acceptance of the fact that those who are to attend to this development must
have some criteria to help them to decide on the direction of this development and on the kind of 'interference' in the growth of children that might
be desirable or permissible. We have already referred to the work of John
Dewey and, in particular, to his view that all our knowledge of the world is
hypothetical and that learning is a matter of framing and testing hypotheses.
From this basis he developed a view of education as concerned to promote
the ability of children to learn in this way and to go on learning and adapting
their knowledge throughout their lives. This approach, he believed, would avoid
imposition by the teacher, which he regarded as indoctrination and as likely
to inhibit real learning; it would also obviate the undirected and possibly
useless learning that might go on if children were left entirely to themselves.
The criterion by which teachers are to evaluate children's activities and direct
them into certain channels is a consideration of the extent to which these
activities are likely to lead to further learning, to progress along what he
called 'the experiential continuum'.[35] Thus education is a matter of
promoting continued experience for children, since it is only from experience
that they will learn in the fullest sense of that term. If we were to proceed in
this way, Dewey felt that we would promote not only the education of the
individual child but also the continued evolution and development of
mankind.

Further support for this kind of view has come more recently from the
work of those psychologists such as Piaget and Bruner who have explored the
process of concept development and in doing so have come forward with a
new view of intelligence, as we indicated in Chapter II, and a new view of
education as the process by which cognitive growth is promoted rather than
propositional knowledge acquired. This view places the emphasis on the kind
of learning that takes place rather than its content, suggesting that it is the
task of education to enable children to acquire a range of concepts which they
they can use in their continuous interaction with the environment. It suggests,
furthermore, as we have seen in Chapter IV, that concepts can only be
acquired by using them both in action and in speech, so that children must be
given opportunities for activity, not always of a physical kind, and for
experiences if they are to be able to acquire these concepts, the teacher's job
being to structure these activities and experiences in such a way as to
promote cognitive growth and conceptual development. This, it is claimed
by Piaget, is particularly important in the early years, at the stage of concrete

operations, when children learn best from concrete activities.[36] This view is reflected also in the often quoted words of the 1931 Hadow Report on Primary Education that the curriculum of the primary school should be thought of 'in terms of activity and experience rather than knowledge to be stored or facts known'. Thus it becomes the task of the educator to get to understand the child's unique ways of thinking and learning and to decide on the content of the curriculum by reference to what will stimulate and promote such thinking and learning.

It will be clear that this approach to curriculum planning is based on a particular view of learning and that if one takes a different view of the nature of learning one will come up with a totally different set of criteria for curriculum planning. A behaviourist theory of learning, for example, such as that of B.F. Skinner,[37] which characterizes all learning in terms of response to stimuli, will lead, as we saw in Chapter III, to a view of education as the moulding of children's minds through a constant input of the appropriate stimuli and the content of the curriculum in such a case will be decided by reference to the sort of responses we want, the sort of adults we want to produce or the kind of knowledge and behaviour viewed as important by the society in which we live. Such learning is unlikely to be very permanent, however, as we also saw in Chapter III, because of the need for constant reinforcement.

To some extent, any approach to curriculum planning that starts from a consideration of child nature will find it difficult to give helpful and positive answers to questions about curriculum content, in the same way and for much the same reasons as the approach that begins from an examination of society. An attempt has been made by some, therefore, to set up the notion of need as the focus of this kind of curriculum planning, to suggest that all decisions as to curriculum content should be made by reference to the needs of the children. Some psychologists have tried to discover for us the needs of children in order to provide us with the basic knowledge we must have to begin to plan a curriculum along these lines. Maslow, for example has proposed a theory of motivation in terms of need reduction.[38] He has identified three sorts of need - primary needs, those for food, air, sleep and so on, emotional needs, those for such things as love and security, and social needs, those for acceptance by a group and the confidence that comes from an awareness that one has something to offer to a group. The theory is that if these needs are reduced, the patterns of behaviour associated with this need reduction will be reinforced and that this is how learning takes place.

Such a theory may help us in our search for effective methods of teaching; it does not help us with questions about the content of our teaching. For all such theories of need or attempts to define need must involve some kind of

evaluation on the part of the person propounding the view and more so on
the part of anyone attempting to implement it. Once one gets beyond the
needs for food, drink, sleep and other physical requirements of this kind, it
becomes increasingly difficult to separate what a child needs from what he
wants or from what someone thinks he ought to have. In other words, 'need'
is a term which has a prescriptive as well as a descriptive connotation. These
two aspects of the meaning of the word must be kept distinct from each
other, since no description can ever give rise to a prescription and no amount
of information about what children do need could ever resolve for us the
question of what they ought to have. We must have other criteria by which
to decide which needs should be catered for since the notion of need cannot
of itself be such a criterion.[39] The same argument applies with equal force to
the claim that curriculum content can be decided by reference to the needs of
society. There is, of course, a trivial sense in which every curriculum is based
on the notion of needs, since no-one would include in it anything that was
not thought to be needed,[40] but in this context the notion is largely otiose
and offers us no practical assistance with the problems of curriculum
planning.

In order to bypass this difficulty with the idea of needs as the basis of
curriculum planning without at the same time losing the advantages that are
thought to be associated with an approach that takes full cognisance of the
psychology of the child, some educationists have stressed the desirability of
using children's interests as the criterion. It is argued that children learn best
through interest, that they are manifestly not interested in much of what is
presented to them by a 'traditional' curriculum and thus do not learn in the
full sense of the word and that we might achieve more success if we were to
find out what interests them and work from that. There are at least two
aspects of this argument that must be distinguished from each other. In the
first place, it may be that what is being advocated here is a change of method
rather than a change of content. For if we accept that children do in fact
learn best when interested in something, we need do no more than improve
our methodology in such a way as to make them interested in what we want
them to learn. This, after all, is no more than many teachers have always tried
to do. However, there is a further, deeper sense in which the interests of
children have been suggested as a basis for curriculum planning. For it has
been proposed (Wilson, 1971)[41] that education is the development of
children's interests in such a way as to help them to pursue them more
effectively and with more discrimination, to organize their experiences and to
gain a clearer view of the intrinsic value of their activities. We have seen that
the notion of education implies that its content must be intrinsically valuable
but we also saw that this assertion does not in itself help us to decide what

activities have this intrinsic value. It is being suggested here that our best approach to the problem of discovering what is intrinsically valuable is to consider what is intrinsically valued, to look for what pupils do in fact value for itself rather than to engage in the essentially metaphysical exercise of attempting to discover intrinsic value inhering in certain activities independently of the way in which human beings view them. Such a view is not, of course, unrelated to the view of Dewey which we considered earlier and it will lead to similar major changes in curriculum content. It also throws up similar difficulties and we must consider some of these now.

It has been argued against this view that we must distinguish what a child is interested in from what is in his interests. In one sense, this assertion reveals more a predilection for the pithy saying than a serious criticism, since those who have argued for an interest-based curriculum have usually been very clear about this distinction, since it lies at the very root of their argument which is that the development of what a child is interested in is in fact what is in his interests. However, it does draw our attention yet again to the central problem of the 'child-centred' approach, whatever form it takes, namely the difficulty of choosing or deciding between competing claims. We have seen the difficulties of equating education with maturation and providing teachers with no clear indication of the role they must play in the process. This view has the merit of giving the teacher a clear directive, that it is his job to identify the interests of his pupils and to develop them by deepening them, widening them, revealing new dimensions to them and so on. However, he is still faced with the problem of deciding which interests can or should be developed and which should be discouraged, and, even if he resolves that problem, he still has to decide on the direction in which he should develop them. Again his own values will impinge on the situation so that this view is no more successful than any other in offering objective criteria by which we can make decisions of this kind.

This difficulty becomes particularly apparent when we ask questions about the origins of children's interests. It must be the case that their origins are to be found in the experience of the child and particularly in his cultural background. It has been argued with some force, therefore, that if the interests of the child are socially determined, then to base the curriculum on those interests is to risk trapping the child in his culture and, in particular, where the child's background is culturally impoverished (if such a notion is acceptable), education through interests is likely to aggravate rather than to alleviate that impoverishment (White, 1968 and 1973).[42] Indeed, it has been claimed that this is likely to result in a kind of social control that is based on not allowing individuals to escape from the cultural environment into which they have been born. The same danger is implicit in the demands we considered earlier of certain sociologists for a curriculum based on the 'common sense' knowledge of the child, the experience he brings to school with him. Furthermore, as we shall see in Chapter VII, if our curriculum is differentiated, knowledge becomes hierarchically structured and those who are allowed access to high status knowledge may come to be deemed more worthy as persons than those offered mere 'common sense' knowledge.

This criticism seems to be based on a somewhat naive and simplistic view of what it might mean to educate a child through his interests and it need not be a serious criticism of a view that stresses the need to develop and extend children's interests in the way we have just discussed. It does draw attention, however, to a serious danger of this approach if it is not allied to an awareness of the need for some adequate basis for curriculum decisions that is independent of the inclinations of the children themselves. It need not lead, as John White seems to think,[43] to the idea of a common curriculum resembling that which derives from a concern only with the nature of knowledge, but we must heed his warning of the dangers of generating one curriculum for an élite and another for the rest of the school population. The notion that there be some kind of common curriculum is an important one. If all pupils are not given access to what is deemed valuable in our culture, then those who are will continue to enjoy many social advantages over those who are not and our society will remain a divided one.

Again, therefore, we come up against the fundamental difficulty of any approach to the curriculum that begins from a rejection of the idea that certain bodies of knowledge are objectively worthwhile and can as a result be imposed upon pupils without qualms. Any such approach must appear process-bound or method-bound, to be more concerned with the 'how' of education than with the 'what', as we noted at the beginning of this chapter, and to offer little help with decisions of content. If taken to its logical conclusion, it is also likely to result in a loss, or at least a devaluation, of much that many would regard as valuable in our culture and this may be particularly to the detriment of those pupils who are not likely to meet these things if they are not introduced to them at school. It is clearly important that we should not ignore the child in planning a curriculum; equally it is true that we need some other, external criteria to appeal to. How can these two positions be reconciled?

It may be that the difficulty arises from too ready an acceptance of this polarization. Education cannot be properly conceived or planned in relation to either the child or society or the subject matter but must pay due regard to all of these.[44] It cannot be centred exclusively on any one of them without being distorted. Education cannot be seen as growth alone or as moulding alone; it must be seen as directed or controlled growth. If this is to be so then teachers need both an understanding and respect for the nature and the interests of the child, an awareness of the social setting in which they are working and a concept of education in the light of which they can promote continued development. Both the means and the ends are equally important and any view that ignores either one must be inadequate as a basis for realistic curriculum planning. Knowledge continues to develop; society evolves; people change; and the curriculum must keep pace with all three. If this is to be possible, if the curriculum is to continue to develop and evolve, then it must be open-ended and not firmly tied to any rigid presuppositions. No extreme position allows for this kind of open-endedness. There is no doubt that a curriculum that is planned out of respect only for certain canons of knowledge is likely to lead to the alienation of many pupils and, therefore, to be self-defeating. There is no lack of empirical evidence to substantiate this view. Some attention must be paid, therefore, to the nature of society and to the many facets of child nature and of individual children. It is equally clear, however, that a curriculum based entirely on what pupils want to learn or what the social order of a given time or place seems to require would lead to the loss of much that seems to have value both for society and for the children themselves. Some reference must be made also to what is felt to be valuable, therefore, in planning a curriculum.

In practice, this is the sort of compromise one can see in the work of most teachers and most schools. It is only at the level of theory that it gives real trouble for it is here that the polarity appears. It can only be solved by an acceptance of the inevitability of the same subjectivity in education that exists in all human activities and endeavours. To expect an objective justification for all educational decisions is to deny that in the last analysis education is a matter of the subjective interaction of minds. In this situation, what distinguishes education from other more sinister activities like indoctrination is not its objectivity nor even the objectivity of its content; it is the intentions of those who practise it. If their intentions are to broaden the experience of children, to enhance their freedom by increasing the range of experiences open to them and to guide them to that autonomy of mind that characterizes being human and which we have seen to be an essential component of the notion of education itself, then any decisions that are made as to the kinds of curriculum content that are most appropriate to these goals are justified by very dint of the intentions they are serving. To say this is not to say that teachers will not make mistakes in the decisions they make; it is to say, however, that they should not be led into error by being required by educational theoreticians to make unnecessary choices between particular ideological positions. The most that any concept of education can lead us to is a respect for the freedom and autonomy of the individual child. How this is to be interpreted in practice is a matter for the professional judgement of every teacher.

A further point must be stressed here, one that we have made before. The problem that we have been discussing at such length is one that concerns only those activities that we encourage in schools on the grounds of their intrinsic value. Many of the things we teach or urge pupils to learn are justifiable by other, perhaps less controversial arguments, since they are seen not so much as valuable in themselves as instrumental in the achievement of other kinds of goal, such as certain social or vocational achievements. Most curriculum decisions are, of course, in practice made by reference to a mixture of both intrinsic and instrumental considerations. Not all decisions of curriculum content, therefore, need to be made by reference to the thorny problems we have been discussing. In many cases it is enough to be able to show reasonably convincingly that what we intend to teach is the most efficient way of achieving certain vocational outcomes, for instance, or certain skills that have a social value, unless, of course, we want to involve ourselves in similar debate about the worthwhileness of the social ends to which these means are appropriate. Education is not socialization, but a good deal of what goes on in schools must be seen as socialization of one form or another and is to be justified in these terms. Education is only one aspect of schooling.

Nor must we allow the polarization that has characterized the discussions of educationists to lead us to believe that even the educational content of the curriculum must be justifiable entirely in terms of one kind of approach or the other. There is plenty of scope in the time-table for a number of different kinds of activity, some involving a great deal of pupil choice, others perhaps far less. If we are to include certain elements in the time-table on grounds of their social or vocational usefulness, there is no reason why we should not also have both interest-based activities and compulsory studies at other times, no reason why the time-table should not offer scope for a whole range of activities, each to be justified in quite different terms (James, 1968).[45] We must not assume that all the purposes of the school, whether they be social, vocational, cultural or educational, will be or can be met by one kind of provision. The curriculum must include a number of quite different elements if it is to achieve a variety of objectives.

This is particularly apposite to the arguments that have raged in recent years over the merits or demerits of integrated studies. Too often these arguments have suffered from the same tendency to polarization, an assumption that to favour the introduction of some form of integrated studies is necessarily to fly in the face of the logical differences that, as we have seen, some have claimed exist between disciplines and *vice versa*. In spite of this, the integrated approach to learning has spread very rapidly through our schools in the last decade and has perhaps been more significant in curriculum change than any other single form of curriculum innovation. No discussion of the curriculum would be complete, therefore, without an examination of some of the main features of this development.

Integrated Studies

Most of the views we have considered that have tried to base their curriculum planning on a concern for the child and his place in society rather than the subject matter have been linked, albeit often in a rather confused way, with some form of integrated studies. There are good reasons for this. Children's experiences do not fall into neat subject areas or into single disciplines, nor do their interests nor their enquiries, nor do most of the things that seem socially or culturally important, so that, once one begins to plan a curriculum from any of these bases, some form of integration almost always follows. This is not inevitable, since it is possible to structure an enquiry or a project, even to develop an interest within one subject area only, as many of the projects of the Schools Council have done. It often happens, however, that a move towards these methods is accompanied by an attempt to establish some kind of integrated studies programme. We must devote some time, therefore, to a consideration of the different kinds of reason that teachers have had for introducing various forms of integrated studies. Not the least important reason for devoting some time to this here is that it illustrates perhaps better than any other recent development in the curriculum the point we tried to make in the last section, namely the kind of development that takes place when we pay due regard in our curriculum planning to the children we are planning for and the society in which they live and not only to the nature of the knowledge we are purveying.

The first thing that must be stressed about integrated studies is that, like all other examples of curriculum innovation, it takes many different forms according to the particular requirements and characteristics of each situation in which it has been introduced (Warwick, 1973).[46] It is absolutely right that all curriculum developments should be adapted to the peculiar conditions of the school into which they are introduced, since each situation is unique and needs its own unique programme. This does, however, make it as difficult to generalize about this particular development as about any other. There are schemes in which integrated studies programmes are based on very careful structuring by the teacher or teachers concerned of both the content of the programme and its methods; there are others, such as the Goldsmiths' College IDE scheme,[47] in which almost complete freedom of choice in matters of content is given to each individual child, often within related areas centred on a common theme, but sometimes entirely free-ranging. In some cases, this kind of development has been associated from the first with some form of team-teaching and thus with the combined working of several classes together; in others it is handled by individual teachers adopting a 'generalist' approach with one class. Sometimes the methods adopted have been largely heuristic, with pupils encouraged to explore and 'find out for themselves' or 'learn by discovery'; on the other hand, often a directly didactic or instructional approach has been used. There are also many variations in the range and type of subjects included in such schemes depending again on the purposes of the teacher or teachers involved and even on their individual preferences, since one crucial factor in all curriculum innovation is that, if it is to be successful, the teachers operating it must believe in its value. Thus there are integrated science schemes, integrated humanities projects and other schemes which have attempted even to integrate scientific and humanistic studies with each other. There are thus so many variables that generalization becomes impossible and teachers have enjoyed a great deal of freedom in planning courses to suit their own purposes within these variables. The particular form of integrated studies that emerges in each situation, however, will depend on the purposes and views of the teachers responsible for it so that the most helpful thing we can do here in attempting to introduce some clarity into discussion of this issue is to examine some of the purposes that teachers have had when adopting this kind of approach to teaching.

The most extreme view that has been taken here, what is sometimes called the 'strong' view of integrated studies, is that which bases itself on the belief that all knowledge is one anyway and that, far from requiring to justify integrating it, we need a better explanation than has so far been given of why it should be 'fragmented'. This is the sort of view that was taken, as we saw earlier, by John Dewey, who saw all knowledge as ultimately of a scientific kind, a result of the experience that each individual has as he solves the problems presented to him by his environment, physical, social, cultural and aesthetic, problems which are solved in all of these spheres by the application of the scientific method of framing and testing hypotheses. Thus for Dewey, subject divisions might appear in the later stages of education when reasons emerged for dividing knowledge into convenient parcels, but there were no fundamental logical reasons, such as those that Paul Hirst puts forward for dividing it up and certainly not for the creation of as many as six or seven discrete 'forms'. The logical positivists too have argued[48] that once we have distinguished between the axiomatic knowledge of Mathematics and Logic and the empirical knowledge that we have in other spheres we have gone as far as we can in dividing knowledge up, although we must remember that on this view many areas such as the moral and aesthetic are regarded as not areas of knowledge as such at all. Views about the wholeness of knowledge in fact have a long history in epistemology from the time when Plato offered us his 'dialectic' as the master science that would weld all knowledge into one supreme system[49] to the more recent claim of A.N. Whitehead that 'you may not divide the seamless coat of learning'.[50]

This view of knowledge is given further support by the difficulties we have already referred to as inherent in the notion of knowledge as divisible into several 'forms' and the manifest fact that knowledge has in practice been organized by man not into logically discrete 'forms' but into convenient 'fields' to suit his particular interests and purposes. Thus an important and necessary field of study has long been Geography, the study of man and his natural environment, a study which has drawn on Mathematics, on Physical Science, on Social Science and so on. Indeed the study of Education itself has little point or relevance to human affairs if it does not include philosophical, psychological, physiological and social dimensions. The suggestion, therefore, that irreducible logical problems are created by the attempt to integrate Geography with, say, History, or Comparative Education studies with, say, Philosophy is in any case nonsensical. If such problems are ever to arise, it will only be in relation to the integration of disciplines not of subjects. Furthermore, it will be a problem not only for new versions of integrated studies but also for those established subjects like Geography or Comparative Education which are and always have been forms of integrated studies in themselves.

Thus one view that some teachers and educationists have taken of integrated studies is that since all knowledge is fundamentally reducible to one, or at the most two types, children especially in the early years of their education, should not be introduced to it in a fragmented form and that subject divisions should emerge only when they have point for the learner in the organization of his own experience and knowledge.

A second and related reason for the introduction of integrated studies has been for many teachers the awareness that many of the things that appear to be of most importance to children and crucial to their development do not fall into neat disciplinary categories anyway. Much of what seems to be important to society and of value in our culture does not fit into these tidy divisions. Live issues in most spheres of human endeavour, like the concerns of the study of education to which we have just referred, straddle the boundaries that are said to exist between the disciplines. Sex education is a good example of a topic that is clearly of importance to pupils but which cannot be adequately tackled within any one of the 'disciplines'. Indeed, much of the inadequacy of what has been done in this sphere is directly attributable to the practice of dealing with it as a part of Biology, while ignoring its social, moral and aesthetic dimensions. Similarly, the Humanities Curriculum Project, to which we have already referred, in recommending that senior pupils should be involved in open discussion of many controversial issues that are of concern in contemporary society, has inevitably been led to an integrated approach. Whether one accepts the arguments put forward in favour of regarding all knowledge as one or not, therefore, it is difficult to argue that some study of an integrated kind is not needed. Many have, as a result, accepted the 'weaker' thesis that even if the arguments for separate disciplines are accepted, we must also recognize the need for knowledge from different 'forms' to be grouped around particular 'topics'. Indeed, Paul Hirst himself, whose name has come to be eternally associated with the notion of 'forms of knowledge' recognizes the need for an inter-disciplinary approach, for studies in the 'fields' as well as the 'forms' of knowledge and stresses the need to devise an interdisciplinary logic that will enable us to operate properly between as well as within the 'forms'.[51]

A second purpose behind the introduction of some programmes of integrated studies, therefore, has been the desire to offer pupils opportunities to study areas of importance and concern that cross the boundaries of the disciplines. In a sense, therefore, this has merely been an extension of a form of integrated studies that has long been with us, since, as we have seen, interdisciplinary studies such as Geography have long been well established on the curriculum of schools, colleges and universities. In fact the question of which combinations of disciplines are regarded as integrated studies and therefore as constituting some kind of new development that needs justification has been more a matter of tradition than of logic at both school and university level. All that has been said so far, then, suggests no more than a concern to base the curriculum on topics rather than or as well as on subjects and to that extent it may be felt to involve little that need necessarily be characterized as new or 'progressive'.

A third consideration that has led many people to favour the introduction of integrated studies schemes into the school curriculum has been the belief that such schemes are likely to lead to a higher level of motivation in pupils and, therefore, to a better level of work satisfaction for both pupil and teacher. We have already referred to the claim that many pupils suffer feelings of alienation in relation to the curriculum. Many teachers have felt that one factor in this is the undue concern with the needs of the subject that has characterized much curriculum planning in the past and that it can, therefore, be overcome if pupils can be engaged in the study of those things that have some point or relevance for them. The difference between this and our second point is that here it is not necessarily the case that what they will be studying will be seen by the teachers as being of value; the crucial consideration is that it is seen as such by the pupils. It is argued, therefore, that if this is so then they will be motivated by what they see as the intrinsic interest or value of the subject matter and the teacher's increasing lack of adequate devices for extrinsically motivating them will not matter so much. In any case, it is argued that intrinsic motivation is more appropriate to education than extrinsic devices, as we saw in Chapter III. This is, of course, the argument that we have already seen being put in favour of regarding the interests of the children as the central concern of curriculum planning, although they need only be accepted as providing an initial motivating factor that the good teacher can use to lead his pupils on to those things that he wants them to learn. Others, as we have seen, would take a stronger position on this issue and regard the interests of children as important not only from a motivational point of view but as the only acceptable determinant of curriculum content. Whichever position one takes, however, as we saw earlier, a commitment to some form of integrated studies becomes more or less inevitable in the practical situation of the classroom. For children's interests do not often fall exactly into recognized disciplines and the areas that are of most concern to them are more often than not of a wider kind. Thus some form of integrated approach to learning must follow if one is committed to taking the interests of children seriously in planning the curriculum. This, then, is a third reason why some teachers have come to accept the integrated studies approach; they have been led inexorably to it from a conviction that their curriculum planning should take full account of what their pupils are interested in and of the need to try to promote an intrinsic form of motivation. This is one reason why such schemes have often been tried initially with the older and less able pupils in their last years of schooling, if only on the grounds that if you can't beat them, you would be well advised to join them, as we have noted elsewhere.

Finally, some teachers have embarked on integrated studies projects because of a desire to promote enquiry methods in their teaching. This is not unrelated, of course, to the point we have just been making, since working from pupils' interests will usually involve allowing the development of enquiries of an individual kind. The enquiry approach also usually leads to the crossing of subject boundaries since a pupil's explorations will seldom be confined within one subject field. The heuristic approach is preferred by many teachers to more didactic methods and, although it can be used within individual subject areas, as many of the Nuffield science projects have shown, it is more often associated with integrated studies. Those who favour this approach often do so, like Dewey, from a conviction not only that this is a more effective way of learning and that it leads to better retention of what has been learnt, but also that it is more appropriate to what they see as being the essential nature of education. If one views education as being essentially experience, as Dewey does, or as involving a dialectical relationship between the pupil and his environment, as Charity James and Dewey both do,[52] or as being concerned with the intentions that lie behind the conscious activity of the pupil, as Paulo Freire believes,[53] or as being an extension of the 'common sense knowledge' that the pupil brings to the teaching situation rather than initiation into anything that can be dubbed objective knowledge, as we have seen a number of contemporary sociologists do, then one must accept that education must be a two-way activity in which the learner must be an active participant rather than a mere recipient of knowledge. If one tries, as a result of this kind of conviction, to promote this sort of active learning in which the pupils' learning consists of genuine experiences, then it will be difficult to confine these experiences within those subject boundaries that we as teachers have found useful for achieving our own purposes and organizing our experience. Some form of integration will, therefore, follow, especially in the early stages of education, and, as we saw above, it is only later that divisions will emerge. Furthermore, these will be divisions that have sense and meaning for the learner himself. They may indeed be divisions based on some notion of logically discrete forms of knowledge, but the significance of the divisions will have become apparent to the learner. In other words, he will have been led to the 'forms' from an initially undifferentiated view of knowledge, so that he can see the point and significance of them for himself. If, for whatever reason, then, we believe that children should have some control over the direction of their education, we will find ourselves being pushed inexorably towards some kind of integrated curriculum. It is for this reason, among others, that, as we will see in Chapter VII, Basil Bernstein has posited a link between this kind of development in schools and certain developments in society at large and in particular changes towards a pluralistic, 'open' society.[54]

There are, then, a number of quite different reasons why teachers may want to introduce integrated studies programmes or, indeed, may find themselves involved in them willy-nilly. It is possible to be led to such a step from a belief in the wholeness of knowledge, from a desire to introduce pupils to interdisciplinary topics that are felt to be important or from a commitment to other positions in education, such as the importance of pupils' interests, enquiry methods or any other route to the full involvement of children in their own education.

We saw also that schemes of integrated studies can take many forms and clearly the form that any particular scheme takes will depend very much on the purposes of the teacher or teachers concerned with it. Obviously, a scheme that is prompted by a desire to promote heuristic methods will involve less teacher direction and more free-ranging pupil enquiry than one which is designed to focus the attention of all pupils on to a particular topic or issue. Similarly, one which is intended primarily to enhance motivation, to get the pupils interested and attentive so that their attention can then be turned to areas of knowledge the teacher wishes them to acquire will be more structured than one that sees children's interests as being more central to decisions concerning the content of the curriculum. There are many variables and, therefore, many variations. Hence, as so often in education, the important thing is to be clear what one is about so that one's practices can reflect this.

In concluding this discussion of integrated studies, we must also repeat what we said when we began it. It is not a matter of having to go all out for one approach or the other. There are many advantages in including a number of different elements, activities or approaches in our curriculum and there is nothing inconsistent in engaging pupils for part of the week in integrated studies and at other times in the 'straight' study of subjects. Indeed, this makes very good sense, since not only does it lead to much needed variety for the pupils, it also ensures that a number of competing interests can be attended to. The curriculum must be a compromise between the competing demands of society and of the individual pupil.

Methods or Procedures

We have said a great deal about the problems raised by discussion of the objectives and the content of the curriculum. It should not be necessary to dwell in as great detail on questions concerning methods or procedures. In part this is because these will follow more or less automatically once we have reached agreement on our aims, our principles of procedure and our approach to decisions concerning content, since it is inevitably bound up with these;[55] in part it is because for the same reason we have touched on several points concerning method in what we have said already. Indeed, it becomes increasingly difficult, even at the conceptual level, to discuss any one aspect of the curriculum without reference to the others. One general feature of educational methodology, however, does merit brief discussion, not only because it has been central to much of the debate over the curriculum that recent years have witnessed but also because we have already referred to it at some length in our discussion of integrated studies and that is the growing commitment to heuristic methods, to encouraging children to 'find out' for themselves, to 'learn by discovery'. Increasingly, even the classrooms of the secondary schools have come to be places of activity rather than centres for instruction and more and more emphasis has been placed on project work of all kinds. The various curriculum schemes sponsored by the Schools Council, the Nuffield science schemes and the Design and Technology projects, for example, have begun from the basic principle that the child must be an active participant in his own education.

We have also seen that learning through some form of enquiry is advocated by some educationists not only as an effective method but also as required by the notion of education itself, as an essential part of the development of understanding and autonomy or as crucial to a process of guided growth through genuine experience.

Whatever reasons one has for advocating such an approach, whether one views first-hand experience as the only source of real education and sees this as the only way of enabling children to have that first-hand experience, or whether one sees this approach merely as an effective device for ensuring that children learn what you want them to learn, it is important to be clear about what is involved, especially as a number of criticisms have been levelled at this technique.

It has been argued, for example, that learning by discovery is not logically possible since it does not make sense to speak of people discovering what is already known. It has also been said that this kind of learning is impracticable since it is not possible for children in the short time of their sojourn in school to discover for themselves all of those many things that man has discovered over the countless centuries of his existence on earth; whereas instructional methods can condense much of this into a quickly assimilable form. Discovery learning is, therefore, dubbed as wasteful and inefficient as well as logically impossible. It has been argued too that while such an approach may be of value for certain kinds of learning, theoretical concepts cannot be acquired in this way, so that in this kind of learning discovery methods are not only slow but useless (Dearden, 1968).[56]

Furthermore, there is also the related point that theoretical concepts learned need to be built up into interconnected systems and learning, if it is to include understanding, must involve a growing awareness of and familiarity with these interconnected systems. In fact, without this growing understanding it will not be possible for children to know what there is to be discovered, to see what questions should be asked about a particular set of experiences, or to recognize the significance of what they have discovered. Learning by discovery, it is argued, therefore, is too naive and unsophisticated a notion to be of any value as a model for the complex process of conceptual development. It is logically nonsensical, impracticable and useless.

On the other hand we referred earlier to some powerful arguments in support of its desirability, not least those derived from the notion of the need for pupils to be active participants in their own learning and the view of education as the development of the individual's awareness and understanding of his world rather than the acquisition of ill-digested and largely propositional knowledge handed on to him by others. Furthermore, we must not lose sight of the arguments of those who like Paulo Freire,[57] see this kind of question as having a significance for society far beyond its implications for the methodology of the classroom , who see an opportunity to attain the skills necessary for problem-solving as being the only viable means of getting the poor of the world to see their own problems in a reflexive perspective and to act on them rather than be 'dopes' whose curriculum content is decided for them by others. Supporters of this method argue, therefore, that if the acquisition of theoretical concepts in a coherent form is not possible when discovery methods are employed, there is ample evidence to illustrate that it does not happen very regularly either when directly instructional methods are used.

Once again the problem seems to arise from too extreme a polarization of the two ideas. There is no doubt that discovery is logically possible for every-one, if we realize that we mean by this only that an individual finds out something that is new to him; it does not have to be taken as implying that one has discovered something new to human knowledge or else we would have very infrequent need to use the word. This is a perfectly normal usage of the term. It is possible for a man to discover that his wife is having an affair with someone else, even though many others have known about it for some time: indeed, we are told that the husband is always the last to know, and, at the very least, it seems reasonable to assume that the wife and the lover have known about it from the first. There is no logical contradiction involved, then, in the notion of learning by discovery, if it is interpreted intelligently.

The arguments that it is impracticable and inefficient are also based on an extreme view of what learning by discovery is to be taken to mean. There is no doubt that if we were to leave children completely alone to find out every-thing for themselves this would be a long and wasteful process and one from which they would be likely to get little of value. Clearly, they would not have the prior knowledge and experience to know what questions to ask, to discriminate between the experiences they had, to see the full significance of what they discovered or to build their growing experience and knowledge into any kind of coherent system. If learning by discovery is to have any value, there is need for a good deal of careful **preparation** by the teacher and of judicious interference in the process, since, as we saw when considering the notion of education as growth or natural development, there is no place for the teacher and no meaning to 'education', if he or she is not to interfere in the learning process in this way in order to ensure its efficiency and its significance for the learner. As Jerome Bruner has said and as we have quoted before, 'discovery, like surprise, favours the well prepared mind'[58] and we must accept that the only intelligible notion is that of guided discovery. As we saw when discussing the content of the curriculum, education must involve the interaction of a number of forces, the pupil, the teacher, society, knowledge and so on so that to plan a curriculum from the point of view of any one of these is to create a caricature of the real thing. This is equally true of the methods we adopt. Any approach that is based on a consideration of only one or two of these elements will be distorted and, as a result, vulnerable to criticism. The process of education is far too subtle to be characterized as simply as it has often been characterized both by some of the proponents of the idea of learning by discovery and by some of its critics who have shown themselves to be equally naive.

Indeed the whole process may be too subtle for the attempts we have been making to discuss objectives, content and methods in isolation from each other ever to be really successful. As our discussion has revealed, these are interwoven in such complex ways that it is very difficult to achieve a coherent examination of any one of them in isolation from the others. The view that we take of education itself will affect the objectives or the procedural principles that we adopt, the decisions we take about content and the methods we choose. In both theory and practice all three are so closely interwoven that in trying to separate them even at the conceptual level we run the risk of forgetting the ways in which they are interrelated. It may well be that this very interconnectedness is a more important area of study than any of these three areas in themselves.

At the very least it should be clear that curriculum development must be an ongoing, open-ended process of a kind that will allow for continuous adaptation and development at all three levels. It is not curriculum innovation that should worry us; the time to start worrying is when innovation stops and the curriculum freezes up again.

Evaluation and Assessment

This is the point from which we must begin our discussion of the fourth aspect of the curriculum that we identified at the beginning of this chapter, evaluation and assessment, since the need for continuous adaptation presents us with particular problems in this area.

There are two aspects to evaluation. Firstly, we must evaluate the curriculum itself, since if we have been right to argue that it should be subject to continuous change and development, it is vital that we examine it regularly and frequently either to ascertain how far we are achieving the goals we have set ourselves or merely to discover what in fact we have achieved in the continuously evolving process we are engaged in. A lot of work must be done to devise techniques and strategies that will enable teachers to engage in this kind of ongoing evaluation of the curriculum.

Secondly, we need to make some evaluation or assessment of the progress of individual pupils both in order to give them a guide to their own attainments and to provide society with some indication of what they have to offer to it. It is on this second kind of evaluation that we will concentrate here both because this is the feature of evaluation that has more direct impact at present on the individual teacher and because it is this that has had most effect in recent years on curriculum planning and development generally. For it is perhaps the assessment procedures that have been most often responsible for inhibiting curriculum change; certainly it is the examination system that most teachers blame for their unwillingness to experiment with new approaches to teaching and learning.

We must start, then, by asserting that decisions about evaluation and assessment should follow decisions about what we are going to do in schools and how we are going to do it. We must discover techniques of assessment which will evaluate what we have done rather than, as so often in the past, make decisions about what we will do in the light of what the assessment procedures available to us can most readily test It is this latter approach that has led to the undue emphasis on subject content in curriculum planning that we referred to at the beginning of this chapter, although it would be, of course, a mistake to assume that assessment procedures can only test factual knowledge.

Examinations have or can have several purposes (Wiseman, 1961).[59] There is no doubt that in many situations an important aspect of these procedures is their administrative purpose. The 11+ assessment procedures are a good example of a process of evaluation the main purpose of which is administrative. Its purpose is to organize the distribution of pupils at the age of transfer to secondary schools into various types of secondary schooling. The CSE and the GCE at both O and A levels perform a similar function in relation to the organization of Further and Higher Education. Examinations such as these often at the same time have a selective role in so far as a part of the administrative duty they perform is the selection of pupils for certain kinds of schooling or occupation. Thus pupils may be allocated to a particular class or stream or ability band or be admitted to a certain kind of career or occupation or training course on the basis of what we believe we have learnt from certain assessment procedures that have been applied to their work. Thus examinations play a major role in what we might call social engineering and this is one aspect of them that we should not lose sight of either in discussing or in planning our assessment procedures.

A third purpose of examinations is that of providing an incentive to both teachers and pupils. Examinations are to both teacher and pupil what a target is to an archer. They represent clearly definable goals towards which both can work. This again is a feature of examinations that should not be taken lightly. Teaching is an occupation whose end result is often so difficult to define or even to recognize that teachers can be excused for wanting to have some positive statistical evidence of their achievements. There is no doubt that in the case of pupils too the kind of achievement motivation that can result from clear statements of their attainments is an important factor in encouraging them to greater efforts. Also although we have seen that for many reasons we should be aiming to bring pupils to value education for its own sake, we also saw when we considered questions of the teacher's authority in Chapter V that no practising teacher can afford lightly to reject the advantages of the 'calculative' methods of control that the extrinsically motivating 'carrots' of examination successes can offer him. This is another aspect of examinations, then, that we must not lose sight of either in our discussions or in our practical provisions.

The most important purpose of evaluation, however, in the context of our discussion of the curriculum, is the setting, measuring and maintaining of standards within the goals, objectives and purposes of our curriculum planning. If public examinations are to have national currency, as they must have if they are to fulfil their administrative and selective purposes, some kind of overall standards must be set and maintained and the attainment of individuals can only be usefully assessed within that sort of context. As we have seen, however, while it is important that they should evaluate the standards reached by individuals in relation to the overall goals of our curriculum planning, they should not themselves control that planning. To allow them to do so is to put the cart before the horse. This raises a number of problems that we must consider.

In the first place, it is often felt that examination techniques can only assess a limited range of curriculum objectives. The objectives of Bloom's affective domain are clearly not easy to evaluate, as he himself is aware, nor are some of the more complex objectives of the cognitive domain. It may be, therefore, that if we want our work evaluated, even if we do not want to allow the evaluation procedures to take charge of our curriculum planning, we may have to accept that the limited range and sophistication of the techniques available to us must limit the objectives we can set ourselves.

However, our discussion of objectives also suggested to us that we may in any case be mistaken if we adopt too rigid an attitude towards our objectives and it may be that such a flexible view of objectives and of the need to allow them to evolve as our work proceeds might be even more difficult to maintain in the light of the need to evaluate what we have achieved. It is one thing to stress the difficulties of assessing complex objectives; the problem becomes compounded once we begin to claim that objectives, complex or not, cannot be clearly specified in advance, that we cannot predetermine the outcome of our endeavours. It would seem that we must either abandon many of the more ambitious things we hope to achieve and let the evaluation procedures available to us decide for us all aspects of our curriculum planning or else give up the idea of evaluating large areas of our work.

If we are not to be left on the horns of a dilemma such as this, we must fashion our techniques of evaluation into more sensitive tools which will be able to meet the complex and sophisticated demands we must place on them. Two things in particular need to be done. In the first place, we need to continue to devise more subtle techniques of assessment than the rather blunt instrument of the 'essay type' examination paper which has for so long been the staple element of our examination procedures, and which, while suitable for many purposes, is certainly not adequate to meet all of the demands that will now be made of these procedures. Comparatively recent developments, such as objective tests, timed essays, 'open book' examinations, orals, practicals, course work assessments, teachers' assessments and the like must be seen not as 'gimmicks' or as 'soft options' but as devices which, if properly used, can extend the range of our assessment procedures to enable them to encompass the increasingly complex objectives we mentioned earlier.[60] We need also to examine these and other techniques in relation to the problem of allowing for the development and refinement of our objectives as our work proceeds. We might perhaps settle for examinations that tell us what in fact we have achieved rather than how successful we have been in attaining predetermined goals.

The second thing that must be done if we are to achieve a greater degree of sophistication here is a development that should also help to solve this difficulty over objectives. There is no doubt that the one factor that is essential to the developments we are discussing is a greater involvement of the teachers themselves in the assessment of their own pupils. This will mean more work for teachers both in the examining itself and in the moderation procedures that must be established to ensure that comparable standards are maintained and that 'halo' effects of neither a positive nor a negative kind are allowed to cloud their judgements. But it should also lead to a more personalized assessment of individual pupils, the production of profiles which will give interested parties far more relevant and useful information about individuals than the present system does and the development of a wide range of examining techniques that will give some hope of assessing the many aspects of the curriculum as it is now conceived. Some progress has been made towards this goal by the development of 'Mode 3' schemes under the aegis of the CSE Boards. We will move further in this direction if more of the GCE Boards follow suit and especially if there is established a common system of examining at 16+ as the Schools Council has suggested.[61]

The most fundamental achievement of such a step will be that effective control of all aspects of the curriculum will be placed in the hands of the teachers in the schools. The way to ensure that the examination system does not control the curriculum of the schools is not to remove it as some would do. There is no doubt, of course, that this solution has worked in relation to the removal of the constraints of the 11+ on the curriculum of the English primary schools. There is equally no doubt that one cannot simply do away with all forms of assessment at the end of the period of compulsory schooling. Assessment at this stage is important for all the reasons we listed earlier. What we can do to ensure that these procedures do not dominate our curriculum planning is to put the teachers in a stronger position to influence them. Teachers are understandably reluctant to undertake curriculum innovation until they can be sure that the assessment procedures will reflect and assess their innovations and will not put their pupils at a disadvantage in relation to pupils from other schools. They can only be fully confident of this if they can directly influence those procedures themselves.

Only if all aspects of the curriculum are in the hands of the same people or if there is constant and close collaboration between all the parties involved can curriculum development be successfully carried out. For, as we have seen, all elements of the curriculum are so closely interwoven that all must develop in phase if there is not to be the kind of distortion that we are only too familiar with. This is the point to which we keep returning; no useful curriculum planning can occur unless it embraces and interrelates objectives, content, method and evaluation. This is perhaps the most important point to be made about curriculum innovation.

This chapter has attempted to reveal some of the many issues that underlie curriculum development at the present time and to show their total interrelatedness. Discussion of these issues will go on and we must try to ensure as great a clarity in such discussion as is possible. Curriculum development must also go on. For, as with any other living thing, once development stops, the process of dying has begun.

REFERENCES

1.   J.F. Kerr (ed.), *Changing the Curriculum,* University of London Press, 1968, p.16
2.   See, for example, P.H. Hirst, 'The logic of the curriculum', *Journal of Curriculum Studies,* 1969

3. See, for example, J.F. Kerr (ed.), *op.cit.*
4. See, for example, P.H. Hirst, *op.cit.*
5. B.S. Bloom (ed.), *A Taxonomy of Educational Objectives,* Longman, 1964, Vols. 1 and 2
6. B.S. Bloom (ed.), *op.cit.,* Vol.2, p.6
7. *Ibid.,* p.7
8. *Ibid.*
9. R.A. Pring, 'Bloom's Taxonomy: a philosophical critique (2)', *Cambridge Journal of Education,* 1971
10. P.H. Hirst, 'The contribution of philosophy to the study of the curriculum' in J.F. Kerr (ed.), *op.cit.*
11. R.A. Pring, 'Objectives and innovation: the irrelevance of theory', *London Educational Review,* 1973, p.49
12. C.M. James, *Young Lives at Stake,* Collins, 1968, Ch.4
13. See *The Humanities Project: An Introduction,* Heinemann, 1970
14. J.H. Gribble, 'Pandora's Box: The Affective Domain of Educational Objectives', *Journal of Curriculum Studies,* 1970
15. J.H. Gribble, *op.cit.*
16. R.S. Peters, 'Aims of education: a conceptual enquiry' in R.S. Peters (ed.), *The Philosophy of Education,* Oxford University Press, 1973
17. Plato, *Republic*
18. P.H. Hirst, 'A liberal education and the nature of knowledge' in R.D. Archambault (ed.), *Philosophical Analysis and Education,* Routledge & Kegan Paul, 1965 and P.H. Hirst, 'The logic of the Curriculum', *Journal of Curriculum Studies,* 1969
19. P.H. Hirst in R.D. Archambault (ed.), *op.cit.,* p.129
20. P.H. Hirst, 'The logic of the curriculum', *Journal of Curriculum Studies,* 1969
21. *Ibid.,* p. 153
22. P.H. Hirst in R.D. Archambault (ed.), *op.cit.,* p.129
23. P.H. Hirst and R.S. Peters, *The Logic of Education,* Routledge & Kegan Paul, 1970, Ch.4
24. *Ibid.*
25. R.S. Peters, 'Education as Initiation' in R.D. Archambault (ed.), *op.cit.,* and R.S. Peters, *Ethics and Education,* Allen & Unwin, 1966, Ch.5
26. R.S. Peters, *Ethics and Education,* Allen & Unwin, 1966, p.160
27. M.F. Young, 'An approach to the study of curriculum as socially organized knowledge' in M.F. Young (ed.), *Knowledge and Control,* Collier-Macmillan, 1971
28. A.F. Blum, 'The corpus of knowledge as a normative order' in M.F. Young (ed.), *op.cit.,* p. 117
29. P. Berger and T. Luckman, *The Social Construction of Reality,* Allen Lane, 1967
30. G.M. Esland, 'Teaching and learning as the organization of knowledge' in M.F. Young (ed.), *op.cit.*
31. See, for example, N. Keddie, 'Classroom knowledge' in M.F. Young (ed.), *op.cit.*
32. D. Lawton, *Social Change, Educational Theory and Curriculum Planning,* University of London Press, 1973, Ch.7
33. J.J. Rousseau, *Emile,* Preface 1
34. cf. R.F. Dearden, *The Philosophy of Primary Education,* Routledge & Kegan Paul, 1968, Ch.3
35. J. Dewey, *Experience and Education,* Macmillan, 1938, Ch. 3
36. B. Inhelder and J. Piaget, *The Growth of Logical Thinking from Childhood to*

Adolescence, Basic Books, 1958

37. B.F. Skinner, 'The science of learning and the art of teaching', *Harvard Education Review,* 1954. Reprinted in abridged form in E. Stone (ed.), *Readings in Education Psychology,* Methuen, 1970 and B.F. Skinner, *The Technology of Teaching,* Appleton-Century-Crofts, 1968

38. A.H. Maslow, *Motivation and Personality,* Harper & Row, 1954, discussed at length in C.N. Cofer and M.H. Appley, *Motivation Theory and Research,* Wiley, 1968

39. cf. R.F. Dearden, *op.cit.,* Ch.2 and P.S. Wilson, *Interest and Discipline in Education,* Routledge & Kegan Paul, 1971, Ch.1

40. cf. B.P. Komisar, ' "Need" and the Needs-Curriculum' in B.O. Smith and R.H. Ennis (eds.), *Language and Concepts in Education,* Rand McNally, 1961

41. P.S. Wilson, *op.cit.,* Ch.2

42. J.P. White, 'Education in obedience', *New Society,* 1968 and J.P. White, *Towards a Compulsory Curriculum,* Routledge & Kegan Paul, 1973

43. J.P. White, *op.cit.,* and J.P. White, 'The curriculum mongers: education in reverse', in R. Hooper (ed.), *The Curriculum: Context, Design and Development,* Oliver & Boyd, 1971

44. cf. K.B. Thompson, *Education and Philosophy,* Blackwell, 1972, Ch.8

45. C.M. James, *op.cit.,* Ch.6

46. D. Warwick (ed.), *Integrated Studies in the Secondary School,* University of London Press, 1973

47. C.M. James, *op.cit.,* Ch.4

48. See, for example, A.J. Ayer, *Language, Truth and Logic,* Gollanz, 1946, Ch.1

49. Plato, *Republic*

50. A.N. Whitehead, *The Aims of Education,* Williams & Norgate, 1932, p.18

51. P.H. Hirst and R.S. Peters, *op.cit.,* Ch.4

52. M. James, *op.cit.*

53. P. Freire, *Pedagogy of the Oppressed,* Penguin, 1972

54. B.B. Bernstein, 'Open schools, open society?', *New Society,* 1967

55. cf. D. Warwick (ed.), *op.cit.*

56. R.F. Dearden, *op.cit.,* Ch.6

57. P. Freine, *op.cit.*

58. J. Bruner, 'The act of discovery', *Harvard Education Review,* 1961

59. S. Wiseman (ed.), *Examinations and English Education,* Manchester University Press, 1961

60. cf. *Secondary Schools Examinations Council, Examinations Bulletin No. 3,* HMSO, 1964 and M. Connaughton, 'The validity of examinations at 16 plus', *Educational Research,* 1969

61. *Schools Council Examinations Bulletin No. 23, A Common System of Examining at 16+,* Evans/Methuen Education, 1971

VII Equality

All that we have said so far in this book and particularly what we have said
about the curriculum in the last chapter illustrates how dramatically both the
theory and the practice of education have changed in the last twenty or
thirty years. One reason for that change has been the increase in our knowledge and understanding of many of the facets of education that we have
been discussing. Another, and perhaps more cogent reason, however, has
been the fundamental change in ideology that recent years have seen. The
most prominent feature of the new ideology is its egalitarianism and the
desire to promote educational equality has been a major theme in those
changes that have been made and are being made in the content, the method
and the organization of education both in the United Kingdom and elsewhere
in the world. The work of every teacher, therefore, has been affected by this
development so that no discussion of the theory and practice of education in
present times would be complete without a careful examination of the
implications that a commitment to this kind of egalitarian philosophy holds
for educational practice.

Much has been done in the name of equality not only in education but
also in other sectors of society. It can be argued that the entire development
of state education has been prompted at every stage by the central desire to
promote equality of educational opportunity and few would be prepared to
admit openly that they were opposed to it. Yet very different and sometimes
conflicting views are expressed on how it is to be achieved in practice and the
practical provisions that have been advocated have varied enormously, from
those that involve careful streaming and selection of pupils to those that
would open the doors of all kinds of institutions to any pupil who wished to
enter them without applying any selection procedures.

The main reason for this discrepancy and confusion is that the notion of
equality in education, and even the apparently more precise notion of
equality of educational opportunity, are too general and vague to provide any
clear directives as to how education should be organized to achieve them. A
system can be said to provide equality of opportunity if all pupils have the
same chance to compete for a place in a grammar school or a university; it is
not necessary that they should all actually gain such places. Indeed, equality
of opportunity would exist in a sense even if it amounted to no more than an
equal opportunity for every child to take a test at 5+ to decide whether he

should be admitted to the school system or excluded from it altogether. For this reason, a distinction has been drawn between the 'strong' or 'meritocratic' interpretation of equality, which would provide educational opportunities for all who are capable of taking advantage of them, and the 'weak' or 'democratic' interpretation, which demands suitable provision for everyone.[1]

The notion of equality is an imprecise one, therefore, and not one upon which any practical proposals can be based without a great deal of further clarification and definition of what is to be taken as its meaning. Until we have achieved this, it will not be possible to make a proper evaluation of those major developments that recent years have seen in the education systems of many countries, such as the comprehensivation of educational provision at a number of levels, the abolition of selective practices such as streaming within the schools, and the introduction and extension of various programmes of what has been called 'Compensatory Education', all of which have been based on some notion of educational equality.

A Historical View of Equality

It is important not to start from an assumption that the notion of social equality is a relatively new one or that it is a product of the twentieth century. It may be that this century has seen man come nearer to the achievement of something like the ideal implicit in the notion, although many would want to dispute even that, but as an idea it is almost as old as man himself; certainly it dates back to the beginnings of organized thought in the western world. From the very beginning, however, the confusion and the tensions between different interpretations of the notion that we have already referred to are apparent. For while there is distinct evidence, particularly in the works of the Greek dramatist, Euripides, that from the beginning for some people equality implied impartial treatment of all human beings, an egalitarianism in the full sense, both Plato and Aristotle accepted the idea of equality as operative only within categories of human being. Thus Plato's 'ideal state', as he described it in the *Republic*, contained three types of citizen - the prototype for many subsequent tripartite systems - and each of these groups had a different role, different responsibilities and, therefore, different rights within the state, 'equality' and 'justice' being achieved by basing membership of each group on talent and suitability rather than on the accident of birth. Plato has also been charged with deliberately opposing egalitarianism in the fuller sense by refusing to discuss it seriously in the arguments he produces to support his view of the ideal state (Popper, 1945).[2] Aristotle too believed that there existed quite distinct categories of being and that, as he is so often quoted as saying, injustice arises as much from treating unequals equally as from treating equals unequally. Each person has his own place; the husband is superior to the wife, the father to his children, the master to his slaves (so long as these are 'barbarians' and not Greeks); to step beyond this place is unjust. 'The only stable principle of government is equality according to proportion'.[3]

However, the other view also took hold, if at a less influential level philosophically. The stoic view of the brotherhood of all men, so well expressed in the words of Pope's *Essay on Man*, 'All are but parts of one stupendous whole, Whose body nature is and God the soul', allied to the Christian doctrine of the equality of all men in the eyes of God, ensured that the idea of human equality without regard to categories should also flourish and so influential was the Church on man's thinking that when, at the time of the Renaissance, philosophers began for the first time almost since the time of Plato and Aristotle to examine philosophical questions independently of theology, the idea of human equality was accepted by most of them as if it were a self-evident truth and was used by them in a largely uncritical manner. John Locke[4] tells us, for example, that the state of nature is 'a state also of equality . . . there being nothing more evident than that creatures of the same species and rank, promiscuously born to all the same advantages of Nature, and the use of the same faculties, should also be equal one amongst another, without subordination or subjection' and also that 'the State of Nature has a law of Nature to govern it, which obliges everyone. And Reason, which is that law, teaches all mankind, who will but consult it, that being all Equal and Independent, no one ought to harm another in his Life, Health, Liberty or Possessions'. This is a view that is clearly reflected in the assertions of the American Declaration of Independence of 1789 that 'all men are created equal' and that 'men are born and live free and equal in their rights', not to mention the 1948 declaration that 'all human beings are born free and equal in dignity and rights'. This was the view that took hold, therefore, and was further developed in the later doctrine of Utilitarianism and in the socialist political philosophy that emerged and grew in the nineteenth and twentieth centuries.

However, we must not lose sight of the fact that, in spite of this, the continued influence of Plato and Aristotle on the thinking of the western world has been enormous, so that the view of equality within categories has never been far away. Furthermore, the egalitarian movement has always had its opponents, particularly after it seemed to have led to the excesses of the French Revolution. For example, the anti-egalitarian view was put strongly in the second half of the last century by the German philosopher, Nietzsche, whose theory that equality led to mediocrity, to the suppression of outstanding individuals who ought to be given their heads and encouraged to be

'unequal' if human evolution was not to be held back, was taken up, albeit in
the context of a nationalism that Nietzsche himself would have rejected out-
right, to be one of the basic tenets of the Nazi version of fascism that led to
the Second World War. The tension, then, is still there and its continued
presence is due in part to the failure of those who advocate egalitarianism to
be clear about what this means. We must now turn, therefore, to a consideration of some of the sources of this confusion in the notion of equality itself,
the lack of clarity over the logical grammar of the word 'equal'.

The Concept of Equality

That all men are equal is clearly not true in any descriptive sense. It is not
even true in a qualified sense - except perhaps at the trivial level of bodily
functioning - since there are no respects in which all men can be said to be
the same. Some of the confusion that bedevils discussions of equality derives
from the fact that some philosophers, such as Locke, and some politicans,
such as those who framed the American Declaration, have used it as if its
meaning were, at least in part, descriptive. We must distinguish the use of
'equal' in mathematical contexts where it clearly signifies that certain things
are descriptively 'the same' and its use in political and social contexts where
its use represents an assertion of an ideal, a demand for certain kinds of
behaviour in our treatment of other people. In other words, in this kind of
context its main force is prescriptive and moral rather than descriptive and
mathematical. A confusion of these uses of the term is one source of many of
the difficulties associated with it.

   The confusion does not end there, however. For, once having accepted
that the notion of social equality constitutes a moral demand for something,
we still have the problem of discovering exactly what is being demanded.
Again confusion results from a failure to answer this question with precision.
Again too the mathematical and descriptive connotations of the word
compound the confusion. For many people accept that all men are not in any
respect the same, but seem to regard the demand for social equality as a
demand that in certain respects they be made the same or be made 'equal'.
There are at least two good reasons why such a view is untenable.

   One difficulty with this interpretation of equality is that it involves a
conflict with other social ideals that many people - even among the
egalitarians themselves - hold equally dear. In particular, it has been suggested
that the demand for equality, if understood in this way, leads to direct
conflict with the demand for freedom (Lucas, 1965).[5] It is clear that to try
to make people equal will involve considerable interference with their
personal liberties. A redistribution of wealth, for example, which many have

regarded as a desirable step towards social equality, can only be effected with a great loss of freedom for individuals. This tension is very much apparent in the arguments for and against the continued existence of private schools. To say this is not to say, of course, that such a position is untenable; it is merely to draw attention to one of its implications.

A more serious objection to this view, however, and one which, if true, does render it untenable is the claim that it is not possible to make everyone equal in any sense of the term. One of the fundamental difficulties with the social philosophy of Karl Marx was that it had as a central concept the notion of the classless society and such a society is unattainable. The kind of redistribution of wealth, for example, which we have just discussed, could only result in a crude form of financial equality and would in any case be only temporary, since the differences in people's attitudes to wealth and uses of it, in part responsible for the original inequality, would very soon lead to new inequalities very like the old. One would have to redistribute wealth so regularly - at least daily as far as most punters and bookmakers are concerned - that the whole process would become meaningless. This is one example of a more general point that must be stressed here, that inequalities are an inevitable part of any kind of society. It has been argued by Ralf Dahrendorf, for example,[6] that, since every human society is a moral society in which behaviour is regulated according to certain norms, there will always be inequalities that will result from the differing degrees to which the behaviour of each individual measures up to these norms. To use one of Dahrendorf's examples, in a society of ladies that is held together by the desire to exchange news of intrigue, scandal and general gossip, individual members will be distinguished according to the quality of the stories they produce and their manner of recounting them, so that inequalities of rank will result. It is not difficult to see how the same principle will apply in larger and perhaps more serious social groupings. 'The origin of inequality is thus to be found in the existence in all human societies of norms of behaviour to which sanctions are attached'.[7] These sanctions will take many forms but they will all lead to inescapable inequalities of rank. The demand for social equality cannot, therefore, be a demand that all should be made equal.

It has been suggested, then, that talk about social equality is a demand not for all to be made equal but for all to be treated equally. Again, however, the descriptive connotations of the term bring confusion. For it looks as though this is a demand that all should be given the same treatment whereas a moment's thought will reveal that such a practice would seldom lead in any context to equality in the moral sense of justice and fairness.[8] It is clearly not just or fair or even desirable, for example, that all patients should be given the same medical treatment or all offenders the same punishment or all

children the same educational diet. Clearly there are differences between
people that require differences of treatment and only confusion can result if
we allow the words we use when we wish to talk about fairness and justice to
obscure this important requirement. Some have suggested that social equality
is a demand for equality of respect for all people but it has also been pointed
out[9] that in this phrase it is the word 'respect' that is doing all the work, the
word 'equality' being entirely otiose. Furthermore, this idea in itself gives us
no help with the problem of deciding what kinds of treatment of others this
equality of respect should lead to nor how we can make decisions about the
appropriateness or inappropriateness of adopting different practices in
relation to different individuals.

What this seems to point to is that equality is not a demand for similarity
of treatment at all but for a justification for differential treatment, a
justification which must take the form of demonstrating that our reasons for
discriminating between people in certain contexts are relevant reasons and,
therefore, arguably, fair, just and impartial reasons. Differential treatment of
patients, therefore, is justified if they are shown to have different diseases or
different constitutions; differences in our treatment of offenders are to be
justified by reference to differences in the nature of their offences or the
circumstances under which they were committed; and differences of
educational provision are to be justified by appealing to differences exhibited
by pupils in their ability to profit from education or what appear to be
differences in their educational needs.

Major difficulties in securing equality in education, however, derive from
the problems of defining 'need' and of deciding what shall count as relevant
differences of educational need or ability. We have already referred to
Aristotle's often quoted dictum that injustice comes as much from treating
unequals equally as from treating equals unequally. We are now saying that
this is the only reasonable interpretation that one can give to the notion of
social equality. However, we must as a consequence face the problem of how
one decides on who is to count as unequal, the grounds on which such
decisions can be taken and justified and the different kinds of provision that
then become appropriate. In education this means an acceptance of the
necessity of making differential provision but at the same time an awareness
of the difficulty of deciding what these differences of provision shall be and
on what basis discriminations between pupils are to be made. Two main
points must be made about this.

In the first place, a difficulty immediately arises if we interpret this as
meaning that we must try to place people into a limited number of categories.
We have already distinguished the notion of equality within categories from
more thorough-going versions of egalitarianism. The main weakness of this

approach is that it does not provide us with the subtle instrument we need to make decisions about differential treatment or provision; it offers only the rather blunt instrument of a limited number of discrete categories - masters and slaves, husbands and wives, fathers and children, bright and backward, grammar, technical and modern, A, B and C and so on. What is wrong with Aristotle's analysis of social equality is not his identification of the need to treat people differently but the lack of subtlety in his interpretation of the practicalities of this. It is the same lack of subtlety that has bedevilled many of our attempts to secure equality in education. We would not regard as just and, therefore, we would not countenance a judicial system which operated by meting out to all offenders one of two or three kinds of sentence. The corollary of the assertion that men are not descriptively equal in any way and that justice requires treatment of them in accordance with the differences between them is that our approach to them must be always an individual approach, so that the educational provision we make for each pupil must be based on what seems to be appropriate for him as an individual and not on the allocation of him to one of two or three broad categories.

This kind of consideration also draws our attention to the irrelevance of the claims we noted in Chapters I and II of certain contemporary psychologists, such as Jensen and Eysenck,[10] concerning the general intellectual capacities of different racial groups. Even if their assertions have any justification or basis, they are meaningless in relation to any practical provision we may want to make, since in practice we will always be dealing with individuals or groups of individuals and never with one racial group as a whole. They merely reveal the fundamental weakness and illogicality of any racist position. Indeed, any comparison of groups, whether offered as a basis for an egalitarian or an élitist system, makes little sense in the context of the individual differences we know to exist between all human beings.

Once we accept this we are nearer to an understanding of what is entailed by demands for equality in education. However, we still have the problems of deciding what are to count as relevant differences between individuals and what differences of provision they should give rise to. The notion of equality itself gives us no help in establishing such criteria of relevance. This, then, is the second point that must be made about this interpretation of social equality in the context of educational provision. We need some criteria by which both of these questions can be answered if we are to be clear about the kinds of educational practice that will lead to the achievement of this kind of equality.

Unfortunately, such criteria are not easy to find. One point must be made, however, and it is a point that has at least two facets that are important to anyone undertaking a search for such criteria. If a difference that can be detected between people is to be regarded as a basis for differential treatment, it must, as we have seen, have some relevance to the context in which we are operating, there must be some connection between the factor we are taking account of and the nature of whatever it is we are trying to distribute justly. Thus in making differential provision of education the only differences we should recognize as relevant to this, if we wish to achieve a fair and just system, are those that can be shown to have a connection with education itself.

To say this is not, of course, to solve the practical problem in any way; it is, however, to point to the direction in which a solution is to be sought. For clearly there are different views of what education is and each will give rise to a different solution to this problem. This has been another source of the confusion that has surrounded the notion of equality in education. For if one sees education as largely or entirely a matter of intellectual growth, this will give rise to one kind of view as to how it should be organized, although for the reasons we gave above it will not suffice to offer only two or three broad types of provision even then. Similarly, views of education as a national investment or as the right of every child regardless of intellectual ability[11] will result in other kinds of answer to questions about relevant differences and kinds of provision. All that is entailed by the notion of equality itself is that we should be able to produce relevant reasons for differences of provision; it does not in itself provide us with the criteria on which these differences are to be based.

However, a further point can be made and a second, very important facet of this general feature of equality highlighted. Whatever view we take of education and, therefore, of what criteria shall be relevant to differential educational provision, the notion of equality itself does require those who accept it to repudiate any suggestion that irrelevant factors can be allowed to take a hand. To some extent all discussions about equality that take place in any practical context are negative pleas against what are regarded as unjustifiable inequalities. In other words, it is usually some form of inequality we are talking about and much of what has been said and written about equality in education has been concerned not so much with its promotion in a positive sense as with the need to put right certain inequalities that were felt to be acting as barriers to its achievement, to remove or to remedy certain factors seen to be giving rise to differences both of treatment and of attainment, which were felt to be unconnected with education itself and were, therefore, regarded as irrelevant, unjust and unequal. We must now consider in greater detail some of these factors unconnected with education in any sense of the term that have nevertheless been affecting the educational achievement of many pupils. For it is on these that recent discussions of equality have

focused and it is these considerations that have given rise to the major
changes in the organization of education we referred to at the beginning of
this chapter, so that no discussion of the realities of educational equality in
contemporary society is possible without a full awareness of the social factors
that have given rise to such impassioned demands for it and the changes in the
education system that some have felt would lead to the achievement of it.

Some Sources of Educational Inequalities

The 1944 Education Act established in England and Wales the concept of
education for all 'according to age, aptitude and ability' and thus a view of
equality that required adequate educational provision to be made for all
children. In particular, it was intended that such provision would be achieved
by making secondary education in some form available to all pupils. Within
a very short time after the implementation of the Act, however, it became
alarmingly clear that the realities of a system offering education for all were
very different from the ideals that had led to its institution. For it became
apparent that many pupils were not finding it possible to take advantage of
the opportunities thus offered. The Report on *Early Leaving* published in
1954[12] revealed some very disturbing statistics concerning the wastage from
the education system of a high proportion of pupils and, most surprisingly,
of those pupils whose intellectual capacities, as measured by intelligence tests,
appeared to be of a very high order. Such a situation was clearly very
worrying not only in the light of what the new deal of the 1944 Act had
hoped to achieve but also in the context of an industrial society dependent
on its human resources for economic survival. The same depressing picture
emerged from the researches of the Crowther committee in 1959.[13] Nor was
Britain alone in this; a similar situation was found to exist elsewhere, not least
in the USA.[14] Equality of educational opportunity existed apparently in
name only; in practice many inequalities persisted. In fine, many irrelevant
factors were coming into play to decide what profit individuals were able to
gain from the educational provision that was made and it was equally clear
that these factors were irrelevant whatever view one took of the aims and
purposes of education, since even if one took a very narrow view of education
as primarily concerned to develop the highest intellects it was apparent that
many pupils of high ability were being excluded from educational success by
factors that had little or nothing to do with intellectual potential.

In general, the reasons for this wastage appeared from the first to be
closely linked with the social class origins of the pupils in so far as the figures
of the *Early Leaving* and Crowther Reports themselves revealed that the
situation was at its most serious among those children who came from

families of low socio-economic status and in the USA a similar situation was seen to exist particularly in relation to coloured pupils, a problem that subsequently became significant in the United Kingdom after the large-scale immigrations of the 1950s and early 1960s. A great deal of attention was immediately directed, therefore, towards these families in an attempt to identify the particular sources of the problem so that appropriate steps might be taken to eradicate them and this has been a source of concern and of continued attention ever since. A number of studies were undertaken from which it quickly became apparent that there were many such factors and that the situation was a highly complex one. Some of the reasons for this failure of pupils to take advantage of the educational opportunities supposedly made available to them were to be found, as one would expect, in the cultural background of the homes in which they were growing up but, more disturbingly, it soon began to emerge not only that the school system was failing to compensate for these disadvantages but that in many ways it was itself aggravating them and introducing additional factors into the situation that worked to the further disadvantage of the 'culturally deprived' child.

The elements in the home background of certain pupils that make it difficult for them to profit from the educational opportunities opened to them were not hard to find. In many cases a straightforward desire on the part of parents for an extra wage-packet to supplement the family income or on the part of the young person himself for a steady wage and the independence that goes with it have led to departure from school at the earliest date on which it was legally possible. The one real argument for the recent raising of the school leaving age to 16 is the need to keep pupils of this kind at school at least until they have had a chance to take some kind of public examination for their own benefit as much as for that of society as a whole. The desire to leave school for reasons of pure economy, then, accompanied sometimes but not always by a reluctance to be 'educated out of one's class', was a prime factor in the situation we have been describing. This one would expect.

It became apparent, however, that this was not the only reason why such youngsters were leaving school early. It was also due in some cases to the fact that neither they nor their parents knew what the opportunities open to them were nor what facilities existed to enable them to take advantage of them. Many were unaware, for example, of the existence of student grants that would enable them to go on to some form of Higher Education. Sheer ignorance was a major factor, then, in discouraging many from continuing their education beyond the statutory leaving age.

It seemed further, however, that many lacked not only a knowledge of but also any real interest in the educational opportunities that were being offered them. One study suggested that only certain identifiable kinds of family in this sector of society could be seen to be really interested in education and, therefore, prepared to support their children, their sons at least if not their daughters, and to encourage them to take full advantage of it (Jackson and Marsden, 1962).[15] Among these families the study identified the 'sunken middle class' family, the family which had, say, once owned a shop or other small business and had fallen on bad times or which was a branch of a largely 'middle class' family and wished to regain that kind of status by way of the education of the children; secondly the families of foremen or others whose work brought them into contact with the more highly educated and gave them thus some inkling of the advantages of this kind of position; and, thirdly, other families, such as those where the mother had herself been educated in a grammar school but had 'married beneath her' and where there was a frustration and a consequent excitement about the possibilities of social advancement through the education of the children. For the rest, a certain apathy was apparent as a result of which there was no encouragement for the children to do well at school and no desire for them to stay there longer than was required by law.

Furthermore the whole ambience of this kind of home seemed to lead to a different view of education from that normally taken by teachers and others who were concerned with its provision and also, it has been claimed, to certain personality traits that made success in the system more difficult for children growing up in such homes. It has been suggested, for example,[16] that in many such families if education is valued at all it is valued only as instrumental towards vocational improvement or the avoidance of exploitation in a competitive and fast-moving world, whereas to some extent at least the ethos of most schools is based on a commitment to the idea of education for its own sake or for the development of self-expression. Such a fundamental conflict of attitudes and values must lead to difficulties. One illustration of this is the interest shown by many pupils in apprenticeships and other courses of vocational training of a kind that are more readily appreciated than the need to learn French irregular verbs or abstruse Latin grammatical constructions.

So far the reasons we have produced to explain why children from certain kinds of family do not get on at school have been those that derive from a fundamental lack of interest in or understanding of what is involved in this. Attention has also been drawn, however, to certain elements in the upbringing of these children that make it difficult for them to cope with the demands of the system even when they are motivated to do so. It has been claimed, for example, that the child-rearing practices usually associated with families of this kind lead to the development of certain character traits that are not conducive to educational success, that the granting of food to babies on demand or giving them comforters and even the quick and immediate smack for any kind of misdemeanour creates a need in children for immediate gratification in all spheres and makes it difficult, if not impossible, for them to direct their energies towards any activity the point of which is to be appreciated only by reference to certain long-term goals, such as examination successes or later career prospects. It has also been suggested that the pace of life is often slower in families of this kind so that children from them do not reveal that quickness in their approach to learning that teachers tend to associate with potential educational success so that they come to be regarded not merely as slow learners but also as poor learners and thus do not succeed in a situation where speed of working seems so often to be at a premium. It has even been argued that the patriarchal ethos of such families makes it difficult for their offspring to accept what is felt to be the largely matriarchal ethos of most primary schools.

The most important single factor, however, that has been identified as contributing to this failure of pupils from such backgrounds to cope success-fully with the demands of the school system is, as we saw in Chapter IV, the nature of the language that they have acquired through their pre-school experiences. The child who has initially acquired his spoken language in a home where a 'restricted' code of language is used will have difficulty in using the formal or 'elaborated' code of the school and thus will not find it easy to learn to read, to extend his vocabulary, to acquire the conceptual under-standing necessary for educational progress especially at an abstract level, in short to attain all of those skills that are fundamental to educational achieve-ment (Bernstein, 1961).[17] Indeed, Bernstein suggested further that this problem of language is the most important single factor in educational disadvantage, leading not only to verbal difficulties but also to a certain rigidity of thinking, a reduced span of attention, a limiting of curiosity, impulsive behaviour in which the interval between feeling and acting is short, an inability to tolerate ambiguity, a preference for the concrete and, in general, a distaste for, not to say a positive suspicion of education as traditionally conceived. There has subsequently been a certain retraction from this extreme position to one which, while maintaining that the language code of such pupils is different, no longer claims that it is inferior or lacking in any way,[18] but, so long as the content of education is couched in a formal 'elaborated' code of language, the pupil whose own language is of 'restricted' or 'public' kind will be at a disadvantage.

This brief discussion of language which was developed more fully in Chapter IV, introduces the suggestion that there are factors in the school itself as well as in the home that need to be looked at if we want to discover what contributes to the difficulties experienced by pupils of the kind we are here concerned with. For it has become increasingly clear not only that schools have not been doing enough to help these pupils but also that there are many ways in which they have been aggravating the problem and themselves creating further barriers to success. We must now consider some of these in more detail.

To begin with, it should be clear that most of these homes will be in poorer districts, especially in the large cities, and that the schools these children attend will also be in these poorer areas. It is almost certainly not the case now, as it once was, that these schools are badly equipped or less generously provided for than those in wealthier neighbourhoods, but in terms of human resources they are often less well endowed since they are not attractive places of work for most teachers and the turnover of staff in them has tended to be very high. Certainly teachers will not be keen to live in such areas themselves so that they will have to be prepared to travel quite long distances to teach in them. Too frequent changes of teacher and too much time spent with supply teachers or well-meaning but inexperienced probationer teachers do not create conditions conducive to educational success.

Furthermore, the attitudes of the teachers themselves often do not help to alleviate these difficulties. Whatever their own origins, teachers by their long education and training have usually developed values very different from those of these pupils and are sometimes less than sympathetic towards those pupils who do not share these values. We have already referred to the problem of confusing slowness in learning with low ability. When this is done, teachers come to expect a low level of performance from such pupils and, as we saw in Chapter I, the demands made by teachers of their pupils and the expectations they have of them seem to be quite crucial in determining the levels of achievement reached.[19] Teachers can also be put off, as we all can, by appearance and dress and will often not expect much from children who are not very well turned out and will not give them as much attention as they need or are entitled to. Difference of language will also lead to difficulties of communication and will thus seriously reduce the efficiency of both the teaching and the learning. Finally, even teachers who are aware of these difficulties and take positive steps to avoid them may unwittingly contribute to the disadvantage. They may quite reasonably fail to answer those important questions that remain unasked, questions like those about grants, careers and other possibilities which we mentioned earlier. Furthermore, in their efforts to do what seems to be best for these pupils they may sometimes talk down to them, lower their standards or take the lack of interest for granted.[20] Teachers in the USA, for example, have been known to advise negro children against aiming too high, doing this honestly in what they see as the best interests of the pupils. This kind of patronization can be in itself a form of discrimination, 'discrimination without prejudice', as Reissman calls it. The attitudes of teachers, then, constitute one major factor within the school that can aggravate the disadvantages that some pupils experience.

It has become increasingly apparent over the last twenty years or so that many elements in the organization of the school system also contribute to the wastage and the inequality of opportunity. In particular, the existence of selective procedures at various stages in the individual's school life have appeared to result in grave disadvantages for many children, but particularly for those who come to school already disadvantaged in the ways we have indicated. Streaming, the practice of grouping children according to measured ability, is one device that creates difficulties of this kind at whatever stage it is used, although clearly the earlier it is introduced the more influential it will be. There are quite clear indications too that it works particularly to the detriment of the child whose home background is not educationally supportive.[21] Similarly, a selective form of secondary education which necessitates some kind of allocation of pupils to different schools or different forms of education at 11+ or at some other equally early stage of a child's school career will result in inefficiencies and errors which will particularly affect such children. In part this is due to all of the factors we have mentioned above, the barriers to achievement created by the home background, teachers' attitudes and expectations, language difficulties and so on, but they all culminate in the difficulties created by the testing procedures used and especially those that involve some attempt to measure intelligence.

The difficulties of doing this have been fully discussed in Chapter II and attempts to base differential educational provision on tests of this kind must for a variety of reasons lead to the misallocation of large numbers of children (Yates and Pidgeon, 1957).[22] It is particularly detrimental to the progress of the socially disadvantaged child for a number of reasons. In the case of verbal tests language differences will clearly play an important part. In all tests the need for speed, often a crucial factor in measuring intelligence, will militate against a high score by the child who sees no particular merit in doing things quickly. A lack of interest or motivation is also unlikely to help a child to show up well in these situations and, where a person is involved as an examiner, the resultant social situation, the relationship with the examiner, will be an added problem for the child who lacks some of the social graces. For all of these reasons children from underprivileged homes can be seen to do themselves less than justice in tests of this kind, so that wherever selection procedures of this type are in use they lead to inequalities of opportunity for such children. The same factors are also resulting in a large proportion of coloured pupils in the United Kingdom, particularly of those of West Indian nationality, being allocated to institutions for the Educationally Sub-Normal, having been 'dubbed' or 'made' ESN (Coard, 1971).[23]

It is perhaps worth noting at this point that many other irrelevant factors come into play when this kind of testing and allocation of pupils to different kinds of school or streamed class are employed, factors which affect the progress not only of pupils from underprivileged backgrounds but many others too. We have heard a lot about the effects of 'nerves' in test situations and interviews and also about the advantages of those who possess 'good examination technique', but these are minor factors when compared with others which are less obvious but equally, and perhaps even more, irrelevant and often far more significant. Sex is one such factor; educational advancement at all levels has always been much more difficult for girls than for boys since, in addition to the greater reluctance of parents to support girls through the system, there have been fewer places for them in all selective institutions. There may be those who would want to argue that sex difference is not an irrelevant factor in differential provision of educational opportunity. It can hardly be maintained, however, that the month of one's birth is relevant. Yet it has been shown[24] that this can and does affect the allocation of pupils to streamed classes in junior schools and thus to different types of secondary school, for the very good reason that the month of one's birth governs the date at which one is admitted to the infant school and consequently the length of time one has spent in full-time education up to the time at which the selection is made. Childhood illnesses and the absences that they involve also play their part in this process. The place of one's birth or at least the part of the country in which one has one's education is another crucial factor in determining the kind of education one has, since provision varies dramatically in both quantity and type from one organizing authority to another. Yet this too would seem to be an irrelevant consideration to the decision about what kind of education an individual can best profit from.

It will be clear, then, that equality of opportunity in education is far from a reality whatever interpretation one puts on the term. Even the most confirmed élitist, committed to nothing more than the education of the intelligent, can hardly believe in the face of this kind of evidence to the contrary that even this hard-line kind of equality is being achieved by the system as it has been organized. Only an elitism based on the advancement of the privileged could leave one satisfied with the situation that the enquiries of the last twenty years or so have revealed and few would want to maintain such an extremist position as that. It has been clear for a long time, therefore, to those with any real understanding of the situation that changes needed to be made and steps taken to rectify the position. Consequently, recent years have seen the introduction of a number of schemes aimed at putting right these deficiencies in the system and at combating the disadvantages of the underprivileged, in order to promote something that could more appropriately be called educational equality. We must now turn to a consideration of the form some of these have taken and the intentions that lie behind them.

Compensatory Education

One major kind of solution that has been suggested to deal with some of the problems we have listed is that of what the Plowden Report[25] called 'positive discrimination'. This amounts to a suggestion that equality does not require that we give all schools and all pupils an equal share of the educational cake but that it is more likely to be attained if we give larger, and therefore unequal, shares to those with greater needs, if we allocate a larger share of resources of all kinds to certain pupils in order to compensate for the disadvantages under which they labour. Certain children must be given unequal treatment if they are to have equal opportunities. This kind of view has led to a number of different forms of 'Compensatory Education', each designed to make good the cultural deficiencies we have referred to and to try to compensate for and to put right those factors that have been hindering the educational success of such pupils. This is an idea that had appeared earlier in the USA in answer to the problem of the education of black children.

One of the solutions offered by the Plowden Report itself, although it had other reasons also for making this particular recommendation, was an expansion of the provision of pre-school, nursery education. One of the arguments adduced in favour of this recommendation was the need to provide early opportunities for children to receive some kind of formal educational provision that might make up for various forms of social deprivation. Certain children, it argued,[26] suffer later in the system because of poverty of language and 'even amongst children below compulsory school age, the growth of measured intelligence is associated with socio-economic features',[27] so that educational provision from the age of three years onwards may offset this. The importance of nursery education in this and other respects is now recognized and the British Government has recently affirmed its intention to expand it on a large scale.[28] In the USA too attempts have been made to introduce compensatory education programmes at the pre-school stage in order to try to ensure that the child from the culturally impoverished background might start his formal school career on a par with his more fortunate colleagues. The 'Headstart' programme was just such an attempt to bring children from poorer homes, especially negro children, up to the starting line level with their fellows.

This, then, has been one form of positive discrimination. Where it has been tried, however, it has not been entirely successful. In part this is due to the fact that when nursery schools or nursery classes are established they are used more by children from 'privileged' than those from 'underprivileged' homes. There is little that can be done about this. One cannot make attendance compulsory at this age nor can one exclude the 'privileged' from it, since the arguments for the provision of education at this age for all pupils are strong. One can only recommend, as the Plowden Report does,[29] that all possible means of persuasion should be used by health visitors and other social workers to encourage mothers of children who seem to be in particular need of nursery education to make greater use of the facilities available.

The attitude that is implied towards the culture of these homes has been another factor in the lack of success of this kind of venture. To regard children from poor homes as culturally deprived is to imply that these homes are fundamentally inferior; this in turn leads to the continuation of a form of education that is linked to a different kind of culture and consequently creates a gap that is difficult to bridge and which does not make any easier the task of convincing the parents, especially the mothers, of these children of the value of what is offered in nursery education. They are unlikely to see it as more than a useful child-minding service which they will use only if they have no more convenient service such as a resident granny.

This latter point draws our attention also to a third difficulty that is being experienced in this area, the problem of establishing nursery education in a form that has more substance to it than a mere child-minding service, the provision of suitable accommodation and resources and the training of suitable teachers for this kind of work, teachers who understand what is needed and have the expertise to provide it. The conversion of accommodation, resources and especially teachers who were originally prepared for teaching older pupils is more important than has often been realized. It is also, at least in the case of the teachers, a long process. If nursery education is to be established properly, it will be a long and expensive task. Only if it is done properly, however, can we hope that it might contribute something towards the solution of the problems we have been discussing.

A second kind of approach that has been adopted in the attempt to provide compensatory education has been directed not at pre-school children but at all of the school population. It has taken the form of putting extra resources into schools in deprived areas, providing extra payments to teachers, larger allowances for materials and other recurrent expenditure, favourable building grants and assistance of this kind in all relevant fields. In suggesting this remedy, the Plowden Report[30] tells us that 'the principle, already accepted, that special need calls for special help, should be given a new cutting edge. We ask for 'positive discrimination' in favour of such schools and the children in them, going well beyond an attempt to equalize resources. . . . The first step must be to raise the schools with low standards to the national average; the second, quite deliberately to make them better. The justification is that the homes and neighbourhoods from which many of their children come provide little support and stimulus for learning.' As a result of this recommendation, many areas in Britain have been officially designated as Educational Priority Areas and the schools in them have been given the kind of preferential treatment suggested. Teachers in these schools have been paid more in an attempt to secure a stability of staffing and to halt the rapid staff turnover that we suggested earlier was a significant factor in the lack of success of the pupils in these schools. Additional money has also been made available in order to make possible the establishment of special programmes either in the schools themselves or in outside centres to remedy the deficiencies in experience, language and other cognitive skills of the children in them. At the same time the back-up services have been strengthened both by increased provision of social services of all kinds and by the appointment of social workers or counsellors to the schools themselves.

While one would not want to deny that this kind of approach has done much to improve the educational lot of certain pupils and to put right some of the inequalities of the system, there are difficulties with it of which we ought to take note. In particular, there are two fundamental problems in this approach. The first of these arises from the difficulty of establishing adequate criteria for designating an area as an EPA. The Plowden Report suggested a number of criteria that should be used,[31] the proportions of unskilled and semi-skilled manual workers in the area, the size of families, the extent of the entitlement to supplementary benefits of all kinds, the amount of over-crowding and sharing of houses, the incidence of truancy, the proportions of retarded, disturbed or handicapped pupils, the number of incomplete families and the proportion of 'children unable to speak English'. Many of these are criteria that can be measured with a high degree of exactitude; others are less easy to determine. Not all of those who are entitled to supplementary benefits actually avail themselves of them, for example, as the Report points out, so that it is not easy to apply this kind of criterion accurately. A criterion such as the incidence of truancy, however, is based not on objectively identifiable conditions in the home background of the pupils but on the way in which they react to their schools. Some cynics have claimed, therefore, that this and other criteria that have been used, such as that of a high staff turn-over, create a situation in which an inefficient or incompetent school is 'rewarded' by additional resources and payments to staff, while a school that successfully tackles problems of this kind as they are presented to it is, in a sense, 'penalized'. A certain amount of tension and dissatisfaction has consequently resulted among teachers from this kind of scheme.

This is one aspect of a wider problem. Whatever criteria are used, they will inevitably be rather rough and ready. A line will be drawn somewhere which must be somewhat arbitrary. This is another example of the problem of establishing categories that we referred to earlier. It will also always be the case that wherever that line is drawn there will be many pupils in the EPAs whose home background is such that they will not need compensatory educational provision and there will always be those outside these areas whose need for it will be every bit as great as that of any of those who are within them, and for the very same reasons. The Plowden Report itself was aware of this and spoke of special groups, such as gypsies and canal boat children whose difficulties would not be met by any EPA scheme.[32] The problem, however, is not only one of special groups; again we find ourselves dealing with categories; the main need is to provide for individual pupils. Attempts have, therefore, been made to identify pupils rather than areas with special needs and to use the additional resources to develop and provide special programmes for them. It is almost certainly true that a judicious combination of these approaches is the only route that is likely to lead to any kind of solution for all such pupils.

A further point that must be stressed is that, to quote the Plowden Report yet again,[33] 'improved education alone cannot solve the problem of these children'. Education cannot compensate for society.[34] To put extra resources only into the education of such children is to attempt to deal with the symptoms without getting at the root causes of their difficulties. The process of equalizing the life-chances of children must begin outside the school and, unless it does, there is little that the school alone can do. Again to quote from the Plowden Report,[35] 'simultaneous action is needed by the authorities responsible for employment, industrial training, housing and planning.' Indeed, it may well be the case that the failure to mount successful attacks simultaneously on these areas has been one factor in the lack of success achieved by some attempts to improve the educational provision of these pupils. This draws attention to the need for a total approach to this problem and this has emerged very clearly from the practical experiences of many of those who have been involved in compensatory schemes of this kind. In many EPAs it has quickly become apparent that little can be achieved by improving the facilities within the schools if no attempt is made to integrate the schools more fully with their communities. Thus compensatory education has appeared to be possible only if the parents themselves can be brought into the picture and only if one can relate what is being provided for and required of pupils in schools to the realities of the environment of the community in which they live for the other seven-eighths of their young lives.

This brings us directly to the major problem of the concept of compensatory education. The schemes we have been discussing have all started out as attempts to make people equal and we suggested earlier that such an approach is fundamentally mistaken. The notion of compensation implies the existence of a deficiency and, while there is no doubt that on any definition of deficiency real deficiencies do exist in many families, the considerations behind programmes of compensatory education have too often assumed that these deficiencies are always cultural ones and that they are an inevitable part of the social background of all children from certain socio-economic or racial groups. It implies that the language and culture of 'working class' or West Indian families, for example, are inferior to the culture that the school is concerned to impart and that pupils from this kind of background must be 'cured' of their linguistic and cultural deficiencies if they are to be brought to a 'proper' standard of educational achievement. The problem with this attitude is that at root it perpetuates and reinforces a conflict which, as we have already seen, is itself a major contributory factor to the educational failure of these pupils. It attempts to do no more than to discover new and more effective ways of imposing an 'alien' culture on them and thus does nothing to overcome the alienation and the conflict of values that we suggested earlier was a major obstacle to the educational achievement of these pupils.

This view of what is needed here is, of course, based on a view of know-ledge and of the intrinsic merits of certain activities, pursuits, culture and values that, as we have seen in Chapter VI, is of questionable validity. It has recently been suggested, therefore, that we should reconsider what we mean by 'education', especially in relation to such pupils.[36] The view that is now taken of what has been called the 'restricted' language code of children from certain kinds of home background is no longer, as we pointed out earlier, that such a code is inferior to that of the school but that it is merely different. It is no longer felt that it need necessarily hinder or limit the development of rationality, since it can be shown itself to be capable of sustaining the most abstract and abstruse relationships (Labov, 1969).[37] If the development of rationality in such pupils is inhibited, it is because the language of teachers and of education is different and no concessions are made to them nor attempts to bridge the gap between the codes, other than to try to push them into using the different and largely 'alien' code of the school.

For this reason, as we saw when discussing the curriculum in Chapter VI, questions are being asked about the content of education. It is being asserted that human knowledge does not have the kind of objective status

often claimed for it and that there is little real foundation for the claim that
certain kinds of knowledge have a value that is superior to that of other kinds
in such a way as to justify an insistence that all pupils acquire such knowledge
and accept the values implicit in it. Views have been expressed about the
'stratification of knowledge',[38] suggesting that decisions about the value of
certain kinds of knowledge are linked to the class structure of society and
that by such decisions the dominant class attempts to impose its own culture
on its society. If there is any truth in this kind of assertion, to engage in
forms of compensatory education such as those we have discussed is to do no
more than to attempt to ease and to make more efficient this imposition of
values by the dominant class on society as a whole. As a result, it is being
suggested that we look again at the content of educational provision and try
to relate this to the existing knowledge and culture of the pupil, that we try
to base our educational provision on the 'common sense' knowledge of the
pupils themselves rather than on the 'educational' knowledge of the teacher.
If we do this, some of the barriers to the education of these children will
disappear - deferred gratification, for example, need create no problem if
there is immediate satisfaction in the subject matter of education here and
now - and there might be some hope that a relevant education might be
provided for pupils from 'working class' and negro homes, so that they will
not become alienated by their experiences at school, at a serious disadvantage
in relation to their own personal development and subsequently perhaps
delinquent and anti-social. In short, it is being claimed that we should not be
attempting to convert such pupils to a new language or a new culture, but
that rather attempts should be made to bridge the gap between the cultures if
education is to cease to play the divisive role it has hitherto played in society.

The same sort of conclusion is being reached by many of those who have
been engaged at a practical level in attempts to deal with the problems of the
EPA areas. As we have seen, they have come to realize that the problem of
the gap between the culture of the home and that of the school requires more
than merely building a bridge from one to the other; the gap itself needs to be
closed by a rapprochement of school and community, an integration of the
school into the community. In order to achieve this, major changes must be
made in what the school regards as its role and function and what it considers
to be the essential content of education.

The problem, therefore, becomes one of introducing modifications to the
curriculum of the school in order to achieve these purposes and we have
already noted in Chapter VI some of the difficulties of ensuring that
curriculum planning achieves an adequate balance between the needs of the
pupil, the needs of society and the demands of knowledge itself. In particular,
we must not lose sight of the dangers of imprisoning pupils in their own

culture and of failing to broaden their horizons by not offering them adequate opportunities for experiencing many things they may come to value that are beyond their immediate environment.[39] But it is clear that many of the current difficulties we are experiencing in our schools arise from a failure to question the validity of much of what we are offering and in particular to do this in the light of the background of many of the pupils we are supposed to be catering for. As we have said, a rapprochement is needed if we are to achieve a form of education that is relevant and, therefore, acceptable to pupils from all kinds of background. What is needed now, therefore, is a careful examination of the form such a rapprochement should take and in particular an awareness that here, as so often, there will be no panaceas. Again it will be necessary to answer these problems at the practical level in relation to the particular contexts of individual schools and it may be that the first-hand experience of those who have worked in Educational Priority Areas will be of more value than the ideas of the theoreticians from this point on. Certainly, one of the weaknesses of the theoretical discussions of these issues has been their failure to offer any clear advice as to how teachers might in practice set about seeking solutions to the problems they have identified.

One way of attempting to achieve educational equality through changes in the educational system, then, is to look very closely at the curriculum and to take account in our curriculum planning of factors other than traditional views about what kinds of knowledge are valuable. Changes must also be made, however, in the organizational structure of the system, since, as we saw earlier, there are factors here that militate against equality. There is little point even in the most sweeping attempts to correct any deficiencies that do exist in the backgrounds of pupils if we do nothing to rectify those features of the system itself which aggravate these problems and create further barriers to the progress of many pupils. Other innovations have been introduced, therefore, designed to meet some of these problems. In particular, attempts have been made to correct the inequalities that have arisen from the use of selective procedures of various kinds and at various points within the system. We must conclude our discussion of equality by considering the two major developments in this area, comprehensive education and the abolition of streaming.

Comprehensive Education

The idea of organizing secondary education in England and Wales on a comprehensive basis had been raised and aired, particularly within the Labour movement, in the years between the two World Wars but it received its first real impetus from the intention made explicit by the 1944 Education Act to provide secondary education for all pupils on an equal footing 'according to age, aptitude and ability'. Once this kind of egalitarianism had been given official sanction in this way, it became increasingly difficult to maintain that this ideal was being realized or could be realized through the provision of two or three different types of secondary school.

Historically, the development of secondary education in England and Wales had resulted for the most part in the emergence of a selective system which allocated pupils at age 11 to two or three types of school on the basis of a diagnostic test or series of tests of attainment and ability that came to be know as the 11+. In some areas an attempt was made to correct some of the inevitable errors of this procedure by arrangements for the further transfer of some pupils at 13+. Children were thus allocated to a grammar school or a modern school at the age of 11. Sometimes provision was made for a third type of school, the technical school, but there were few of these and, where they did exist, transfer to them was usually at 13+ rather than 11+, so that effectively, although known as tripartism, in most parts of the country this resulted in a bipartite system.

This was a natural development from an earlier scheme in which all pupils went to an all-age elementary school and those who were successful in the 'scholarship' at 11 were offered free places in grammar schools or sometimes in 'central' schools, the others remaining in the elementary schools until the age of leaving. It was a system that was given the official blessing of the Hadow Report of 1926,[40] the Spens Report of 1938,[41] albeit with a few sympathetic comments on the idea of the multi-lateral school, and the Norwood Report of 1943.[42] The latter even went so far as to posit the existence of three types of mind for which these three types of school, conveniently enough, were ideally suited to cater. In spite of this official view, the 1944 Education Act, which was the culmination of these discussions, did not impose this system on the country but gave the local authorities the freedom to organize secondary education in whatever way they felt appropriate to their particular situations. One would like to feel that it took this line because it accepted the implications of its own fundamental egalitarianism; it is more likely, however, that it was the result of the pressures of the Labour Party participants in an Act that was the work of the wartime coalition government.

The immediate reaction of many authorities to the requirements of the 1944 Act was to develop and extend the selective system of secondary education they had been building up before the Second World War started. Indeed, the more progress an authority had made with its plans in the thirties, the more committed it was to proceeding along similar lines now. Clearly, this made good sense in terms of the economic use of existing plant and the conservation of resources in what was a time of great economic stringency. Others, however, did begin to experiment with comprehensive schools. In particular, where new schools had to be built anyway to put right the effects of bombing, as in London and Coventry, it was no extravagance to build a completely new system and, indeed, where very large schools were built there might even have been some saving. The years immediately following the Act, therefore, saw the emergence of a number of different systems, bipartism, tripartism, comprehensivism of a number of different kinds, 'all-through' and 'two-tier', and even systems which attempted to reconcile selective and non-selective methods by having grammar and 'comprehensive' schools in the same scheme.

Throughout this time, however, the pressures against selective systems were mounting, backed not only by the ideological arguments of the Labour Movement but also by the growing evidence of the hidden effects of such systems, some of which we have already referred to, so that comprehensiviza tion slowly spread. In 1965, a Labour government issued Circular 10/65 which requested all local authorities to submit to it plans for the comprehensivization of secondary education in the areas under their jurisdiction, and, although some of them refused to do this and the request was subsequently withdrawn by a Tory government, many of them did respond to the request and had gone too far towards implementing their schemes to draw back later, even if they had wanted to.

The most unfortunate feature of the development of comprehensive secondary education in this country has been that it has in this way been debated almost entirely at the level of political ideology and prejudice and has been implemented for political rather than educational reasons, so that emotion has tended to play a larger part than reason both in the discussion and the development of it and the educational issues at stake have thus been often lost or ignored. It is due in no small part to this feature that we have made so many mistakes in the development of the comprehensive system so that we have so few comprehensive schools that one can approve of either on political or on educational grounds. We must look now at some of the educational issues involved here and at some features of both the notion and the realities of comprehensive education itself.

The first thing we must note is the problem of any kind of selectivity in education. Selective systems have been criticized on ideological grounds as being socially devisive and as resulting in inequalities of all kinds. Parity of esteem between types of school which was stressed as a vital concomitant of any selective system was never a realistic aim, since no matter how hard any- one tries to ensure that all types of school have equality of provision, there is no doubt in anyone's mind that different types of school are not on a par, if only by reference to the kinds of career their pupils enter, a criterion that is very commonly applied by both parents and teachers in evaluating schools.[43] Thus inequalities result as the 'best' teachers choose to go to the 'best' schools and parents choose to send their children to these schools if they can.

However, ideological arguments of this kind have no force with those who reject the ideology itself and to say that selective procedures result in inequalities between different types of school is not to condemn the system in the eyes of those who would argue that such inequalities are acceptable, even right and proper. As we saw earlier, the notion of equality in itself requires no more than this. The educational arguments against selection, however, are more cogent. At basis they are the same arguments we have seen as applying to any attempt to use broad and rather crude categories in planning our educational provision. It is impossible to allocate pupils to categories of this kind with any acceptable degree of accuracy or efficiency. Some of the reasons for this we have encountered elsewhere. It is worth briefly bringing them together here.

The belief that one can use tests of any kind to assess educability and thus to allocate pupils to certain kinds of educational institution was criticized at a very early stage in the development of such tests. The Hadow Report of 1931[44] questioned the use of intelligence tests for these purposes and earlier than that, in 1924, a report on 'Psychological Tests of Educable Capacity' described the use of such tests for transfer at 11+ as 'gravely unreliable'. Nor is the problem merely one of devising more accurate and sophisticated techniques of assessment. The difficulties are much more complex than is recognized by those whose solution to it is to abolish the 11+ test and replace it with a series of tests supported by teachers' and headteachers' assessments.

One aspect of this issue that we have already noted is the extent to which irrelevant factors such as sex, date and place of birth, socio-economic background and other such features influence the allocation of pupils. But the problem goes even deeper than this. Yates and Pidgeon[45] suggested that even at its most efficient any system of selection must result in an error of 5 per cent each way, that 10 per cent of any age cohort will be wrongly placed even by the most accurate system, these being the pupils who fall on either side of the borderline wherever we draw that line. An error slightly in excess of 10 per cent which the same study claimed to have discovered in the practice of local authorities at that time represented a very creditable performance and yet, in human terms, it meant that a lot of children were being placed in educational institutions that were not necessarily the most suited to them. The prime reason for this is that intellectual growth is a constantly changing and developing process and the rate of such growth varies so much from one child to another. It is possible to test with reasonable accuracy the level of an individual's attainment at any given time but to use this as a basis for assertions about that individual's potential for further growth, to try to predict future performance on the evidence of present achievement, to assume that one has measured ability rather than attainment is fraught with danger, as we saw in Chapter II. Furthermore, to do this is to make no allowance for what we know about the importance of achievement for motivation and the effects of both success and failure in raising or lowering the motivational level of pupils and therefore their standards of performance, points which we discussed in detail in Chapters I and III. There is clear evidence of this in tests given to pupils shortly after 'success' or 'failure' in the 11+.[46] Finally, we must remember the effects of teacher expectation here. As we saw in Chapter I, teachers will raise or lower the demands they make of their pupils according to whether they view them as 'bright' or 'average' or 'backward' and this will itself contribute to a widening of the gap between those who 'succeed' and those who 'fail' in a selective system, so that the process becomes a 'self-fulfilling prophecy', an expression that has been used to describe the comparable practice of streaming.[47] It was for this reason, among others, that the 'fail-safe' device of the 13+ transfer between schools did not work. The fundamental argument for comprehensive education, then, is the besetting difficulty of any system of selection, its inability to select with accuracy or to correct errors once they have been made.

A growing awareness of the many facets of this problem has reinforced the increasing ideological and political pressure and has brought about a rapid expansion of comprehensive or non-selective secondary education in recent years. This has taken a number of different forms, which can be broadly grouped into two main types, the 'all-through' comprehensive school (a term that has a sad ambiguity) and the 'two-tier' system. The 'all-through' comprehensive schools are those schools, usually rather large in size, that have been established by some authorities to take pupils of all abilities on their transfer from junior schools at 11+ and provide for them until they leave school at 16, 17 or 18. In some cases these schools have been purpose-built or have been developed from an existing grammar, technical or modern school, where the site offered scope for building development. In other places, units of this kind have been created by the amalgamation of several existing schools of different types, even where in some instances these have been widely separated geographically. This seemed to some authorities to be the most economical way of responding to the request of Circular 10/65 and there has resulted a number of 'botched up' schemes that have done the concept of comprehensive education little good and in some cases much harm.

The main difficulty with any kind of 'all-through' system is that it gives rise
to educational units of a size that some people have argued is too great to
cater adequately for aspects of education other than intellectual development. This is a view that has support too from many who have first-hand
experience of the realities of these institutions. Such large units cannot easily
provide the secure, warm, face-to-face environment that many pupils need
and attempts to break the school down into smaller units by the creation of
houses, year groups, tutor groups or some other such device can only work
where the physical structure of the school is such as to make these sub-
divisions real and meaningful to the pupils and this is possible only in a few,
fortunate cases. On the other hand, it has been argued that unless the school
is of a certain minimum size it will not be capable of producing from a fully
comprehensive intake a viable sixth form, even allowing for the new and
wider concept of sixth form studies that has emerged since the appearance of
the comprehensive school, nor will it make possible the variety of courses
that it is felt should be made available, especially at sixth form level. The
problem of size is, then, a very serious one and has created problems for
many schools the failure to cope with which has led to severe criticisms of the
notion of comprehensive education itself.

For this reason, some authorities have introduced various forms of two-tier
system on the assumption that to break the large all-through school into
two units will give all the advantages of a non-selective scheme without the
attendant problems of great size, and that it will avoid both the need for
expensive new buildings and the 'botched up' amalgamations that might
otherwise result. Thus some authorities have introduced schemes in which
transfer from the junior school at 11+ is followed by further transfer to a
'High' school or a grammar school at 14+. Others have established Sixth
Form Colleges which pupils who choose to stay on at school beyond 16 may
attend for a variety of courses. Besides removing from the secondary school
the sixth form which, as we saw just now, has led to the need for very large
schools, this kind of scheme has the additional advantage that it makes
possible the education of early maturing teenagers in a 'college' rather than
a 'school' environment, where they can be given more freedom and
responsibility and may thus be encouraged to persevere with their education
more willingly. The trend that seems to be developing of late, as sixteen-year-
olds increasingly leave their schools for the A level classes of the technical
colleges, would seem to support the need for some development of this kind.
Lastly, some authorities have taken up yet another suggestion of the Plowden
Report and have decided to reorganize the whole of their educational
provision into three phases, First, Middle and Secondary, with transfer at
8+ or 9+ and at 12+ or 13+. The main advantage of this kind of scheme, again

apart from the smaller units that it makes possible, would seem to lie in the opportunities it creates for allowing twelve and thirteen-year olds to continue to enjoy some of the best features of our primary education, although no clear philosophy of the Middle school has yet emerged and some would see it as an opportunity to extend downwards the age at which children can begin some of the learning associated with the secondary stage of education.

Many of these developments are still in their infancy, so that it is difficult to evaluate them in any helpful way. Some have, of course, been in operation for some time, but even here the evidence is unclear and even conflicting. One or two general points can be made, however. In the first place, a great deal of concern has been expressed about the fact that the introduction of comprehensive education in the full sense can only be achieved at the cost of abolishing the grammar schools as such, regarded by many people as the jewel of the English system. This is put by many people with an eye for an elegant turn of phrase as being equality at the expense of quality. There is no doubt that this is a serious issue. It must, however, be put into a proper perspective. While it is true that the work of many English grammar schools has been of a very high order, no one could begin to maintain that this has been true of all of them. The reputation of the very best ones too derives more from their academic record than any ability to cater for the wide spectrum of educational need that is generally recognized today. Furthermore, if the evidence we have considered concerning the inaccuracies of the selective procedures has any weight at all, it is difficult to argue that this quality of educational provision should be the preserve not of those who in educational terms most deserve it or are most able to profit from it but of those who for a variety of irrelevant reasons have been lucky enough to be offered it. The aim of comprehensive education should be to achieve this kind of quality of both breadth and depth in the education it offers to all pupils. If educational equality can really only be achieved with an attendant loss of quality, then we must think again about its desirability. Before we do so, however, we must ask whether it is in fact inevitable and, indeed, we must also ask some searching questions about how we are to define quality in education.

A second major criticism of comprehensive education is that it results in the growth of neighbourhood schools and thus does not achieve the social mix that some supporters of the idea feel is important nor even, perhaps, a fully comprehensive mixture of abilities. Attempts to ensure an adequate spread of abilities have resulted in schemes for admitting to each school a fixed proportion of pupils from each of three or four ability bands. This kind of approach may in turn result also in a certain social mix, since it invariably involves bringing in pupils from outside the immediate neighbourhood of the school. More positive attempts to ensure a social mix have been made through various schemes for 'bussing' children, sometimes from long distances, as has been done in some parts of the USA in an attempt to ensure a balanced racial mixture in schools.

The advantages of such schemes are doubtful. For one thing they necessitate the continuation of selective procedures even within the comprehensive system with all the difficulties and tensions for pupils and parents that that creates. The strain on pupils who have to travel long distances to school must also not be minimized. Finally, if there are any advantages in the development of the community school, the use of the facilities of the school by pupils in the evening, the involvement of parents in the work of the school and, in general, the integration of the school with the community to which it belongs, as we suggested earlier, then the school must be a neighbourhood school; it must draw its pupils from its own community. No community school can develop if its pupils are drawn from several areas.

This seems, then, not to be as serious a problem in the context of current educational thinking as was once felt to be the case. Provided that the parent's right to choose another secondary school for its offspring is safe-guarded (although, of course, if this right were extensively asserted the whole system would break down), there seems little to be lost and perhaps much to be gained, not least from the loss of the stress and strain on children and parents, by transfering pupils from their Junior or Middle schools directly to their neighbourhood or community comprehensive secondary school. It is perhaps enough if the schools can avoid creating social barriers; we may be asking too much if we expect them also to destroy for us those that already exist, since this may deflect them from doing their own job properly.

The last comment that must be made about comprehensive education in the context of a discussion of educational equality is one that may have some bearing on the problem we noted earlier of the inadequacy and conflicting nature of some of the evidence that has so far emerged as to its success or failure. In trying to evaluate comprehensive education, we must maintain the very important distinction between the notion of comprehensive education and the realities of comprehensive schools as they have been established. If the evidence is not conclusively in their favour, we must remember that this may reflect on the inadequacies of the schemes that have so far been tried rather than on the idea itself. We have already noted, for example, that many authorities have kept some or all of their selective schools in existence alongside what they have called 'comprehensive schools'. In such situations, it is clearly unfair and unhelpful to judge such schools on their academic achievements, unless one regards any achievement in this sphere as a success. Similarly, where comprehensive schools are the result of 'botched up' amalgamations of existing schools or where the units created have been too large or housed in buildings too badly designed for them to have any real chance of success, we must beware of condemning the idea of comprehensive education because of the inept way it has been put into practice in many places.

Finally, comprehensive education does not follow merely from joining several schools together nor even from abandoning selective procedures, particularly if the old divisions remain within the school, as they have done in so many cases. Comprehensive education, if it is to mean anything, must involve a much more fundamental rethinking of the whole of education. It cannot be discussed or planned in isolation from the kind of rethinking about the curriculum we have referred to earlier in this chapter and elsewhere in this book, nor can it be undertaken without a fundamental reappraisal of the internal organization of the school. If we adopt a system of schools that is based on an abandonment of selective procedures, we must look very hard at any such procedures it is proposed to use within the school. This is why we must now conclude our discussion of equality by considering the process of streaming, itself an 'education system in miniature',[48] which may be creating within some comprehensive schools the very difficulties that those schools have been established to overcome.

Streaming

Streaming is the grouping of pupils according to both age and intellectual ability. It is a system that was first introduced in England and Wales in the 1920s. The method of grouping which it replaced was that of 'Standards', grouping by attainment but not by age, a system under which pupils moved from one Standard to the next only when and if they reached an appropriate level of attainment. Such a system worked satisfactorily when most pupils remained in the same all-age elementary school throughout their school careers and it was little affected by the 'creaming off' of the very bright few to the grammar schools at 11+.

Two factors led to the change to streaming. The first of these was the move towards establishing secondary education for all which began with the Hadow Report of 1926.[49] The 'decapitation' of the all-age elementary school which this entailed resulted in the disruption of the Standards system and the emergence of the dull and backward in the new junior and secondary schools. Secondly, psychologists were beginning to concern themselves with the characteristics of age-groups and to suggest that it might be unwise to group children without reference to their chronological ages. Indeed, this was one of the factors that had led to the Hadow Report's recommendation for separate primary and secondary schools. At the same time, the work of other psychologists such as Binet and Simon on intelligence[50] and Burt on backwardness,[51] was encouraging the view that intellectual ability was largely innate, relatively static and readily measurable and that, as a result, it could be used as a basis for grouping pupils, not least in order to make possible the provision of special treatment for the less able. These factors together suggested that in the new schools Standards should be replaced by streams and and in fact a 'triple track system of organization' of pupils into A, B and C classes was explicitly advocated by the Hadow Report on Primary Education in 1931.[52] In 1937 this official view was reiterated in the Board of Education's 'Handbook of Suggestions for Teachers' and the same system was suggested as appropriate for the multi-lateral school in the Spens Report on Secondary Education in 1938.[53] As a result, streaming began to appear in primary, elementary and, where they were introduced, modern schools throughout the 1930s.

The assumptions of this system are several. Firstly, it assumes that intellectual ability is relatively fixed and static; secondly, that it can be measured with a high degree of accuracy; and thirdly, that to use this as a basis for grouping pupils will give homogeneous teaching groups. It further assumes that the central concern of the school is the intellectual development of its pupils through certain kinds of subject content and that a class teaching approach is the most effective and suitable method of attending to this. It also assumes that such a method of grouping is best for all pupils, not only the bright but also and equally the less able. Indeed, there are many teachers who today advocate this method of grouping primarily from the conviction that more can be done for the less able if they are kept together in small groups and not exposed to the discouragement of working next to their brighter peers (Daniels, 1961).[54]

However, the years since the Second World War have seen a reaction against streaming and a developing trend towards the introduction of mixed ability groupings in schools. As early as 1945, the newly formed Ministry of Education questioned the desirability of streaming in a pamphlet, 'The Nation's Schools' and by 1959 its report on Primary Education,[55] although not explicitly condemning the practice, did stress the value of the mixed ability form of organization in the primary school, a form of organization that it claimed had begun to appear in the previous decade. Indeed, although the immediate post-war years had seen, if anything, an increase in the incidence of streaming in both primary and secondary schools, as they dealt with an enlarged school population along with a shortage of resources and increased demands for educational success both at 11+ and in public examinations at 16+, the late 1950s and early 1960s saw a move away from streaming in primary schools, particularly in those areas where the introduction of some form of comprehensive secondary education removed the pressures of the 11+, and recent years have seen this trend spreading into the lower forms of secondary schools and, in some cases, the upper forms too

Several reasons can be adduced to explain this trend. For the most part they are the same reasons as those we saw behind the movement towards the comprehensivization of secondary education. The assumptions about the nature of intelligence upon which selection of any kind is based have been strongly questioned by psychologists and educationists, and as we saw in Chapter II, few would now feel justified in claiming that intelligence is a faculty, let alone that it can be measured with any accuracy. Consequently, it has become increasingly apparent that selective procedures are no more possible within a school than between schools. The problem of categories again comes into play in respect of establishing both adequate theoretical criteria and efficient practical devices. The idea that it is acceptable within the school because of the supposed ease of transfer between classes has little credence in the light of the extent to which transfers do in fact take place in streamed schools. Transfer between streams happens at a rate far below that which even teachers who support streaming believe to be necessary (Daniels, 1961)[56] and the reasons for this are those that we saw also resulted in the failure of the 'fail-safe' device of transfer between schools at 13+. The expectations teachers have of pupils labelled A, B or C again affects the pupils' performances, a point we discussed in detail in Chapter I, as do the effects of success or failure, achievement or non-achievement, on the motivation of pupils, as we also saw in Chapter III. In fact, it has become apparent that streaming has the effect of creating differences where none need exist, that it is a 'self-fulfilling prophecy'.[57]

Furthermore, many irrelevant factors of the kind we have already discussed again affect the selection of pupils[58] and the evidence that mounted from a clutch of studies undertaken during the 1950s and 1960s suggested not only that streaming did not help schools to alleviate the inequalities that we referred to earlier but also that, as we also suggested, it was doing much to aggravate them and, indeed, itself creating further inequalities. In particular, it emerged as a major factor in the wastage of talent we noted above.

Another factor in this reassessment of the merits of streaming has been the changes we have commented on elsewhere in the view taken of education and of the purposes of the school. We saw just now that one of the underlying assumptions of streaming is that the main, even the sole, concern of the school is or should be with the intellectual development of its pupils. If one views education in wider terms than that, one will want to consider the implications of streaming for other aspects of schooling. In particular, concern has been expressed about the effects of streaming on the development of divergent thinking and creative abilities in pupils and also on their personal, moral and social development.

There is some evidence that more divergent thinking is to be found in unstreamed than in streamed schools (Ferri, 1972)[59] and there is also some indication, as we saw in Chapter II, that schools which use formal, conventional methods are less successful in promoting creative abilities than schools where the learning is more self-initiated (Haddon and Lytton, 1968).[60] This evidence is far from conclusive, not least because of the difficulties of measuring these kinds of ability, and many other factors may be involved too, such as the attitudes of the teachers, which may be even more influential than the method of grouping (Barker-Lunn, 1970).[61] However, this is an aspect of the problem that must not be ignored if we consider the development of these kinds of ability to be an important part of the school's task. It is thus an area that is worthy of further investigation.

There is little doubt, however, about the adverse effects of streaming on the social and emotional development of pupils. The study of streaming in the primary school mounted by the NFER[62] devoted a lot of attention to these aspects of streaming, starting from the assumption that they are as important a part of education as 'more formally attained skills'. The study claimed that in unstreamed schools pupils of average ability and boys of below average ability developed better relationships with their teachers, that relationships and friendship patterns between pupils correlated less highly with ability levels, that average and below average pupils revealed more positive attitudes to school and that there was generally a higher level of participation in school activities. The studies of Hargreaves and Lacey revealed similar advantages to the social and emotional development of pupils, especially the less able pupils, in unstreamed schools or corresponding disadvantages when classes were streamed.[63] There is little evidence of friendships between A and D stream pupils in streamed schools and, as we saw in Chapter III, streaming seems to encourage the formation of delinquescent sub-cultures within the school (Hargreaves, 1967).[64] It was once argued, as we saw, that the less able pupils should be grouped separately because they would become discouraged if required to work in the shadow of their brighter colleagues. It seems in fact that discouragement comes more from the official rejection that being placed in a lower stream implies. This results in harmful effects on the self-concept of the child, a negative attitude to school and all that school stands for and the kinds of behavioural problems that all teachers are familiar with in lower streams, especially in the secondary school (Rudd, 1958).[65] Nor must we forget the effects of streaming on parental attitudes to the school. Little research has been done on this, but it would not be surprising to discover that the experience of many headteachers of lack of cooperation from the parents of their less able pupils was to some extent explicable in terms of the loss of interest, ambition and involvement that must follow the allocation of one's child to a lower stream.

A further and significant factor in the move away from streaming has been the lack of any positive evidence as to its efficacy in promoting even the intellectual development of pupils, its original *raison d'être*. The most interesting feature of all the attempts that have been made to assess the relative merits of streaming and unstreaming in relation to intellectual attainment has been the lack of evidence that streaming makes any real difference. Such evidence as there is suggests either that there is no real difference (Barker-Lunn, 1970)[66] or that pupils do slightly better overall in the unstreamed school (Daniels, 1961).[67] There is also a suggestion that unstreaming leads to a reduction in the spread of attainment between the bright and the less able (Daniels, 1961).[68] A survey undertaken by the UNESCO Institute of Education in Hamburg in 1962[69] noted the widely varying results of English schoolchildren when compared with those in eleven other countries. It suggested that this was due to the fact that English educationists expect a wide difference in performance. It has further been suggested that this wide spread of achievement is a direct result of having streamed classes within a streamed system[70] and the findings of Daniels lend support to this view since he detected a significant reduction in the dispersion of attainment scores in the unstreamed primary schools which he studied.[71] It seems fairly clear, therefore, that the less able, for whose benefit in the view of many people streaming was introduced, do better in an unstreamed situation.

It may be, however, that the gifted children do less well and it is this possibility that gives pause to many people for whom the other evidence might well be conclusive. Clearly, this is a very important consideration. Pupils should not have to pay for their intellectual education at the cost of their social education, but it is equally important that we should not be too ready to adopt on social grounds a system of grouping that is likely to be detrimental to the academic achievement of any pupil. The same problem arises here, then, that we saw when discussing the comprehensivization of secondary education. We must not purchase equality at the cost of quality of any kind nor should we accept an equality that can be achieved only by holding back the more able.

It is here that another finding of the NFER study perhaps has particular significance. One of the most interesting findings of that study was that the success of either system of grouping, at least in relation to intellectual development, depended more on the attitudes of the teachers involved than on any other single factor. Both systems worked more effectively when the teachers believed in them than when they did not. Here may lie a clue to the solution of the dilemma we are faced with. If unstreaming, with the advantages it obviously has for the social and emotional development of pupils, is to attend with equal success to the intellectual needs of all pupils, it must be in the hands of teachers who believe in it and this in turn implies that it must be in the hands of teachers who are willing to adapt their methods to the totally new situation that an unstreamed class presents them with. It may well be not only the attitudes of teachers but the resulting unsuitability of their methods that leads to lack of success. In other words, if unstreaming is not to result in holding back the very bright pupils and if it is to ensure that all pupils get full value from their education, we must make sure that we get right the methods we use in attending to the work of unstreamed classes.

This means, in the first place, that we should examine the possibilities of flexible groupings in schools, especially with older pupils, accepting that one rigid form of grouping to which we adhere unflinchingly for every purpose is no better when it is an unstreamed form than when it is a finely streamed grouping, that different purposes require differently constituted groupings and that for some purposes, again particularly with older pupils, a system of setting or grouping according to specific abilities and attainments might be desirable. The main difficulty of a streamed form of organization stems from the fact that it groups pupils on the basis of a limited set of criteria for all purposes. Again it is the polarization, the apparent need to choose one or the other system, that leads to difficulties and again what seems to be required is a much more subtle and flexible scheme, if we are to provide each child with the kind of education he or she needs.

Secondly, a lot more attention needs to be given to questions about the methods appropriate to the unstreamed class. Quite clearly the class-teaching approach in which an attempt is made to take all pupils through the same material at roughly the same pace, which we saw was one of the basic desiderata that led to the introduction of streaming, although it will still have a part to play, must for most purposes give way to more subtle methods and it would seem that those methods must be individual methods.[72] The streamed class is intended to be homogeneous so that all of the pupils in it can be taught almost as one, although in practice, of course, such homogeneity can never be achieved. The unstreamed class by contrast is overtly heterogeneous and the logic of this is that each individual must be catered for on his own terms. If we believe that the social advantages of the unstreamed class are important and worth having, then we must try to ensure that there are no concomitant disadvantages in the academic sphere. We can only do this by a complete change of approach which will involve us in adopting more individual methods. Perhaps it is because many teachers have not been prepared for this kind of teaching that some experiments with unstreamed classes have not been entirely successful.

If this is so and it can be put right, certain advantages would seem likely to accrue in relation to the achievement of equality in education. For such a system makes it unnecessary to exercise selective procedures from an early stage within the schools so that we can avoid the errors and consequent inequalities that we have seen to be an unavoidable concomitant of such procedures. We no longer have to devise categories which we have seen bring inevitable difficulties in relation to both the theoretical criteria by which they are to be established and the practicalities of putting them into operation. This is a problem which we have seen dogs all attempts to achieve equality. It can only be avoided if we cease to look for categories and recognize that every individual is different and entitled to be catered for on his own merits. To say this is not to suggest, of course, that it is an easy process; it is to suggest, however, that it may be a more fruitful way of working towards equality than the provision of two or three or any number of types of curriculum or school or class or any other kind of educational offering.

For this kind of approach may make more readily possible the adaptation of the content of education to the individual's needs, interests and requirements. We have seen some of the inequalities that can result from attempts to fit 'off-the-peg' curricula or programmes to all pupils and we have considered some of the demands that pupils should not have an 'alien' culture imposed upon them. All of this would seem to point to the desirability of individually tailored provision. The paradox of equality in education is that it is only when the educational diet of every child is different from that of every other that we can really hope that we are near to achieving it.

REFERENCES

1.　A. Crosland, 'Some thoughts on English education', *Encounter,* 1961
2.　K.R. Popper, *The Open Society and its Enemies,* Routledge & Kegan Paul, 1945, Vol.1, Ch.6
3.　Aristotle, *Politics,* 1307a
4.　J. Locke, *Second Treatise on Civil Government,* para. 6
5.　J.R. Lucas, 'Against equality', *Philosophy,* 1965
6.　R. Dahrendorf, 'On the origin of social inequality' in P. Laslett and W.G. Runciman (eds.), *Philosophy, Politics and Society,* Second Series, Blackwell, 1962
7.　R. Dahrendorf, *op.cit.,* p.102
8.　cf. R.S. Peters, *Ethics and Education,* Allen & Unwin, 1966, Ch.4 and S.I. Benn and R.S. Peters, *Social Principles and the Democratic State,* Allen & Unwin, 1959, Ch.5

9. J.R. Lucas, *op.cit.*
10. A.R. Jensen, 'How much can we boost IQ and scholastic achievement?', *Harvard Education REview*, 1969 and H.J. Eysenck, *Race, Intelligence and Education*, Temple Smith, 1971
11. cf. *15 to 18*, HMSO, 1959, Ch.6
12. *Early Leaving*, HMSO, 1954
13. *15 to 18*, HMSO, 1959, Ch.1
14. See, for example, F. Riessman, *The Culturally Deprived Child*, Harper & Row, 1962
15. B. Jackson and D. Marsden, *Education and the Working Class*, Routledge & Kegan Paul, 1962
16. See, for example, F. Riessman, *op.cit.*
17. B.B. Bernstein, 'Social structure, language and learning', *Educational Research*, 1961. Reprinted in M. Craft, J. Raynor and L. Cohen, *Linking Home and School*, Longmans, 1967
18. B.B. Bernstein, 'Elaborated and restricted codes: their social origins and some consequences', *American Anthropologist: Ethnography in Communication*, 1964 and W. Labov, 'The logic of nonstandard English', *Georgetown Monographs in Language and Linguistics*, 1969. Reprinted in A. Cashdan (ed.), *Language in Education*, Routledge & Kegan Paul with Open University Press, 1972 and in N. Keddie (ed.), *Tinker, Tailor: The Myth of Cultural Deprivation*, Penguin, 1973
19. cf. D.A. Pidgeon, *Expectation and Pupil Performance*, NFER, 1970
20. See, for example, F. Riessman, *op.cit.*
21. See, for example, B. Jackson, *Streaming: An Education System in Miniature*, Routledge & Kegan Paul, 1964
22. A Yates and D.A. Pidgeon, *Admission to Grammar Schools*, Newnes, 1957, Ch. 10
23. B. Coard, *How the West Indian Child is Made Educationally Sub-normal in the British School System*, New Beacon Books, 1971
24. See, for example, B. Jackson, *op.cit.*
25. *Children and their Primary Schools*, HMSO, 1967
26. *Ibid.*, paras 301-2
27. *Ibid.*, para. 302
28. *Education: A Framework for Expansion*, HMSO, 1972
29. *Op.cit.*, paras. 318-9
30. *Ibid.*, para. 151
31. *Ibid.*, para. 153
32. *Ibid.*, para. 155
33. *Ibid.*, para. 157
34. cf. B.B. Bernstein, 'Education cannot compensate for society', *New Society*, 1970. Reprinted in A. Cashdan (ed.), *op.cit.*
35. Plowden Report, para. 151
36. cf. N. Keddie (ed.), *op.cit.*
37. W. Labov, *op.cit.*
38. M.F.D. Young (ed.), *Knowledge and Control*, Collier-Macmillan, 1971
39. cf. J.P. White, 'Education in obedience', *New Society*, 1968 and J.P. White, *Towards a Compulsory Curriculum*, Routledge & Kegan Paul, 1973
40. *The Education of the Adolescent*, HMSO, 1926
41. *Spens Report*, HMSO, 1938
42. *Curricula of Secondary Schools and Examinations*, HMSO, 1943

43. O. Banks, *Parity and Prestige in English Secondary Education,* Routledge & Kegan Paul, 1955, Ch. 14
44. *Primary Education,* HMSO, 1931
45. A. Yates and D.A. Pidgeon, *op.cit.,* Ch. 10
46. J.W.B. Douglas, *All Our Future,* Davies, 1968, Chs. 6 and 7
47. cf. B. Jackson, *op.cit.*
48. *Ibid.*
49. *The Education of the Adolescent,* HMSO, 1926
50. A. Binet and T. Simon, *The Development of Intelligence in Children,* Williams & Wilkins, 1916
51. C. Burt, *The Backward Child,* University of London Press, 1937
52. *Primary Education,* HMSO, 1931
53. *Spens Report*, HMSO, 1938
54. J.C. Daniels, 'The effects of streaming in the primary school - what teachers believe', *British Journal of Educational Psychology*, 1961
55. *Primary Education*, HMSO, 1959
56. J.C. Daniels, *op.cit.*
57. B. Jackson, *op.cit.*
58. See, for example, B. Jackson, *op.cit.* and J.W.B. Douglas, *The Home and the School*, MacGibbon & Kee, 1964, Ch. 14
59. E. Ferri, *Streaming: Two Years Later*, NFER, 1972
60. F.A. Haddon and H. Lytton, 'Teaching approach and the development of divergent thinking abilities in primary schools', *British Journal of Educational Psychology*, 1968
61. J.C. Barker-Lunn, *Streaming in the Primary School*, NFER, 1970
62. *Ibid.*
63. D.H. Hargreaves, *Social Relations in a Secondary School*, Routledge & Kegan Paul, 1967 and C. Lacey, *Hightown Grammar: The School as a Social System*, Manchester University Press, 1970
64. D.H. Hargreaves, *op.cit.*
65. W.G.A. Rudd, 'The psychological effects of streaming by attainment', *British Journal of Educational Psychology*, 1958
66. J.C. Barker-Lunn, *op.cit.*
67. cf. J.C. Daniels, 'The effects of streaming in the primary school: a comparison of streamed and unstreamed schools', *British Journal of Educational Psychology*, 1961
68. *Ibid.*
69. UNESCO Institute of Education, *Educational Achievements of Thirteen-Year-Olds in Twelve Countries*, UNESCO, Hamburg, 1962
70. B. Jackson, *op.cit.*
71. J.C. Daniels, *op.cit.*
72. cf. A.V. Kelly, *Teaching Mixed Ability Classes,* Harper & Row, 1974 and A.V. Kelly (ed.), *Case Studies in Mixed Ability Teaching*, Harper & Row, 1975

Index